THE TEXT
OF
THE OLD TESTAMENT

THE TEXT
OF
THE OLD TESTAMENT

An Introduction to the Biblia Hebraica

by

ERNST WÜRTHWEIN

TRANSLATED BY ERROLL F. RHODES

WILLIAM B. EERDMANS PUBLISHING CO.
Grand Rapids, Michigan

Translated from the fourth edition of *Der Text des
Alten Testaments,* © 1973 Württembergische
Bibelanstalt Stuttgart.

Library of Congress Cataloging in Publication Data

Würthwein, Ernst, 1909—
    The text of the Old Testament.

    "This translation is based on the expanded and
thoroughly revised fourth edition of Der Text des Alten
Testaments (Stuttgart, 1973)."
    Bibliography: p. 221.
    Includes index.
    1. Bible. O.T.—Criticism, Textual. 2. Bible.
O.T.—Manuscripts, Hebrew. I. Title.
BS1136.W813   1979   221.4   79-15492
ISBN 0-8028-3530-9

PREFACE TO THE FIRST EDITION

THIS BOOK HAS BEEN WRITTEN TO MEET A PRACTICAL
need. It becomes clear again and again, when Hebrew texts are being read
with students, that many of them do not avail themselves of the wealth of
material provided in Kittel's *Biblia Hebraica*. They disregard it, or feel
uncertain how to use it, and, as a result, it serves them no useful purpose.
This is because they are not sufficiently familiar with the history, the
characteristics, and the problems of the various witnesses to the text; nor
with the methods of textual criticism. The Prefaces to the *Biblia Hebraica*, valuable as they are, cannot provide a complete introduction, nor
can it be expected that textbooks on Old Testament introduction should
give an account of all the material which is referred to in *Biblia Hebraica*.
It seemed convenient, therefore, to propose to the Privilegierte Württembergische Bibelanstalt the publication of a supplement to *Biblia Hebraica*,
which would provide the reader with the necessary information for this
purpose. I am greatly indebted to the Bibelanstalt for the readiness with
which it has accepted this proposal.

In carrying out the plan, the writer has found it necessary to go
considerably beyond the original scope proposed. Even so he has often
had to compress the material more than was desirable. In many sections
of the book, it would have been easier to write a much larger textbook in
which the problems could be fully set out and a detailed account given of
the discussions on them. But the attempt has at least been made to give
the reader not merely the basic facts, but also, so far as space allowed,
some insight into the most important problems. Only by so doing can the
right attitude be adopted towards the actual problems of textual criticism.
There must be freedom from prejudice, without mere subjectivism.

The addition of the fourth chapter on textual criticism seemed
particularly desirable in view of the practical purpose of the book. The
points raised there, necessarily in mere outline, make no claim to provide
the book of rules for textual criticism which Paul Volz once said was so

desirable. But I hope that they will serve to help the student towards a certain clarity and reliability of method in textual criticism.

I acknowledge with special gratitude the decision of the Bibelanstalt to include forty plates which make it possible to present a good selection of illustrative material. In the choice of the plates I have preferred to use less accessible manuscripts. Some of the points which could only be briefly touched on in the sections on the history of text have been elaborated in the explanatory notes to the plates.

Vocalization has been used sparingly, in view of printing problems. The reader, it is assumed, will refer to his *Biblia Hebraica* as he reads, and can easily supply what is omitted.

Finally, I wish to place on record my gratitude for the assistance I have received. Professor Otto Eissfeldt was good enough to read a proof of pages 1-82 and made many valuable suggestions. I have been advised on individual points by Professors Albrecht Alt, Artur Weiser, and Karl Elliger. In obtaining photographs for the plates I have been greatly helped by Professors Paul Kahle of Oxford, and H. H. Rowley of Manchester, and by Fathers Alban Dold and Johannes Schildenberger of the Benedictine Abbey of Beuron. Last but not least I am grateful for the encouragement and interest shown by the President of the Bibelanstalt, Dr. Schlatter, and its business manager, Dr. Diehl. It is a pleasure to me to express my gratitude to all those whom I have named.

Tübingen, Advent 1952   ERNST WÜRTHWEIN

PREFACE TO THE FOURTH EDITION

THIS FOURTH EDITION, LIKE EARLIER EDITIONS, HAS BEEN thoroughly revised to include recent publications of texts as well as of studies in the field of textual history.

In 1968 publication of the *Biblia Hebraica Stuttgartensia* was begun in fascicles, edited by K. Elliger and W. Rudolph (BHS), to take the place of the *Biblia Hebraica* edited by R. Kittel and P. Kahle (BHK). It should be completed by 1976. The principal differences are noted in the Foreword to *Liber Jesaiae* (1968). I have tried to include discussions of the witnesses it adds to those used in BHK, as well as of other differences, to make this book useful as an introduction to both BHK and BHS (note especially the appended comparative list of sigla for both editions).

I am sincerely grateful to my British colleagues Professor P. R. Ackroyd, Professor B. J. Roberts, and Dr. S. Brock, for their most kind assistance with suggestions and bibliographical references. My thanks are also due to all who have assisted me in the preparation and printing of this new edition.

The manuscript was completed in December 1971. Later publications have been noted in only a few instances.

Marburg, October 1972   ERNST WÜRTHWEIN

FOREWORD TO THE ENGLISH EDITION

THIS TRANSLATION IS BASED ON THE EXPANDED AND thoroughly revised fourth edition of *Der Text des Alten Testaments* (Stuttgart, 1973). At many points it has been further supplemented with more recent bibliographical references.

Dr. Erroll F. Rhodes has earned my gratitude not only by his careful work of translating, but also by making many valuable suggestions.

Marburg, May 1978   ERNST WÜRTHWEIN

TRANSLATOR'S NOTE

THE PUBLICATION OF THE FIRST FASCICLES OF *Biblia Hebraica Stuttgartensia* under the editorship of K. Elliger and W. Rudolph beginning in 1967 prompted Professor Würthwein to produce a fourth edition of his introduction to the text of the Old Testament, changing its subtitle from "An Introduction to Kittel-Kahle's Biblia Hebraica" to "An Introduction to the Biblia Hebraica." The completion of the *Biblia Hebraica Stuttgartensia* now also makes a revision of Peter R. Ackroyd's translation of the first German edition a desideratum. For the reader's convenience the sigla of BHK are indicated in square brackets where they differ from those of BHS. The translator is indebted to Prof. Ernst Würthwein for his generous cooperation, especially in making available his own notes toward a revision of the fourth German edition, to Prof. Ackroyd for kindly reading the manuscript and suggesting many improvements, and also to Dr. Eugene A. Nida, Translations Research Coordinator of the United Bible Societies, to Dr. Gernot Winter of the Deutsche Bibelstiftung, and to Mr. Allen Myers of Willam B. Eerdmans Publishing Company, for their encouragement and sympathetic assistance in making this English edition possible.

Riverside, Connecticut, June 1978   ERROLL F. RHODES

CONTENTS

PLATES

INTRODUCTION

WHEN WE READ A MODERN BOOK, PRINTED FROM A MANU-
script which has been prepared by the author himself and produced under
his own supervision, we can study it with confidence that its text represents the author's intention in its wording and even in the details of its
punctuation. We can be sure of the text we interpret. With works produced
hundreds or even thousands of years before the invention of printing the
situation is quite different. Almost without exception the original documents have been lost. The texts are available only in copies separated
from their autographs by several centuries and an unknown number of
intermediary copies. We know how easily errors can occur in copying a
text. By accident a word may be missed or repeated, groups of words may
be inadvertently transposed or replaced by similar or synonymous words,
and if the handwriting is difficult to read, an element of guesswork may
enter.

Many errors may be due to carelessness, especially if the copyist
is a professional scribe who works rapidly and becomes casual, and
further may not be familiar with the subject of the text he is copying. But
even the scribe who approaches his text with interest and devotion may
introduce corruptions. He may find an expression in his exemplar which
in his view reflects an earlier scribe's misunderstanding of the author, and
in his concern for the meaning of the text he naturally corrects it, just as
we would correct a typographical error in a printed book. But his correction itself could very well reflect his own misunderstanding! It is not only
the casual or absentminded scribe who introduces errors, but the con-
scientious scribe as well. The next stage in the process is obvious. A
scribe copying a faulty manuscript—and no manuscript is without
errors—will deal with his predecessor's errors either by guesswork or
with ingenuity, with the result of a series of intended improvements
leading away from the original text.

All the writings which come to us from antiquity, including the writings of the Old and New Testaments, have suffered from just such (mis)adventures.[1] The interpreter of these materials cannot proceed from assumptions which would be accepted without question in the study of a modern book. The text to be interpreted must first be established—it is not already defined. The available witnesses to the text must first be examined in order to reconstruct a single form of the text which we can assert with confidence to be as close to the form of the autographs as scientific principles can lead us, if not (ideally) identical with them. The work of textual criticism is both a preliminary and an integral part of the task of interpretation; its role may once have been overrated, just as now it tends to be overlooked, yet its service remains indispensable.

The purpose and goal of our critical editions of the Bible is to assist in achieving an objective understanding of the text. They bring together in a convenient form a vast array of material, well beyond the capacity of individual scholars to assemble for themselves, to provide the first requirements for a systematic study of the text. But to deal with all this material and use it effectively we must understand its peculiarities and the value of its various elements. When faced with a difficult passage we cannot simply gather together the various readings and select the one which seems to offer the simplest solution, at times preferring the Hebrew text, at other times the Septuagint, and yet other times the Aramaic Targum. Textual witnesses are not all equally reliable. Each has its own character and its own peculiar history. We must be familiar with these if we hope to avoid inadequate or false solutions. Accordingly we shall first survey the available witnesses to the text in three sections: A. transmission of the text in the original language; B. translations from the original language; and C. the remaining translations. A final fourth section will outline the purpose and the procedures of textual criticism.

1. It is true, as we shall see, that efforts to protect the Hebrew text of the Old Testament from accidental and intentional changes were successful. But this was only after a certain date, and in the preceding centuries it was subject to the common vicissitudes of all ancient texts.

A
THE TRANSMISSION OF THE TEXT IN THE ORIGINAL LANGUAGE

I

SCRIPT AND WRITING MATERIALS

1. *SCRIPT*

EXCAVATIONS AND DISCOVERIES OF THE LAST HUNDRED years have revealed an unexpected wealth of literary activity in Palestine and Syria. Several different writing systems were invented there during the second millennium B.C., and even foreign systems of writing such as the cuneiform script were in use as well. Here also, presumably, the first step was taken in the transition from complex writing systems with hundreds of characters to the alphabet, that simplest of all forms of writing, with only some twenty-odd letters—a step so significant for man's intellectual history. All this was certainly not without significance for the formation of the Old Testament, and must receive due recognition in any consideration of the roles of oral and written tradition among the Israelites and the Jews. We can only allude to this in passing, limiting ourselves here to some comments on those systems of writing which were directly related to the initial writing of the Biblical texts and their continuing transmission.

All the manuscripts and fragments of the Hebrew Old Testament which have come down to us from Jewish sources, from the earliest examples, e.g., the Qumran texts (cf. pp. 30ff.) and the Nash Papyrus, are with few exceptions written in the script still in use today known as the *square script* (כְּתָב מְרֻבָּע) or the Assyrian script (כְּתָב אַשּׁוּרִי) from its place of origin. This script was in general use in the time of Jesus: the allusion to the letter *yodh* as the smallest in the alphabet (Matt. 5:18) would be true only of the square script. This script was derived by a gradual process of development from the Aramaic script, which was used extensively (pl. 5). The earliest recorded examples are the 'Araq el-Emir inscription in East Jordan from the fourth or early third century B.C.,[1] and the earliest

---

1. W. F. Albright, *The Archaeology of Palestine* (1949, revised 1960), pp. 149f.

Qumran fragments from about 200 B.C. (4QSam[b] and 4QJer[a]).[2] The Jews were aware, however, that this script was not their earliest. One Jewish tradition attributes its introduction to Ezra, about 430 B.C. The later rabbis were embarrassed by the implication that it was a post-exilic innovation. Accordingly they told how the Torah was first given in the square script, but because of Israel's sin the script had been changed, and then in Ezra's time the original form was restored. Although this was obviously special pleading and without any historical value, it clearly reflects the awareness of a change of script in the post-exilic period. Most probably the Jews' gradual adoption of the Aramaic language, the lingua franca of the ancient Near East, was followed by their adoption of the Aramaic script, so that by inference it was this script that the sacred writings were first written in, and only eventually in the square script which developed from it.[3]

When the earlier parts of the Old Testament were first written down in the pre-exilic period, another script was in use in Palestine and Syria. This was the *Phoenician-Old Hebrew script,* the ancestor of all the alphabets of past and present. It is known to us in a later, more developed form in a series of texts, the earliest dating from the twelfth or eleventh century. Apart from the recently discovered abecedary of Izbet Ṣarṭah (cf. pl. 49 and discussion), the best-known examples are:[4] the Ahiram sarcophagus from Byblos (*ca.* 1000 B.C.), the farmer's calendar from Gezer (*ca.* 950), the Moabite stone (*ca.* 840; pl. 2), ostraca from Samaria (ink on clay, eighth century), a palimpsest papyrus from Murabbaʿat (eighth or seventh century), the Siloam inscription (*ca.* 700; pl. 3), and ostraca from Lachish (*ca.* 588; pl. 4).

Its origins must lie far earlier than any of the examples yet discovered. Early examples of alphabetical inscriptions include the *Sinai script* found in a group of inscriptions in the mines of Serabit el-Ḥadem on the Sinai peninsula and dated by Albright *ca.* 1500,[5] the (related?) *proto-*

---

2. F. M. Cross, "The Oldest Manuscripts from Qumran," *JBL* 74 (1955), pp.147-176 (= *QHBT,* 1975, pp. 147-176); *idem,* "The Development of the Jewish Scripts," in *The Bible and the Ancient Near East* (1961), pp. 133-202.

3. Cf. also G. R. Driver, *Semitic Writing* (Schweich Lectures 1944, revised 1976, p. 250: "This כתב אשורי or simply אשורית 'Assyrian script' was so called because it was the originally Aramean form of the 'Phoenician' script which had been coming into use in Assyrian and Babylonian commercial houses since the 8th century B.C. and which was brought back by Jews returning from the Exile. The 'square script' (כתב מרבע) was derived from this form of the alphabet."

4. The texts have been collected and annotated in H. Donner and W. Röllig, *Kanaanäische und aramäische Inschriften* 1-3 (1962-64); D. W. Thomas, ed., *Documents from Old Testament Times* (1958, 1961[2]); and in J. C. L. Gibson, *Textbook of Syrian Semitic Inscriptions* 1, *Hebrew and Moabite Inscriptions* (1971); 2, *Aramaic Inscriptions* (1975).

5. *BASOR* 110 (1948), pp. 6-22.

Palestinian script found on artifacts from middle and southern Palestine of the period from 1700 to 1200 B.C. (Gezer, Lachish, Shechem, etc.; pl. 1),[6] and the cuneiform alphabet of Ugarit in north Syria, *ca*. 1400 B.C. There is no need to discuss here the relationship of these scripts to the Phoenician-Old Hebrew script, because it is still largely a prehistory, obscure in its details. Deciphering the scripts, except for Ugaritic, is still at the beginning stages. Only the Phoenician-Old Hebrew script and the later square script are directly related to the earliest written forms of the Old Testament texts and to their preservation as written documents. We need only observe here that when the Israelites settled in Palestine they found in the Phoenician alphabet (although without vowels) a script which was easy to learn and required hardly any improvement; more than four hundred references in the Old Testament attest that the art of writing was widely practiced in Israel.[7]

The transition from the Old Hebrew script to the square script occurred between the fourth and second centuries B.C.—it is impossible to be more precise. For a long while the Old Hebrew script remained in use beside the square script. The coins of the period of Bar Kochba's revolt (A.D. 132-135) bear Old Hebrew letters. Among the texts found in the Dead Sea caves are some written in the Old Hebrew script (pl. 14).[8] "This script . . . derives from the old pre-exilic Hebrew script. Apparently it survived as a book hand and enjoyed a renascence in the period of Maccabean nationalism and archaism. In any case, at Qumrân it appears in documents contemporary with the Jewish hand."[9] Jewish accounts in the Mishna and the Babylonian Talmud imply that although manuscripts of the Bible in the old script were still circulating in the first two centuries of the Christian era, they were ascribed an inferior degree of holiness— they did not "defile the hands" levitically as did scrolls written in the square script. And yet for a while the Old Hebrew script must have been regarded as especially holy. This would at least explain a peculiar feature of some recently discovered texts: in the Habakkuk Commentary (pl. 13), the Hodayoth, and the Psalm scroll from Cave 11 (11QPs[a]), the square script is used except of the divine name YHWH and both אל and אלי,

6. The so-called Sinai Inscriptions have been collected and studied recently by W. F. Albright, *The Proto-Sinaitic Inscriptions and Their Decipherment, Harvard Theological Studies* 22 (1966); on the proto-Palestinian inscriptions cf. also F. M. Cross, "The Evolution of the Proto-Canaanite Alphabet," *BASOR* 134 (1954), pp. 15-24.

7. Cf. D. Diringer, *CHB* 1 (1970), p. 13.

8. According to present reports there are five Pentateuch manuscripts and some fragments of Job (Cross, *ALQ*, 1961², p. 43; cf. p. 146, pl. 14). Of special interest is an Exodus scroll with fragments of Exod. 6:25–37:15 which preserves the Samaritan text type throughout although it is not of Samaritan origin (it lacks the characteristic addition after 20:17). Cf. P. W. Skehan, *JBL* 74 (1955), pp. 182-87, and *JBL* 78 (1959), pp. 22f.; also R. S. Hanson, "Palaeo-Hebrew Script in the Hasmonean Age," *BASOR* 175 (1964), pp. 26-42.

9. F. M. Cross, *ALQ* (1961²), p. 34.

which are written in Old Hebrew. Again, the Tetragrammaton is found in Old Hebrew letters in a fragmentary leather scroll containing the Greek text of the Minor Prophets which was discovered in August 1952 by bedouin at Naḥal Ḥever in the Judean desert (cf. p. 180). It was probably written between 50 B.C. and A.D. 50, and confirms Origen's account of the treatment of divine names, that in the more careful copies of the Greek Old Testament the Old Hebrew script was used for the Tetragrammaton.[10] As late as the fifth century A.D. the divine name was written in Old Hebrew letters in a fragment of Aquila's Greek version.

The *Samaritans* (pl. 27), who contrary to traditional beliefs (cf. p. 42) did not separate themselves from the Jews completely until the Hasmonean period, also preserved their sacred book, the Torah, in *Old Hebrew script,* probably because they claimed to preserve the older and purer tradition, and they may have regarded the introduction of the new script as a flagrant innovation.[11]

2. WRITING MATERIALS

Many different kinds of material were used for writing in Biblical times. Job wished his words were chiseled in *stone* (Job 19:24); and the successful achievement of the tunnel of Siloam (pl. 3) in the late eighth century B.C. was recorded on the smooth surface of a rock in an inscription discovered in 1880. We read in Exod. 34:1 of *stone tablets* with the commandments of God written on them, and in Deut. 27:2f. stones were covered with a plaster on which letters were presumably painted. *Wooden tablets*[12] for brief notes may be intended when the prophets Isaiah and Habakkuk were instructed to record their oracles on tablets (Isa. 30:8; Hab. 2:2; perhaps also Isa. 8:1). The *clay tablets* so popular in the rest of the ancient East were ideal for the straight lines of cuneiform script, but hardly adapted to the curved lines of the Hebrew script. But the excavations in Palestine demonstrate that *potsherds* or *ostraca* (pl. 4) inscribed with ink were as popular there as elsewhere for routine daily matters. While excavating Tell ed-Duweir (ancient Lachish) in 1935, archaeologists found some ostraca in a room by the city gate; these proved to be military dispatches from the last years of Judah, *ca.* 588 B.C. It has already been suggested that individual prophetic statements, proverbs, and the like may have been written on such potsherds before they were collected into

---

10. Edition: D. Barthélemy, *Les devanciers d'Aquila: Première publication intégrale du texte des fragments du Dodécaprophéton trouvés in de Désert de Juda, précédée d'une étude sur les traductions et recensions grecques de la Bible réalisées au premier siècle de notre ère sous l'influence du rabbinat palestinien, VTS* 10 (1963); cf. pl. 30.

11. According to F. M. Cross, *ALQ* (1961²), p. 34, the Samaritan script was derived from the (archaizing) Old Hebrew script of the Hasmonean period.

12. Excavations in Egypt and Mesopotamia show that these could be prepared for writing with a coat of plaster or wax.

books. While this could well account for the lack of continuity found in the order of some Biblical books, it remains only a theoretical possibility.

A special exception is the *copper scroll* found in Qumran Cave 1; it does not contain a Biblical text.

The materials mentioned above were appropriate only for texts of very limited length, and would be relevant only to the earlier stages of the formation of our Biblical books. *Papyrus* and *leather* were more suitable materials for the books themselves; these must be intended where the Old Testament refers to a scroll, whether מְגִלַּת־סֵפֶר or simply מְגִלָּה (Jer. 36:2ff.; Ezek. 2:9; 3:1-3; Zech. 5:1f.; Ps. 40:8), because only these are adapted to the scroll format.

Papyrus[13] was already in use in Egypt in the third millennium B.C. We know from the famous travel narrative of the Egyptian Wen Amon (*ca.* 1090 B.C.) that this convenient material was exported from Egypt to Phoenicia in exchange for wood. We may infer from the fact that Wen Amon took with him five hundred scrolls of fine grade papyrus (several qualities were distinguished) that the commodity was being manufactured commercially. Egypt was later to supply the whole Mediterranean world. Papyrus was made from the stem of the papyrus reed. It was cut into thin strips. A vertical layer was placed upon a horizontal layer; the two were pressed together (the natural gum provided adequate bonding), dried, and rubbed smooth. The sheet was then ready for use. A number of sheets could be glued together to form a scroll of a desired length. The Israelites wrote on such scrolls in columns, from right to left. Usually the inner side of the scroll (recto) with its horizontal grain was used for texts, but some scrolls were inscribed on both sides (cf. Ezek. 2:10). It was probably a papyrus scroll which Baruch wrote on at Jeremiah's dictation, and which King Jehoiakim burned in the open brazier sheet by sheet (Jer. 36).[14] On the whole, papyrus must have been used quite commonly in Palestine. It was cheap and more durable than has generally been recognized, "at least as durable as the best hand-made paper, if not more so."[15] But of course favorable climate and soil, as in the desert sands of Egypt, were required for it to survive through the centuries. This is why very few papyrus fragments have been discovered thus far in Palestine, and these were found in the caves of Qumran and Murabba'at (cf. pp. 30f., 134f.), where the conditions were suitable for their preservation. Among them were found only a few Biblical texts (Kings and Daniel).

The palimpsest of Murabba'at deserves mention as the earliest

---

13. Cf. also D. J. Wiseman, *CHB* 1 (1970), pp. 30-32; T. C. Skeat, *CHB* 2 (1969), pp. 54-61.

14. Others suggest it was of leather because a knife was needed to cut the sheets apart.

15. T. C. Skeat, *CHB* 2 (1969), p. 59.

known Hebrew papyrus, ascribed to the eighth (Milik) or seventh (Cross, Gibson, and others) century B.C. The almost illegible underwriting seems to be a letter, while the overwriting seems to be a list of persons.[16]

As a writing material, *leather*[17] undoubtedly played as important a role in Palestine as it did elsewhere in the Near East. The advantage it had over papyrus of not wearing out so quickly made it an ideal material for writings which were intended for long or constant use. Jewish regulations still require that a copy of the Torah intended for liturgical use be written on leather made from a clean animal, and this surely represents ancient usage.[18] The Letter of Aristeas, at the end of the second century B.C., alludes to a magnificent Torah scroll with gold writing on leather (parchment?); and the Isaiah scroll found in 1947 (pl. 10, 11) provides an actual example of an ancient Biblical scroll which is not much later than this literary evidence. It comprises seventeen sheets of carefully prepared leather (not parchment, as often stated). These were sewn together to make a scroll 7.34 m. long (26 cm. wide). It contains all sixty-six chapters of Isaiah in fifty-four columns, averaging thirty lines of 12.8 cm. width. The lines were marked in the leather with a dull knife, also in accordance with Jewish regulations. This scroll and others found with it were wrapped in linen and sealed in clay jars (pl. 8)—a method of preservation mentioned in Jer. 32:14, and common also in Egypt.

From about 200 B.C. a special technique of treating leather (was lime mordant already known?) was used to produce **parchment** (Greek *pérgamon*), named after the city of Pergamon in Asia Minor. This became the principal material for books from the fourth century, and the dominant writing medium of the medieval period, while the use of papyrus declined. In contrast to the earlier materials, parchment offered great advantages. It is durable, with a smooth writing surface, accepting writing on both sides, and with a light color that lends clarity to the ink. It could be used several times by erasing the text; there are many examples of its use in palimpsests (literally "rescraped," Latin *codex rescriptus* = a rewritten book; pl. 34, 42). The material of the important fragments from the Cairo Geniza (cf. pp. 33f.) was also parchment. **Paper** made its appearance beside parchment in the ninth century. Paper was invented in China in the first century A.D. or perhaps earlier, and by the eighth century the

---

16. Benoit-Milik-de Vaux, *Les Grottes de Murabba'ât: Discoveries in the Judaean Desert* 2 (1961), no. 17. Text and translation in J. C. L. Gibson, *Textbook of Syrian Semitic Inscriptions* 1, *Hebrew and Moabite Inscriptions* (1971), pp. 31f., where the papyrus fragment is dated *ca.* 650 B.C.

17. T. C. Skeat, *CHB* 2 (1969), pp. 61-65.

18. On the preparation of Torah scrolls the Jerusalem Talmud states: "It is a rule [*halakah*] that was given to Moses at Sinai: write on leather, write with ink, and line with a reed" (*Meg.* 1.9).

knowledge of its manufacture came first to the Near East through Chinese prisoners of war, and thence to Europe.

3. *SCROLL AND CODEX*

The common book format of antiquity was the papyrus or leather scroll—a rather inconvenient form. It takes both hands to use it: one to hold the scroll (the left hand for Hebrew scrolls, because of the right-to-left script), while the other hand draws the sheets out slowly, column by column, and rolls them up again as they are read (cf. Latin *volvere* "to turn," whence *volumen* "volume" to designate a scroll). After a scroll has been read, it must be wound back on the original roller to prepare for its next use, with the first sheet on the outside again. We noted that the sixty-six chapters of Isaiah required a scroll about 7.5 m. long. For practical reasons a scroll could not be made much longer.[19] Only in exceptional instances of very large scrolls with very small script could the entire Old Testament, or even several of its longer books, be included in a single scroll. Most of the Biblical books circulated in separate scrolls, and in some instances, as in the Pentateuch, the division into books seems to have been made with the normal capacity of a scroll in view.[20]

It was the invention of the *codex* in the first century A.D., and especially the parchment codex, that made it possible to produce many or all of the books of the Bible in a single volume. Remains of *papyrus* codices (pl. 31, 32) containing Greek texts of the Old and New Testament books have survived from the second and third centuries A.D.[21] In the fourth century the codex came into common use. The scroll did not disappear completely, but its importance diminished. The role of the Christian church in this development is of interest. It was the victory of the church which led to the dominance of the codex, which had been used by Christians from the beginning, over the scroll format. Scrolls came to be used only for official records and contracts, while the codex became

19. The longest surviving scroll is the 40 m.-long Harris Papyrus in the British Museum, which was never intended for practical use. This is far greater than the average, which was between 6 m. and 10 m. for Greek papyrus scrolls. In the Qumran caves there were also found scrolls "of very small format with a tiny script" (H. Bardtke, *Die Hand-schriftenfunde am Toten Meer* 2 [1961²], p. 83).

20. Conversely, the joining together of the two parts (ch. 1–39 and ch. 40–66) of the book of Isaiah which come from completely different periods may best be explained on the assumption that these two books were originally independent (though related in vocabulary and ideas), and came to be regarded as a single book because they were written on a single scroll.

21. C. H. Roberts has shown how completely the codex form came to dominate Biblical manuscripts (in complete contrast to pagan literature) in the second and third centuries: *Proceedings of the British Academy for the Promotion of Historical, Philosophical and Philological Studies* 40 (1954), pp. 169-204; *idem, CHB* 1 (1970), pp. 48-66; T. C. Skeat, *CHB* 2 (1969), pp. 65-74.

the normal form for books.[22] Its advantages over the scroll format are obvious: an increased ease of browsing and rapid reference, as well as the use of both sides of the sheet to receive texts. Even the Jews adopted the codex, retaining the use of leather and parchment scrolls for copies of the Torah and of Esther designated for liturgical use. The major part of the fragments from the Cairo Geniza represent codices (cf. pp. 12f., 33); only a few are from scrolls.

4. WRITING IMPLEMENTS AND INK

Writing implements mentioned in the Old Testament include the חֶרֶט (Isa. 8:1) and the עֵט (Jer. 8:8; 17:1; Ps. 45:2; Job 19:24). חרט corresponds to a *pen* or *stylus* with which characters are inscribed on prepared materials. The same tool is probably intended by עֵט בַּרְזֶל, the iron pen with a diamond point of Jer. 17:1, and the iron chisel of Job 19:24[23]. But again the עֵט סֹפְרִים of Jer. 8:8 and עֵט סוֹפֵר of Ps. 45:2 refer to the *reed pen* of the professional scribe, used with ink on leather, papyrus, and ostraca. In ancient Egypt rushes were used with their ends crushed and frayed like a small brush, or later cut at an acute angle like a quill pen; we may infer similar practices in Palestine. The reed pen (*kalamos*), formed like a quill pen with a split point that permitted a flowing cursive script, can be traced to the third century B.C. It has continued in use in the East until modern times.

    Ink (Hebrew דְּיוֹ) was used for writing on ostraca, leather, and papyrus. The only mention of it in the Old Testament is at Jer. 36:18 (605 B.C.), where it is referred to as something well known. There were two kinds: *nonmetallic* ink made from lamp black (the soot from an olive oil lamp) in a solution of gum (resin) or oil, and *metallic* ink, usually a compound of gall nuts and vitriol.[24] The use of metallic ink, which was not permanent and was damaging to the writing material, was opposed by Jews in the early Christian centuries, but it became common in the medieval period in spite of Talmudic prohibition. The ink of the Qumran manuscripts was not metallic, but vegetable or carbon.[25] The fact that these inks long continued in use alongside the metallic ink (and are still prescribed for use in Torah scrolls) makes these inks of little use in dating

    22. Cf. W. Schubart, *Einführung in die Papyruskunde* (1918), p. 56; *idem, Das Buch bei den Griechen un Römern* (1921²), pp. 122f.; C. H. Roberts, *CHB* 1 (1970), pp. 48-66, esp. 56-60.

    23. Cf. J. J. Stamm, *ZAW* 65 (1953), p. 302, on this passage.

    24. The ink used on the Lachish ostraca has been analyzed as metallic (cf. p. 126). According to G. R. Driver, *Semitic Writing* (rev. ed. 1954), p. 86, nonmetallic ink was used for parchment, metallic for papyrus. According to T. C. Skeat, *CHB* 2 (1969), p. 61, the practice among Greek scribes was practically the reverse.

    25. Cf. H. J. Plenderleith in Barthélemy-Milik, *Qumran Cave I* (1955), p. 39.

manuscripts, other than favoring an earlier over a medieval date. The inks used by the early scribes did not penetrate deeply, but could be washed off with a sponge or something similar. When it faded the script could be restored. Yet both the Egyptian papyri and the Qumran manuscripts show that the ancient world could produce an ink of remarkable permanence, far more enduring than the later metallic ink.

II
THE MASORETIC TEXT

1. GENERAL CONSIDERATIONS

THE HEBREW TEXT OF THE OLD TESTAMENT IS CALLED *Masoretic* because in its present form it is based on the Masora (Hebrew מָסוֹרֶת,[1] the textual tradition of the Jewish scholars known as the Masoretes. It is designated by the symbol 𝔐 in both the *Biblia Hebraica* edited by Rudolf Kittel (BHK) and the *Biblia Hebraica Stuttgartensia* (BHS).

(a) In BHK since the third edition, 𝔐 has represented the text of the Leningrad Public Library Ms. B 19ᴬ, written in 1008 A.D. (L, Leningradensis; pl. 24). The fourth edition of *Biblia Hebraica,* the *Biblia Hebraica Stuttgartensia* (BHS), edited by K. Elliger and W. Rudolph, is also based on the same manuscript. The first two editions, like most other editions (e.g., C. D. Ginsburg, 1908ff.), followed the edition of Jacob ben Chayyim (𝔅) printed by Daniel Bomberg in Venice, 1524/25, which was based on late medieval manuscripts. In BHK and BHS, then, we have a text that is centuries older than that of any previously printed edition. But even this manuscript which underlies BHK and BHS is remarkably recent when we consider the age of the Old Testament and compare it with the important fourth- and fifth-century manuscripts of the Greek Old and New Testaments. In fact, we do not have any Hebrew manuscript of the entire Old Testament written earlier than the tenth century. The oldest dated codex (pl. 20) contains only the Prophets and dates from A.D. 895 (Codex Cairensis, cf. p. 34). In the latter half of the nineteenth century many fragments from the sixth to the eighth century were found in an *Old Cairo* synagogue which had been St. Michael's Church until A.D. 882. They

---

1. This broad use of the word Masora to include the whole "philology of the Hebrew Bible," including all the varied activities which go into the transmission of the text (transcription with all its special features, pointing, and the Masora in the narrow sense, cf. p. 30), seems to derive from the Jewish scholar E. Levita (1469-1549), while in the golden age of the Masoretes it had a special meaning (cf. pp. 15, 30); cf. R. Edelmann, "Soferim-Massoretes, 'Massoretes'-Nakdanim," *In Memoriam P. Kahle, BZAW* 103 (1968), pp. 116-123. M. Gertner proposes a complex development of the term in "The Masorah and the Levites," *VT* 10 (1960), pp. 241-284.

were discovered there in the *Geniza,* a kind of storage room where worn or faulty manuscripts were kept hidden until they could be disposed of formally (Aramaic גָּנַז "to hide") to avoid misusing or profaning a manuscript containing the holy name of God. Periodically the contents of a Geniza would be buried in the ground with due ceremony. It was only by accident that the Cairo manuscripts escaped this fate: at some time the Geniza was walled over and its existence forgotten.

It is even more coincidental that a number of substantially earlier Hebrew manuscripts, some dating from the pre-Christian era, were hidden during the first and second centuries A.D. in various caves in the Judean desert, especially in the vicinity of the Essene settlement of Khirbet Qumran (pl. 7-15b) near the Dead Sea, and remained there for nearly two millennia to be found in a succession of discoveries since 1947. Among them are found the Biblical book of Isaiah in its entirety, the first two chapters of Habakkuk, and fragments of all the other Old Testament books except Esther (cf. pp. 30f.). But despite the importance of these discoveries for scholarly research, the fact remains that for the entire Old Testament we are dependent on manuscripts of the tenth century and later. This is to be expected because Jewish regulations required the destruction of worn and defective manuscripts. And when scholars had finally established the text in the tenth century, all older manuscripts which represented earlier stages of its development were naturally considered defective, and in the course of time they disappeared. It is also true that manuscripts were often destroyed during the medieval persecutions of Jews, sometimes by their adversaries, but sometimes also by the Jews themselves to prevent their sacred books from falling into the hands of infidels.

In evaluating the significance of the surviving manuscripts for textual studies we should remember that although most of them are relatively late, their age is neither the sole nor primary criterion of their worth. When papyrus fragments of the Greek classical authors were discovered which were centuries older than the medieval manuscripts previously known, they aroused high expectations especially in lay circles; but on examination their texts proved to be inferior. This was because the medieval manuscripts were based on the careful studies of the great Alexandrian philologists, while the papyri which circulated in the provinces of Egypt represented the range of textual corruption which made the critical work of the Alexandrian scholars so necessary. More important than age, then, is the *textual tradition* represented by a manuscript (Georgio Pasquali: *codices recentiores—non deteriores—*"later manuscripts, but not inferior").[2] This holds for the Hebrew text of the Old

---

2. Cf. G. Pasquali, *Storia della tradizione e critica del testo* (1932[1], 1952[2]), pp. xvff.

Testament as well; the history of the transmission of the text must be considered when forming a judgment.

(b) Until the Age of Humanism and the Reformation the Hebrew text and its transmission remained primarily a Jewish concern. In the first millennium A.D., during which the basic lines of transmission were set, we should distinguish between the Jews of Palestine, the *Western Maso-*

Occ *retes* (Occidentales, מַעֲרְבָאֵי), and the members of the great Jewish colony

Or in Babylonia, the *Eastern Masoretes* (Orientales, מַדִינְחָאֵי). The Western school centered at Tiberias until the end of the third century, and again from the eighth to the tenth century; the Eastern centers were the schools

Sor at Sura,[3] Nehardea (destroyed A.D. 259), and later at Pumbeditha, which were authoritative in matters of Jewish scholarship for centuries. Finally the Babylonian schools lost their significance, and in the tenth and eleventh centuries they disappeared. Once again the West assumed the spiritual leadership of Judaism, and the Western Masoretes sought to eliminate all traces of textual traditions that differed from their own. The views of the school of Tiberias became determinative for the future, and the Eastern tradition was forgotten for a millennium.

(c) It is well known that for many centuries the Hebrew text of the Old Testament existed as a purely consonantal text. Vowel signs were not added to the text until a later stage, when the consonantal text was already well established with a long history of transmission behind it. The history of the consonantal text and of its vowel pointing therefore must be considered separately.

(d) In the golden age of the Masoretic tradition the men who devoted themselves to the textual transmission of the Old Testament were apparently designated by their special functions. The *Sopherim*[4] wrote out the consonantal text proper, the *Nakdanim* (from נקד "to point") added vowel points and accents to the manuscript, and the *Masoretes* added the marginal and final Masoretic notes (cf. pp. 27f.).[5] The same person could serve more than one function; for obvious reasons the vowel points and the Masoretic notes were frequently added by the same scholar. For example, Shelomo ben Buya'a wrote the Aleppo Codex, and Aaron ben Asher was responsible for its pointing and Masoretic notes (cf. p. 162); the same Shelomo ben Buya'a wrote a Torah manuscript in A.D. 930 (cf. p. 166), to which Ephraim, the son of Rabbi Buya'a, added the points and Masora. According to its colophon, the Leningrad Codex was the work of

3. The Masoretes of Sura (Sorae) are indicated in BH by the siglum Sor.
4. For the history of the word *sopher*, cf. J. Jeremias, *TDNT* 1, 1964, pp. 740f. (*ThWNT* 1, 1933, pp. 740f.) During the Israelite kingdom the word *sopher* indicated the incumbent of a high political office; in Judaism it took the meaning of "legal scholar, one who knows the Torah, an ordained theologian." For Josephus (37/38–early second century A.D.) it has the meaning of "scribe."
5. R. Edelmann, *op. cit.* (cf. p. 12, n. 1).

one man: Samuel ben Jacob not only wrote it, but pointed it and added the Masora as well.

2. *THE CONSONANTAL TEXT*

The consonantal text which is preserved in the medieval manuscripts and forms the basis of our present editions goes back to about A.D. 100. As part of the great Jewish revival which marked the decades after the catastrophe of A.D. 70, the canonical status of certain disputed books of the Old Testament was defined at the Council of Jamnia (late first century A.D.), and an authoritative text of the Old Testament was also established. Such a text became a necessity once the canon was defined, and Rabbi Akiba (*ca.* A.D. 55-137) popularized an exegetical method which found significance in the smallest details and peculiarities of the text. "Thus there came into existence an authoritative text of the Torah, substantially the consonantal text of our present Masoretic text. This text was established with the aid of early manuscripts that were then available, and in contrast to the widely used popular texts of the period, of which the Samaritan Pentateuch survives as an example, it gives the impression of greater age and value. The remaining books of the Bible followed. We cannot trace all the stages of the work in detail, but the result is quite evident."[6] Manuscripts already in use were at first corrected to conform to the text designated as standard, until finally in the course of time they were replaced by correct copies.

Attempts have been made to trace the standard text to an earlier date. Josephus (*ca.* A.D. 100; cf. *Contra Apionem* 1.42) claimed that despite the length of time since the Old Testament books were first written no one had ever presumed to add to, remove from, or in any way alter the text of the Bible. This has been understood to imply that an official standard text had already been long in existence and was regarded as sacrosanct.[7] B. Albrektson has demonstrated, however, that Josephus was speaking here of the *content* of the Holy Scriptures of the Jews, which was regarded by every Jew from the day of his birth as the commandments (*dogmata*) of God, which he would observe faithfully, and which he would gladly die for if it became necessary. Josephus' words in no way imply the existence of an established text, fixed in its smallest details.[8] Even the exegetical method Rabbi Akiba mentioned above does

---

6. P. Kahle, *Die hebräischen Handschriften aus der Höhle* (1951), pp. 28f.

7. M. H. Segal, "The Promulgation of the Authoritative Text of the Hebrew Bible," *JBL* 72 (1953), pp. 35-47; M. Greenberg, "The Stabilization of the Text of the Hebrew Bible, reviewed in the Light of the Biblical Materials from the Judean Desert," *JAOS* 76 (1956), pp. 157-167. In the third edition of this book the theses of these authors were reviewed so uncritically that Albrektson (cf. next note) received the (unintended) impression of agreement with them.

8. B. Albrektson, "Josefus, Rabbi Akiba och Qumran," *Teologinen Aikakauskirja Teologisk Tidskrift* 73 (1968), pp. 201-215.

not point with any certainty to a standard text of long standing, if indeed it
even suggests it. So we must conclude that the establishment of the text
was not achieved until about A.D. 100 in connection with the definition of
the scriptural canon. Naturally we may assume that this standard text was
not completely a new creation: the Rabbis obviously relied on earlier
traditions. This fact is demonstrated in an interesting way by the manuscripts from Qumran because there are some among them which are quite
close to the Masoretic text. The second Isaiah scroll from Qumran Cave 1
(1QIsa[b]), for example, does not differ essentially from the Masoretic text
any more than do its representatives in the late medieval tradition. This
would seem to justify Roberts's reference to the "likely existence of a
pre-Massoretic 'Massoretic' text."[9] But despite all the superficial
similarities there is one decisive difference: the Qumran text of the
Masoretic type was only one of several types in common use (see below),
and there is no indication that it was regarded as more authoritative than
the others. We may infer that for Qumran, and evidently for the rest of
Judaism as well, there was not yet a single authoritative text. It was not
until the Jewish revival that one of the existing texts, or a recension of one
of these texts, gained a position of authority, eventually displacing almost
completely the other forms of the text which were in use among the Jews
before A.D. 70. The texts from Murabba'at show that by A.D. 132/35 this
text had prevailed (cf. p. 152). We would know nothing about the varieties
of text which circulated in the previous centuries if it were not for the
Samaritan Pentateuch (cf. pp. 42ff.), the Nash Papyrus (p. 33), the Septuagint (pp. 49ff.), and above all the Biblical texts from Qumran. At Qumran three groups of text may be distinguished; these are related to the
Samaritan Pentateuch, the Septuagint, and the Masoretic text
respectively.

How this plurality of text types is related to the history of the text
has not yet been fully explained. Following W. F. Albright, F. M. Cross
has interpreted them (provisionally, he emphasizes) as local Palestinian,
Egyptian, and Babylonian (?) textual forms. S. Talmon has responded
with the objection that the theory of three local texts can hardly explain
satisfactorily the plurality of text types at the end of the pre-Christian
era.[10] For the present F. M. Cross's observation stands: "The ground is
not yet sure, and many missteps will be taken before sure results can be
hoped for."[11] The surviving non-Masoretic texts belong in differing de-

9. B. J. Roberts, *BJRL* 42 (1959), p. 144.

10. *CHB* 1 (1970), p. 198 (=*QHBT*, 1975, p. 40).

11. *ALQ* (1961), p. 188. For further discussion cf. C. Rabin, "The Dead Sea
Scrolls and the History of the Old Testament Text," *JTS* n.s. 6 (1955), pp. 174-182; S.
Talmon, "Aspects of the Textual Transmission of the Bible in the Light of Qumran Manu-
scripts," *Textus* 4 (1964), pp. 95-132 (=*QHBT*, 1975, pp. 226-263); F. M. Cross, "History of the

grees to the popularizing type, distinguished by the following characteristics (to a certain extent a similar relationship obtains between the Chronicler and the books of Samuel and Kings): they tend to use matres lectionis more frequently than does 𝔐, they assimilate words to contemporary spoken forms, e.g., they Aramaize (sometimes using עַל for אֶל), they prefer hiphil forms, they replace the imperative use of the infinite absolute with the simple imperative form, and so on. They also frequently supplement the text with material from parallel passages.

In contrast to the popular texts, the Masoretic text gives the impression of greater age and reliability. Its relationship to the *original form of the text,* however, is quite another matter. This becomes evident from a comparison of texts which have a double transmission (2 Sam. 22 = Ps. 18; 2 Kgs. 18:13–20:19 = Isa. 36–39; 2 Kgs. 24:18–25:30 = Jer. 52; Isa. 2:2-4 = Mic. 4:1-3; Ps. 14 = Ps. 53; Ps. 40:14-18 = Ps. 70), and the books of Samuel and Kings with their related passages in Chronicles.

The conservative principles of those who established and preserved the text may be observed in some of the features which have survived in 𝔐 to the present day.

(a) *Special points* (*puncta extraordinaria*). In fifteen passages there are special points found over particular letters or words: Gen. 16:5; 18:9; 19:33; 33:4; 37:12; Num. 3:39; 9:10; 21:30; 29:15; Deut. 29:28; 2 Sam. 19:20; Isa. 44:9; Ezek. 41:20; 46:22; Ps. 27:13. These points register textual or doctrinal reservations on the part of scribes (*sopherim*) who dared not alter the text because they held it to be sacrosanct.

(b) *Inverted nun* (*nun inversum*). This occurs nine times: before Num. 10:35; after Num. 10:36; and in Ps. 107:21-26, 40. Kahle agrees with Blau in understanding it as an abbreviation of נָקוּד "pointed." The נ is inverted to distinguish it from the letters in the text: the question may be concerned with the position of the particular verses.

(c) *Sebirin.* In numerous instances (Ginsburg notes altogether Seb about 350 in different manuscripts) a marginal note to an unusual word or usage in the text is introduced by סְבִיר (passive participle of Aramaic סְבַר "to suppose") and proceeds to give the usual form or the expected expression, e.g., Gen. 19:8 הָאֵל for הָאֵלֶּה, Gen. 49:13 the meaning עַל for עַד, Gen. 19:23 the masculine יָצָא for the expected feminine יָצְאָה, etc.

(d) *Kethib and Qere.* In many instances the traditional text was K, Q felt to be unsatisfactory on grammatical, esthetic, or doctrinal grounds. The solution was found in providing an alternative reading to that found in

Biblical Text in the Light of the Discoveries in the Judaean Desert," *HTR* 57 (1964), pp. 281-299 (=*QHBT*, 1975, pp. 177-195); *idem*, "The Contribution of the Qumran Discoveries to the Study of the Biblical Text," *IEJ* 16 (1966), pp. 81-95 (=*QHBT*, 1975, pp. 278-292); P. W. Skehan, "The Biblical Scrolls from Qumran and the Text of the Old Testament," *BA* 28 (1965), pp. 87-100 (=*QHBT*, 1975, pp. 264-277).

the text: the distinction was made between the כְּתִיב, the written form which could not be altered, and the קְרֵי, the form to be read, with its consonants written in the margin and its vowel points written with the consonants of the כְּתִיב. But not all the instances of Kethib-Qere, which number more than 1,300, represent corrections of this kind. In many instances they preserve *textual variants* which were regarded as too important to ignore or forget when the official text was established.[12]

Yet the restoration of the early traditional text, reconstructing and preserving it even where it is open to criticism, is only one of the characteristics of this textual recension or tradition. A second characteristic is an opposite tendency. There is clear evidence that no qualms were felt in altering the text when there appeared to be adequate doctrinal reasons. For example, proper names which include the abhorred name of בעל as an element usually retain their original form in the Chronicles while they were altered in the parallel passages of Samuel and Kings.[13] This shows that the second part of the Old Testament, the Prophets, ranked higher in canonical esteem than the Writings, and was subjected to a more thorough revision with doctrinally objectionable elements consistently purged. Jewish tradition preserved the record of these textual alterations in notes known as the *Tiqqune sopherim* and the *Itture sopherim*.

Tiq soph   (a) The *Tiqqune sopherim* (תקוני ספרים "scribal corrections").[14] The tradition of their number is not without ambiguities: a Masoretic tradition indicates eighteen instances, but it is hardly exhaustive. The primary purpose of these corrections was to remove objectionable expressions referring to God. The context of Gen. 18:22 indicates that the original reading was "but YHWH remained standing before Abraham." The idiom "to stand before someone," however, can also mean "to stand in service before someone, to serve" (e.g., Gen. 41:46; 1 Kgs. 1:2), and as

---

12. G. Gerleman has concluded that some of the Qeres represent popular variants, based on his observation that many of the Qeres in Samuel and Kings are found in the text in Chronicles, which preserves a more popular type of text (*Synoptic Studies in the Old Testament,* Lund, 1948). On the Variant Theory cf. further: R. Gordis, *The Biblical Text in the Making: A Study of the Kethib-Qere* (1937); A. Rubinstein, "A Kethib-Qere Problem in the Light of the Isaiah-Scroll," *JSS* 4 (1959), pp. 127-133; H. M. Orlinsky, "The origin of the kethib-qere-system—a new approach," *VTS* 7 (1960), pp. 184-192. Orlinsky suggests that the Jewish scholars of about A.D. 600 who attempted to establish a firm text for vocalization worked with three manuscripts. When these differed, the reading of the majority was automatically accepted for vocalization (Qere), and that of the minority was left unvocalized (Kethib). Yet there are many questions that remain even in Orlinsky's proposal, although there is much in favor of the Variant Theory. Cf. G. E. Weil, "Qere-kethibh," *IDBS* (1976), pp. 716-723.

13. Cf. 1 Chr. 14:7 בעלידע—2 Sam. 5:16 אלידע; 1 Chr. 8:33; 9:39 אשבעל—2 Sam. 2:8ff. איש־בשת; 1 Chr. 8:34; 9:40 מריב בעל—2 Sam. 4:4, etc. מפיבשת. Cf. Gerleman, *op. cit.*, p. 23.

14. D. Barthélemy, "Les tiqquné sopherim et la critique textuelle de l'Ancien Testament," *VTS* 9 (1963), pp. 285-304 (=*EHT*, pp. 91-110); cf. C. McCarthy, "Emendations of the Scribes," *IDBS* (1976), pp. 263f., with bibliography.

this would be inappropriate at Gen. 18:22, it was changed to the present form. The other corrections: Num. 11:15; 12:12; 1 Sam. 3:13; 2 Sam. 16:12 (בעיני for בעוני); 20:1 (לאהליו for לאלהיו, similarly 1 Kgs. 12:16; 2 Chr. 10:16); Jer. 2:11; Ezek. 8:17; Hos. 4:7 (כבודם בקלון אמיר for כבודי בקלון המירו); Hab. 1:12; Zech. 2:12; Mal. 1:13; Ps. 106:20; Job 7:20; 32:3; Lam. 3:20 (for details cf. BH apparatus).

(b) The *Itture sopherim* (עטורי ספרים "scribal omissions"). The Babylonian Talmud (*Ned.* 37b) records that the scribes omitted a ו four times with the word אחר (Gen. 18:5; 24:55; Num. 31:2; Ps. 68:26), and once more with משפטיך (Ps. 36:7). Seven passages are also named where certain words are to be read although they are not in the text (קרי ולא כתיב: 2 Sam. 8:3; 16:23; Jer. 31:38; 50:29; Ruth 2:11; 3:5, 17), and five passages where the words in the text are not to be read (כתיב ולא קרי: 2 Kgs. 5:18; Jer. 32:11; 51:3; Ezek. 48:16; Ruth 3:12). Most of these are noted in the Masora of BH.

We can scarcely err in regarding the evidence of these traditions as merely a small fragment of a far more extensive process (cf. also pp. 108ff.).

The designation of a particular form of the text as authoritative, to be transmitted thenceforth to the practical exclusion of all other forms, marks a critical turning point in the history of the Old Testament text. The existence of various forms of the text alongside each other, as we find in the situation at Qumran, now became as impossible within Judaism as the free treatment of the text which had given rise to that situation. From this time onward the transmission of the text was to be governed by strict regulations. No pains were spared in preventing errors from entering the sacred text, or in discovering and eliminating them if they should creep in. This was the function of the tradition, the Masora, and it is in this sense that R. Akiba says of it: "The Masora is a (protective) fence about the Law."[15] This was the purpose of the scribes' meticulous work. They counted the verses, words, and letters of the Law and other parts of the Scriptures as a procedural aid in preparing manuscripts and in checking their accuracy. One Talmudic passage even derives the name "scribe" from this very practice: "The ancients were called Sopherim because they counted (סופרים) all the letters of the Torah." They found, for example, that the letter ו of גחון in Lev. 11:42 was the middle letter of the Torah, that the word דרש of Lev. 10:16 was its middle word, etc. It is due to these

15. It is not certain, however, whether in Rabbi Akiba's statement (*Pirqe Aboth* 3:13) the word "Masora" refers to the activities of textual transmission, as it is usually understood (cf. e.g., W. Bacher, *Die exegetische Terminologie der jüdischen Traditionsliteratur*, 1 [1899; reprint 1965], p. 108). Strack-Billerbeck, *Kommentar zum NT aus Talmud und Midrasch*, 1 (1922), p. 693, interprets "Masora" here as the Oral Law. R. Akiba would mean that the Tradition of the Fathers (the Oral Law) was intended to prevent the violation of the Written Law.

scribes and their successors that many letters are written in some peculiar way, such as the raised letter of מְנַשֶּׁה Judg. 18:30 (to be read מֹשֶׁה; cf. the marginal note *in loco*), מִיַּעַר Ps. 80:14 (the middle letter of the Psalter), etc. In fact, it is to them that we may trace the beginnings of those textual studies that later found their formulation in the Masora.

Their greatest importance for the history of the text, however, was their contribution to the universal acceptance of an authoritative, established text which must have appeared to be an innovation to many at the time despite its continuity with an earlier form of the text. The Hebrew manuscripts of the medieval period show a remarkably consistent form of the text, even in the forms of certain peculiarly written letters, and other minor details. The most plausible explanation of this was long considered to be Paul de Lagarde's theory first published in 1863, that the Hebrew manuscripts of the medieval period all derived from a single exemplar, an *archetype* made in the second century A.D. E. F. C. Rosenmüller was more accurate in 1797 when he traced the surviving manuscripts of the Hebrew text to a *recension*, but his insight remained ignored even though he repeated it in 1834 in the introduction to the Tauchnitz edition of the Hebrew Old Testament.[16] Yet we have learned today, especially from the material found in the Cairo Geniza, that for centuries there existed texts with variant readings (granting the variants were few); the same inference may be gathered from the Biblical quotations (which differ from the text of 𝔐) in the writings of Jewish scholars as late as the eighth century and beyond. Similarly, the fact that a group of medieval Masoretic manuscripts agrees with the Samaritan text in many details, as Hempel has demonstrated for Deuteronomy,[17] can be explained, in my opinion, by the long-continuing influence of the above-mentioned popular texts in the transmission of the text. We should therefore assume that the consonantal text which was established *ca.* A.D. 100 did not result in the immediate suppression of all other forms of the text, but that manuscripts with variant texts continued to circulate for a long time, especially in private hands. The impressive unity of tenth-century and later manuscripts is due, as Kahle in particular has shown, to the work of the earlier and later Masoretes who championed the established text and assisted it to victory over all the variant forms of the text.

Divisions. BH indicates various divisions of the Old Testament books which were customary among Jews to a certain extent even at an

---

16. The theories of Rosenmüller and Lagarde were long confused with each other; for clarification cf. M. H. Goshen-Gottstein, *Bibl* 48 (1967), pp. 254-273, on the forerunners of Lagarde, pp. 261f. (=*QHBT,* 1975, pp. 53-72 and 60f. respectively).

17. *ZAW* 52 (1934), pp. 254-274; idem, *Der textkritische Wert des Konsonantentextes von Kairener Genizafragmenten in Cambridge und Oxford zum Deuteronomium, NAG, Phil.-Hist. Kl.,* 1959, no. 10, pp. 207-236.

early date,[18] long before the text was divided into chapters. We should note first the division of the entire Old Testament (except the Psalter)[19] into *open* and *closed paragraphs* (Parashah, pl. Parashoth). An open paragraph (פְּתוּחָא) is one that starts a new line after an empty or incomplete line; a closed paragraph (סְתוּמָא) is separated from its preceding paragraph by a short space within the line. Eventually this distinction was ignored in the actual written format, but a prefixed פ (פתוחא) or ס (סתומא) continued ‏ס, פ‏ to indicate the distinction. BH follows this usage.

A second division of the text was into somewhat larger sections of some 452 *Sedarim* (סֶדֶר "order, sequence"). This was of Palestinian origin: it provided a sufficient number of Sedarim (weekly lessons) for the three-year lectionary cycle which was the original Palestinian usage. In Babylonia, where the Torah was read through each year, the division was made into fifty-four (or fifty-three) *Parashoth* (weekly lessons). BH indicates the beginning of a Seder by ס, and the beginning of a Parashah by ‏ס‏ פרש in the margin (BHS: the inner margin). ‏פרש‏

Verse divisions were also already known in the Talmudic period, with differing Babylonian and Palestinian traditions, but they were not numbered by chapters until the sixteenth century. The division into *chapters*, a system derived from Stephen Langton (1150-1228), was adopted in Hebrew manuscripts from the Latin Vulgate in the fourteenth century.

3. *POINTING*

In the matter of vocalization the situation was quite different because there was no written tradition to rely on. This task was engaged by the Masoretes from about the fifth century. It was found inadequate to establish merely the consonantal text and the matres lectionis, the vowel letters which were used to a limited extent to indicate pronunciation, because even with due consideration for the stabilizing influence of oral tradition the possibility still remained open for reading and interpreting many words in more than one way.

There was evidently a need felt at an early stage for aids to reading the sacred text. Before the consonantal text was authoritatively

18. Even in the manuscripts at Qumran a division into Parashoth may already be observed, although it agrees only partly with the Masoretic divisions and occurs with differences in the individual manuscripts (e.g., 1QIsa[a] and 1QIsa[b]); cf. H. Bardtke, *Festschrift Franz Dornseiff* (1953), pp. 33-75; *idem, Die Handschriftenfunde am Toten Meer* 2, pp. 91ff. Maimonides (1135-1204) still complained that manuscripts were inconsistent in observing the open and closed Parashoth. In order to remedy the situation he prepared a kind of model Torah scroll, basing it on the authority of the well-known Cairo Codex, which is probably to be identified with the Aleppo Codex (cf. p. 34). Cf. I. Ben-Zvi, *Textus* 1 (1960), p. 7; M. H. Goshen-Gottstein, *Textus* 5 (1966), pp. 55f.

19. I. Yeivin (*Textus* 7, 1969, pp. 76-102) reports on a list of open and closed paragraphs in the Psalter which he found among the Geniza fragments at the Bodleian Library, Oxford.

established, while it was still possible to treat it with freedom, the proper reading could be indicated by a frequent use of *vowel letters*.[20] A valuable witness for this stage is provided not only by the Samaritan text, but also by the Isaiah scroll (1QIsa^a = 𝔐^a; cf. p. 32), with its abundance of scriptio plena forms. The authoritative text of the second century followed the earlier usage in reducing significantly the use of the scriptio plena, and ended the practice of inserting vowel letters at will. It seems that another solution was then found. Transliterations were prepared for those Jewish believers who needed them, giving the proper pronunciation of the Hebrew text in the Greek alphabet. Christians also made use of this practice: an example is found in the second column of Origen's *Hexapla*, but Jewish sources also seem to refer to the practice. Eventually the Jewish tendency to avoid anything Greek made this solution impossible, and from the fifth century A.D. a system of vowel signs written above and below the consonants was adopted, patterned perhaps after Syriac usage. This system was called *pointing*, from the Jewish technical term (Hebrew נָקֵד). At the first stage vowel signs were inserted occasionally in the Biblical text to indicate the proper pronunciation required by the liturgical usage of the time (Kahle). This situation is reflected in many of the Geniza fragments, and the Samaritans never advanced beyond it. The next stage was to point the entire text fully. Different systems of pointing eventually developed in the east and the west: the Babylonian, the Palestinian, and finally the Tiberian. The following signs were used.[21]

Babylonian	⟝ ā	⟝ } ä	— e	— i	— o	⟝ u
Palestinian	— å	— a	⟝ e / ⟝ æ / ⟝ e	— i	⟝ o	— u
Tiberian	⟝ å	— a	— æ	— e	— i	— o	⟝ ו u

The *Babylonian* system is supralinear. Originally the consonants א, ע, י, and ו were used for the vowels ā, a, i, and u, and in a simplified form they later became the regular vowel signs. This system developed in two stages, an older and simpler stage represented in the fragments of the

---

20. The use of vowel letters is very ancient; the earliest evidence is in Aramaic documents of about the ninth century B.C. (Cross-Freedman, *Early Hebrew Orthography*, AOS 36, 1952), and they are found, although sparingly, in the Siloam inscription (cf. pp. 126f.) and the Lachish ostraca (cf. pp. 128f.).

21. Adapted from P. Kahle in Hans Bauer and Pontus Leander, *Historische grammatik der hebräischen Sprache des Alten Testaments* (1922), p. 102.

seventh century (E),[22] and a later, more complex stage appearing in [E]
fragments from the eighth and ninth centuries (K). The development of a [K]
more complex system may have been related to the appearance of the
Karaites, the sect founded about A.D. 760 by 'Anan ben David. They
rejected the Talmud for a more literal interpretation of the text, giving rise
to a new interest in the text of the Bible and the necessity for determining
its pronunciation as closely as possible. In BHK, pp. xliv-xlvii, Kahle has
compiled a list of the Babylonian fragments known to him, derived from
more than 120 manuscripts.[23] Variants from the manuscripts which Kahle
collected and in part published in *Masoreten des Ostens* (1913) are cited in
BHK as V(ar)^{Ka}. The quantity of known material containing Biblical texts [V(ar)^{Ka}]
with Babylonian pointing (but lacking in any uniformity) has been significantly increased by A. Díez Macho,[24] I. Yeivin,[25] and A. Navarro-Peiro.[26]

The Babylonian tradition was preserved in Yemen into the twelfth
and thirteenth centuries. Under the influence of Tiberian pointing a
characteristic *Yemenite* tradition was later developed reflecting a simplified
Tiberian system with supralinear signs.

The *Palestinian* system, also supralinear, remains imperfect. A
system found in some Samaritan manuscripts from the twelfth to the
fourteenth century is clearly derived from it. Kahle published the relatively few and textually varying Biblical fragments (seventh to ninth
century) in *Masoreten des Westens*, 2 (1930); they are cited in BHK as
V(ar)^{pal}.[27] Their significance lies in showing how the vocalized Hebrew [V(ar)^{pal}]
manuscripts of the Bible first appeared when the Masoretes of Tiberias

22. Manuscripts with this pointing were presumably still available to the editors of
the Complutensian Polyglot (1514-1517); cf. pl. 47 and comments.
23. Cf. also the list in *ZAW* 46 (1928) with seventy magnificent facsimiles. Kahle
concludes from the fragments Eb 4 and Eb 8 (from a single manuscript) that an older system [Eb]
using only dots and related to the system of the Eastern Syrians antedated the Babylonian
system discussed here (*The Cairo Geniza*, 1959², pp. 65f.).
24. *VTS* 4 (1957), pp. 27-46; *idem, Textus* 1 (1960), pp. 132-143.
25. *Textus* 2 (1962), pp. 120-139.
26. *La Biblia Babilónica, Proverbios: Edición crítica según Manuscritos de Pun-
tuación Babilónica, Textos y Estudios "Cardenal Cisneros"* 13, Madrid, 1976. A catalog of
all known (Hebrew and Aramaic) Biblical fragments was published by L. Diez Marino in *La
Biblia Babilónica*, Madrid, 1975.
27. Díez Macho has published some further fragments from the Library of the
Jewish Theological Seminary of America in *Estudios Biblicos* 13 (1954), pp. 247-265. Besides
the Biblical texts there are fragments of Targums, Mishna, Midrash, Masora, and liturgical
texts, thus suggesting that this pointing was widely known in Palestine. For further material
and a sketch of Hebrew grammar in the Palestinian tradition we are indebted to A. Murto-
nen, *Materials for a Non-Masoretic Hebrew Grammar*, Akad. Diss. Helsinki, 1, 1958; 2,
1960; 3, 1962. Further: M. Dietrich, *Neue palästinisch punktierte Bibelfragmente: Veröf-
fentlicht und auf Text und Punktation hin untersucht, Publications de l'Institut de Recherche
et d'Histoire des Textes, Section biblique et massorétique: Massorah, collection éditée par
G. E. Weil, Serie 2, Etudes, Premier Volume* (1968); I. Yeivin, *Textus* 3 (1963), pp. 121-27;
E. J. Revell, *Textus* 7, (1969), pp. 59-75. Cf. also P. Kahle, *Der Hebräische Bibeltext seit Franz
Delitzsch* (1961), pp. 24-31. A list of Biblical manuscripts with Palestinian or related pointing
is given in E. J. Revell, *Biblical Texts with Palestinian Pointing and Their Accents, Masoretic Studies* 4 (1977), pp. 7-34.

began their work. Basically they lack the strict consistency of the Tiberian Masoretes in indicating pronunciation.

Masoretic activity flourished again in the west in the period A.D. 780-930, evidently stimulated by Karaite influence.[28] Tiberias was the center of these studies. The incomplete Palestinian system was inadequate to the demands of this period, nor was it found as adaptable as the Babylonian system. So a new *Tiberian* system was created, based on the experience of the Palestinian system, which combined the accent system with a means of indicating finer nuances, and permitted control of pronunciation and intonation of the Biblical text in its minutest details. This Tiberian system supplanted its two predecessors so thoroughly that their very existence was forgotten for centuries and rediscovered only in the nineteenth and twentieth centuries.

Within the Masoretic center of Tiberias there were several different parties or schools. The Ben Asher family was outstanding among them: its last two members are known today for the model manuscripts Codex Cairensis and the Aleppo Codex (cf. pp. 34f.). But we know that there were other Tiberian Masoretes besides the Ben Ashers; Ben Naphtali is the best known among them. The Jewish scholar Mishael ben 'Uzziel in his famous tractate *Kitab al-Khilaf* (eleventh to twelfth century) discusses the differences *(khillufim)* between the text of Ben Naphtali and that of Aaron ben Moses ben Asher.[29] It was once thought that these two schools were diametrically opposed, because Ben Naphtali's text was identified with manuscripts that have nothing to do with him (see below). But if we read carefully the statement by Mishael, which is our only reliable source for Ben Naphtali's text (ignoring as less significant the occasional marginal notes in some manuscripts), it appears that Ben Asher and Ben Naphtali are quite closely related. They differ only eight times in their consonantal text, and these differences are slight. The majority of their differences are concerned with minutiae of vocalization and accent. Specifically, Ben Naphtali influenced the further development of the text by using the metheg far more frequently. There were occasionally differences also of pronunciation. The prefixes בְ, וְ, and לְ before a יְ were pronounced differently, e.g., בְּיִשְׂרָאֵל by Ben Asher, בִּישְׂרָאֵל by Ben Naphtali. Considering that the differences are limited to such minor details, we must agree with Goshen-Gottstein's judgment that both of

---

28. The Ben Asher family itself apparently belonged to the Karaite community. The arguments demonstrating this relationship have been assembled by N. Wieder, *JQR* 47 (1956/57), pp. 97-113, 269-292, and P. Kahle, *The Cairo Geniza* (1959²), pp. 80-82. I. Ben-Zvi, *Textus* 1 (1960), pp. 1-16, challenges this in a reference to A. Dotan, *Sinai* 41 (1957), pp. 280-312, 350-362 (English tr. *Ben Asher's Creed: A Study of the History of the Controversy,* 1977); cf. also D. S. Loewinger, *Textus* 1, pp. 88-92. In his study of the vocalization of the Qere-Kethib in A (cf. pp. 34f., 162), I. Yeivin also concludes "that the vocalizer of A was most certainly a Karaite" (*Textus* 2, 1962, p. 148).

29. Edited by L. Lipschütz, *Textus* 2 (1962), pp. א-עה; cf. *idem,* "Kitab al-Khilaf, The Book of the Hillufim," *Textus* 4 (1964), pp. 1-29.

these Masoretes represent one and the same school,[30] but that, interestingly enough, Ben Naphtali preserves the text of the older Moses ben Asher more faithfully than does his son Aaron ben Asher (cf. p. 34). This close relationship is also attested by Mishael, who mentions more than four hundred instances where Ben Asher and Ben Naphtali stand in agreement, apparently against other Masoretes.

A tenth-century discussion of the shewa mentions five members of the Ben Asher family and the names of several other Tiberian Masoretes, with an account of their differences over qameṣ and pataḥ, ṣere and seghol, shewa mobile and shewa quiescens.[31] More than this we do not know. Kahle considers it possible that their pointing was "the predecessor of that found in Codex Reuchlinianus and the large number of related manuscripts"[32] which he edited in *Masoreten des Westens* 2 (1930), pp. 45-68, as the Biblical text of Ben Naphtali, but which are regarded today, with all their differences, as representing a system quite different from that of Ben Asher and Ben Naphtali.[33] Thus Codex Reuchlinianus (written in Italy in A.D. 1105)[34] does not distinguish between long and short vowels, writing the qameṣ and pataḥ, the ṣere and seghol indiscriminately;[35] even the daghesh does not have the same function. R. Meyer says of this pointing system that "in many respects it is better and more precise, and occasionally more original than anything we have found to date in the best of the Ben Asher manuscripts. Yet it remains true that the Reuchlinian pointing system is based upon different principles, and that its linguistic approach is quite different from Ben Asher."[36]

30. M. H. Goshen-Gottstein, "The Rise of the Tiberian Bible Text," *Studies and Texts* 1 (1963), p. 112.

31. K. Levy, *Zur Masoretischen Grammatik, Bonner Orientalist. Studien* 15 (1936), p. 8; P. Kahle, *The Cairo Geniza* (1959²), pp. 78f.

32. P. Kahle, *The Cairo Geniza* (1959²), p. 79.

33. This has been rightly pointed out by many, including S. Morag, "The Vocalization of Codex Reuchlinianus: Is the 'Pre-Masoretic' Bible Pre-Masoretic?" *JSS* 4 (1959), pp. 216-237; M. H. Goshen-Gottstein, *op. cit.*, pp. 108ff., with further bibliography; and others.

34. Facsimile edition: A. Sperber, *Codex Reuchlinianus with a General Introduction: Masoretic Hebrew* (Corpus Hebraicorum Medii Aevi, redigendum curavit Rafael Edelmann: Pars 2/1), Copenhagen, 1956.

35. R. Meyer, "Die Bedeutung des Codex Reuchlinianus für die hebräische Sprachgeschichte," *ZDMG* 113 (1963), p. 55.

36. R. Meyer, *op. cit.*, p. 60. For further characteristics of this group of manuscripts, see below, p. 170. M. H. Goshen-Gottstein, *op. cit.*, pp. 113f., calls this text the "Tiberian non-receptus" in contrast to the Ben Asher (and Ben Naphtali) text which he calls the "Tiberian proto-receptus" in order to express the view that this tradition was in its own way just as Masoretic as "our" Tiberian text. I believe that this describes the facts more accurately than any such terms as "pre-Masoretic" (Sperber), "post-Masoretic" (Morag), or "non-Masoretic" (Yeivin). A. Díez Macho prefers to regard these as "proto-Tiberian manuscripts deriving from the Palestinian tradition" (in "A new list of so-called 'ben Naftali' manuscripts, preceded by an inquiry into the true character of these manuscripts," *Hebrew and Semitic Studies,* Driver Festschrift, 1963, pp. 16-52). For further examples of these manuscripts wrongly attributed to Ben Naphtali, see J. Prijs, *ZAW* 69 (1957), pp. 171-184.

The fact that such a text was not only circulated widely in the tenth century,[37] but was still being preserved at the beginning of the twelfth century, shows that the text of Aaron ben Asher, the last member of his family, achieved only through the course of several centuries the status of an authoritative text, supplanting all rival forms of the text. The esteem in which the great Jewish philosopher Maimonides (1135-1204) held it may have contributed to its acceptance as authoritative. This text, influenced by Ben Naphtali only in such matters as the insertion of the metheg which Aaron ben Asher had used sparingly, and other minor details of pointing and accent, became accepted by the fourteenth century as a kind of textus receptus and was used, for example, by Jacob ben Chayyim for his edition (cf. pp. 37f.).

From this historical survey it appears that we may assume a fairly constant consonantal text even from the beginning of the second century A.D., but that the pointing and accents of the present text were first formulated in the course of the ninth and tenth centuries as the culmination of centuries of study, research, and experimentation.

There remains finally a question of the relationship between the Masoretic and the older Hebrew pronunciation. A number of observations have been made questioning the authenticity of the Masoretic pronunciation. More than a millennium separates the Masoretes of Tiberias from the days when Hebrew was a living national language, and it is altogether probable that the pronunciation of Hebrew had undergone some change in this interval, especially because it was written without vowels. In fact, Greek and Latin transliterations of the early Hebrew texts do reflect some differences from the pronunciation of the Tiberian Masoretes, as does also the Samaritan tradition. Within the tradition itself there were variations of pronunciation evidenced by differences among the Masoretes, as in the few texts with Palestinian pointing which do not always agree with ℳ, and also the differences between Ben Asher and Ben Naphtali noted above. It would seem necessary, then, to expect a fair number of artificial forms in the Tiberian system, related to the Masoretes' desire to produce a correct pronunciation which made them susceptible to such outside influences as Syriac and Islamic philology. For example, the almost consistent stress on the ultima derives from the Tiberian Masoretes, as does also the double pronunciation of *BGDKPT* (a Syriac influence). But again, the Tiberian pronunciation agrees with certain forms which were regarded as very late until their antiquity was unexpectedly attested by the free use of vowel letters in the Qumran manuscripts, especially in the first discovered Isaiah scroll (1QIsa[a] = ℚ[a]).

---

37. R. Meyer, *Hebräische Grammatik* 1 (1966³), p. 35, where he calls this school "Pseudo-Ben Naftali."

For example, the Masoretic pronunciation of the second person singular masculine suffix as -^{e}ka is found in the Isaiah scroll, whereas the other pre-Masoretic texts have the pronunciation -ak. In other instances the Isaiah scroll's pronunciation is found among the Samaritans where the Masoretes clearly use later forms, e.g., the second and third person plural masculine pronouns and suffixes are pronounced 'attimma, lakimma, bahimma, '^{a}lehimma, etc., in the Isaiah scroll and the Samaritan, where the Masoretes have 'attem, lakem, bahem, 'alehem, etc. The Tiberian pronunciation therefore must not be regarded as absolutely authoritative. Much may be said rather for the thesis that "the Tiberian system is related historically to the early medieval period, and should never be adduced as direct evidence for Canaanite-Hebrew usage without careful examination. For between them lies that great complex, of such tremendous importance for the history of the language, which is commonly called pre-Masoretic."[38]

Further, the introduction of pointing met with scattered opposition. In the ninth century it was still rejected by the head of a Babylonian school, Gaon Natronai II, on the ground that it did not derive from Sinai. Later its recent origin was disputed. About A.D. 1100 the Karaite Hadassi stated that God did not create the Torah unpointed, a position revived in an adapted form by Johan Buxtorf the Elder (1564-1629). Following the above discussion no further evidence is necessary to show that the pointing does not possess the same authority as the consonantal text. While this is significant for textual criticism, it should also be remembered that when the Masoretes pointed the text they were not attempting to be original, but rather to preserve with accuracy the tradition they had received.

4. THE MASORA[39]

The Masoretic notes which are usually referred to as the Masora in the narrow sense are printed beside the text in BH. Among the Western Masoretes a distinction is drawn between the *marginal Masora* (Masora marginalis) written in the four margins, and the *final Masora* (Masora finalis), an alphabetical arrangement at the end of the Bible. The marginal

---

38. R. Meyer, *TLZ* 75 (1950), col. 726. On the whole problem, cf. especially P. Kahle, *The Cairo Geniza* (1959²), pp. 141-188; Z. Ben-Hayim, "Traditions in the Hebrew Language, with Special Reference to the Dead Sea Scrolls," *Scripta Hierosolymitana* 4 (1958; 1965²), pp. 200-214; Kl. Beyer, *Althebräische Grammatik* (1969), p. 33, characterizes the Tiberian system in the following way: "Reflections of Old Hebrew, all the stages of Aramaic, and false reconstructions as well are found here mingled together inseparably. And yet the Masoretic material continues to be indispensable, because on the strictest examination it still surpasses all else in its wealth of information."

39. G. E. Weil, "La nouvelle édition de la Massorah (BHK IV) et l'histoire de la Massorah," *VTS* 9 (1963), pp. 266-284.

Mp   Masora is divided into the *Masora parva* (Mp) in the side margins, and the
Mm[Mas.M]   *Masora magna* (Mm[Mas.M]) in the upper and lower margins. BHK includes only the Mp reproduced from manuscript L, its textual base. The
first volume of Mm, issued as a supplement to BHS, appeared in 1971.[40]

The *Masora parva* offers observations on the literal form of the
text designed to assist in preserving the form unaltered. Wherever the text
is readily open to transcriptional error there is a note, e.g., when a word
could easily be written plene but is written defective, and vice versa; or
when the multiple occurrence of a word like את in a single verse might
give rise to an omission by oversight. Singular expressions are not simply
recorded as such: it is also noted if a similar form or a parallel construction is to be found elsewhere. Thus enumerations are frequent, giving the
number of times a particular form occurs or identifying hapax legomena.
Thus, for example, it is noted at Gen. 1:1 that בראשית occurs five times,
of which three are at the beginning of a verse, ברא אלהים occurs three
times, and the combination את השמים is found here alone; at Gen. 1:11
that ויהי כן is found six times in the same pericope; at Gen. 1:12 that
ותוצא occurs three times, twice plene and once defective. Occasionally
certain incidental peculiarities are noted, as at Deut. 31:3, that this and
two other verses begin and end with the divine name יהוה. Also noted in
the Mp are the Sebirin, Qeres, etc. Frequently the Masoretic notes may
seem strange, trivial, and of no practical value. But we must remember
that these are the result of a passionate desire to protect the text, guarding it
from willful or careless scribal errors, even in such matters as the use of
the vowel letters ו and י, where the writing of a form plene or defective
is completely fortuitous, involving neither consistency of usage nor
significance for the meaning of the text. The Masora witnesses to an
extremely exact revision of the text which demands our respect even
though it risks the danger of losing the spirit of the text while concen-
trating on the letter.

With regard to the Masora in BHS, these facts should be noted:
although the text of BHS reproduces manuscript L with the greatest
fidelity, the editor of the Masora, G. E. Weil, is much freer with it. The
notes of the Mp in the margin of BHS are still based on the Mp of L, but
its terminology and abbreviations are made consistent in a standardized
form, and its references are filled out where the manuscript itself is
incomplete. In other words, when the Mp of L indicates multiple occurrences of a word or expression in the text, and a corresponding note is
lacking at the parallel passages in L, the editor has supplied corresponding
notes at the parallel passages in BHS. The expansion of the Mp in BHS to
three times as many entries as in BHK, which reproduces only the

---

40. *Massorah Gedolah iuxta Codicem Leningradensem B 19a, elaboravit edidit-
que Gerald E. Weil* 1, *Catalogi*. Rome (Pontificium Institutum Biblicum), 1971.

references found in L, suggests how frequently such supplements were necessary. The larger part of the Mp in BHS, then, was supplied by the editor who filled in the pattern of L where it was incomplete.

Where the Mp gives statistics on the frequency of a word or an expression's occurrence, the *Masora magna* provides specific lists of these instances; in the early manuscripts these lists are in the upper and lower margins, but in BHS they are given in a supplementary volume. Thus at Gen. 1:1 the Mp reads "בְּרֵאשִׁית five times: three times at the beginning and twice in the middle of a verse." The notes in BHS refer to tables 1 and 2 in Weil's edition of the Mm, where the specific instances are spelled out as in a concordance: Gen. 1:1; Jer. 26:1; 27:1; and Jer. 28:1; 48:34. *Massorah Gedolah* 1 contains a total of 4,282 such lists (including the 11 lists added while the volume was at press). For further information cf. BHS, Foreword II, pp. xiii-xviii.

In the *Masora finalis* the Masoretic material is arranged alphabetically. As the base for the final Masora in his famous Rabbinic Bible, Rabbi Jacob ben Chayyim used a medieval collection entitled *Okhla weOkhla* (Okhl [Ochla]). This begins with "an alphabetical list of words which occur twice only in the Holy Scriptures, once without and once with ו at the beginning." The collection derives its name from its first entry, which is אָכְלָה (1 Sam. 1:9) וְאָכְלָה (Gen. 27:19). It was edited by S. Frensdorff from a Paris manuscript in 1864. [Okhl [Ochla]]

The Masoretic material was transmitted orally at first, but as it continued to grow it was progressively entered in the manuscripts themselves.

The language of the Masora is primarily Aramaic, but with some Hebrew as well. Obviously the Masora must be adapted to the particular form of the text for which it is intended. There was accordingly an independent Babylonian Masora[41] which differed from the Palestinian in terminology and to some extent in order. The Masora is concise in style with a profusion of abbreviations, requiring a considerable amount of knowledge for their full understanding. It was quite natural that a later generation of scribes would no longer understand the notes of the Masoretes and consider them unimportant; by the late medieval period they were reduced to mere ornamentation of the manuscripts. It was Jacob ben Chayyim who restored clarity and order to them (cf. pp. 37f.).

Christian D. Ginsburg made a survey of these manuscript materials in an unfinished work of four folio volumes entitled *The Massorah compiled from manuscripts alphabetically and lexically arranged* (1, 1880; 2, 1883; 3, Appendices, 1885; 4/1, Supplement, 1905). [Ginsb(urg Mass)] G

---

41. G. E. Weil, *Textus* 2 (1962), pp. 103-119; 3 (1963), pp. 74-120, 163-170; 6 (1968), pp. 75-105.

5. MANUSCRIPTS

In view of the purpose of this book the present chronological survey includes only those manuscripts, of the large number that exist, which are used in BH or which deserve mention because of their special importance, such as the Nash Papyrus and the Ben Asher Codex of Aleppo.

We may note that Hebrew manuscripts of the Bible from the tenth and eleventh centuries are very rare. The overwhelming majority of manuscripts are from a later period. The most comprehensive collection of Hebrew manuscripts, and the most valuable because of its wealth in early manuscripts, is in the Russian Public Library in Leningrad. Two collections were brought there in 1863 and 1876 by the Russian Karaite Abraham Firkowitsch (1785-1874), who had shown an unparalleled zeal in assembling them, mainly from Karaite synagogues of the east.[42] Firkowitsch was also a notorious forger, frequently adding new colophons or altering the dates in early manuscripts in order to prove the antiquity of Karaite Judaism, which was for him the only true Judaism. Yet the manuscripts which he assembled are of very great importance. The Biblical part alone of the second Firkowitsch collection comprises 1,582 items on parchment and 725 on paper. Another collection in the same library includes about 1,200 fragments, probably derived from the Cairo Geniza, which were assembled by Antonin, a Russian archimandrite in Jerusalem.

The most important phenomenon in the recent history of the Old Testament text is the successive discoveries of manuscripts at ***Qumran*** (𝕼) by the Dead Sea since 1947. These discoveries have put us in possession of manuscript materials several centuries older than any we had known before, and coming from a time and a group for which there was no single form of the text which was regarded and transmitted as exclusively authoritative. These texts presented us for the first time with a large number of variants. After the chance discovery of the first cave in 1947, search parties of archeologists and bedouin between 1952 and 1956 led to the discovery of texts in ten more caves. Especially productive were Cave 4 with fragments of more than 380 manuscripts, and Cave 11 which contained (like Cave 1) relatively undamaged texts. Along with the Qumran texts which may be dated by archeological evidence before A.D. 70,[43] the discoveries at ***Murabba'at*** (Mur) including Biblical texts from the second century A.D. deserve special attention (cf. p. 31, n. 46 for the edition).

𝕼

ˁ

Mur

---

42. The first collection was described by A. Harkavy and H. L. Strack, *Catalog der hebräischen Bibelhandschriften der kaiserlichen Öffentlichen Bibliothek in St. Petersburg* (1875); in this some variants of the individual manuscripts are noted (cited in BHK as Vᶠ). On the criticisms of Firkowitsch mentioned next, cf. now S. Szyszman in *Akten des XXIV. Internationalen Orientalistenkongresses München 1957* (1959), pp. 194-96; on the significant collections of Hebrew manuscripts in the USSR, cf. A. I. Katsh, *ibid.*, pp. 202-205.

[V(ar)ᶠ]

43. The dating of the texts has now been confirmed, primarily by archeological evidence. The jars found in the caves are from the Roman period (cf. p. 136). The age of a piece of linen found in Cave 1 has been determined by its radioactive carbon-14 content to be

Also important are the remains of fourteen scrolls with Biblical texts from the period before A.D. 73, discovered while excavating the rock fortress of *Masada* in the Judean desert in 1963-1965. These agree extensively with the traditional Biblical texts—only in the text of Ezekiel are there a few insignificant variants.[44]

The scrolls found in Cave 1 in 1947 were acquired at the time partly by the Hebrew University of Jerusalem and partly by the Syrian Monastery of St. Mark in Jerusalem. The scrolls belonging to St. Mark's Monastery were taken at the time of the Israel-Arab war to the United States, where they were published with the exception of the Genesis Aprocryphon.[45] These scrolls were acquired for the Hebrew University for $300,000 in 1954, bringing the texts from Cave 1 together again in a single collection.[46] All the other texts are the property of the State of Jordan, and are preserved in the Palestine Archaeological Museum in Jerusalem, where they are being edited by an international team. Their publication will require several more years. The published manuscripts from Caves 2-11 have yielded fresh evidence of the great value of the Qumran texts.[47]

---

between 167 B.C. and A.D. 233. The results of the excavation of Khirbet Qumran since 1952 under the direction of L. Harding and R. de Vaux make it most probable that the manuscripts were hidden during the first Jewish war (A.D. 66-70; cf. now R. de Vaux, *Archaeology and the Dead Sea Scrolls,* Schweich Lectures 1959, rev. ed., 1973). They must all, therefore, have been written before then. This dating is supported by the texts from Wadi Murabba'at, which may be dated with certainty at the time of the revolt of Bar Kochba (A.D. 132-135): "The script is more developed, the Biblical text is definitely that of the Masora, and it must be concluded from this that the documents from Qumran are older, earlier than the second century" (de Vaux, *RB* 60, 1953, p. 267).

44. Y. Yadin, *Masada* (1967²), pp. 168-179, 187.

45. *The Dead Sea Scrolls of St. Mark's Monastery,* edited by M. Burrows with the assistance of J. C. Trever and W. H. Brownlee, published by the American Schools of Oriental Research; 1, *The Isaiah Manuscript and the Habakkuk Commentary* (1950); 2/2, *The Manual of Discipline* (1951).

46. The texts acquired by the Hebrew University in 1947 and edited by Sukenik were published under the title אוצר המגילות הגנוזות שבידי האוניברסיטה העברית (1954); in English: *The Dead Sea Scrolls of the Hebrew University* (1955). It was followed by N. Avigad and Y. Yadin, ed., *A Genesis Apocryphon* (1956).

The Qumran manuscripts in the possession of the State of Jordan are published in the series *Discoveries in the Judaean Desert of Jordan,* edited by the Palestine Archaeological Museum and the Ecole Biblique et Archéologique Française. Volumes already published include: 1, *Qumran Cave I* (1955) (includes the smaller fragments found on reinvestigating Cave 1); 2, *Les Grottes de Murabba'ât,* edited by P. Benoit, J. T. Milik, and R. de Vaux (1961); 3, *Les Petites Grottes 2Q, 3Q, 5Q, 6Q, 7Q, à 10Q. Le rouleau de cuivre.* Edited by M. Maillet, J. T. Milik, and R. de Vaux, with an essay by H. W. Baker (1962); 4, *The Psalms Scroll of Qumran Cave 11,* edited by J. A. Sanders (1965); 5, *Qumran Cave 4 I (4Q158– 4Q186),* edited by J. M. Allegro with the collaboration of A. A. Anderson (1968).

47. We can mention here only a few of the major manuscripts. For the material thus far published, see the valuable annotated survey by J. Hempel, *Die Texte von Qumran in der heutigen Forschung* (1965²), pp. 290-95 (reprinted from *NAG* 1/10 [1961]; cf. also Sellin-Fohrer, *Introduction to the Old Testament* (1968¹⁰), pp. 494-97 (*Einleitung in das Alte Testament,* 1968¹¹, pp. 587f.); J. A. Sanders' lists of published texts in "Palestinian Manuscripts, 1947-1972," *QHBT* (1975), pp. 401-413.

As a result of the discoveries made in 1947, the first place among all Old Testament manuscripts must be given to:

𝔔ᵃ   (a) The *Isaiah manuscript from Cave 1* (1QIsaᵃ = 𝔔ᵃ; pl. 10, 11). For the physical characteristics of the scroll, see p. 8. It is remarkable that two different text types are represented in the scroll, dividing the book into precisely two halves (ch. 1–33, 34–66). In the second half the plene forms and full suffix forms are found far more frequently than in the first half. Either a single scribe was copying from two different exemplars, or there were two scribes with different characteristics working at the same time, as also happened with papyrus scrolls in Egypt. The scroll has a popular type text (cf. pp 16f.) which supports 𝔐 essentially, but which also offers a great number of variants. In a number of instances these coincide with variants found in the early versions or with emendations proposed by modern scholars. Some of the variants may be attributed to an interest in a particular interpretation of the text. The third apparatus of BHK exhibits about 1,375 readings which remain after setting aside approximately 4,500 orthographic variants. A second Isaiah manuscript (1QIsaᵇ
𝔔ᵇ   = 𝔔ᵇ; pl. 12)[48] is fragmentary, but stands much closer to the Masoretic text.

(b) The *Habakkuk Commentary from Cave 1* (1QpHab; pl. 13). This scroll comprises two sheets of leather sewn together, and only the upper (larger) part has been preserved. Sentences of varying length from the first two chapters of Habakkuk are cited and followed by the formula "this means . . ." to introduce an interpretation adapted to the period of the commentary, showing how the present national and religious scene had been foretold by the prophet Habakkuk. A group of variants in Hab. 1–2 is worth serious consideration (cf. the third apparatus of BHK and the apparatus of BHS). The sacred name Yahweh is written in the Old Hebrew script (cf. pp. 5f.).[49]

(c) The *Psalm Scroll from Cave 11* (11QPsᵃ) contains forty-one canonical psalms from the last third of the Psalter and seven apocryphal psalms including one known from the LXX translation (Ps. 151), two from Syriac translations, and one from Sir. 51:13-30. The order of the psalms differs largely from the Masoretic text, with the apocryphal psalms placed among the canonical psalms; in Ps. 145 each verse is followed by the refrain: "Praise be to Yahweh! May his name be praised always and for ever!" The evidence would indicate that this is not a proper Psalter, but a

---

48. Edition 1954: אוצר המגילות הגנוזות; in English, 1955.
49. Cf. the thorough study by K. Elliger, *Studien zum Habakuk-Kommentar vom Toten Meer* (1953).

collection with a liturgical purpose.[50] Also in this scroll the name Yahweh is written in Old Hebrew script.[51]

(d) The *Nash Papyrus* (Pap. Nash; pl. 6).[52] Until 1947 the oldest known witness to the Hebrew Old Testament text was the papyrus sheet acquired in 1902 by W. L. Nash in Egypt and donated to the Cambridge University Library. The Nash Papyrus, as it is called, contains a somewhat damaged copy of the Decalogue, following mostly the text of Exod. 20:2-17, partly Deut. 5:6-21, and also the Shema' from Deut. 6:4f. The sequence of the text shows that it is not derived from a Biblical scroll, but from a liturgical, devotional, or instructional collection. The papyrus was dated in the second or first century A.D. by its first editors. On the grounds of its paleographical traits (which were not undisputed at the time, and have since been confirmed by the Qumran texts), Albright assigned it to the Maccabean period,[53] while Kahle assigned it on internal grounds to the period before the destruction of the Temple.[54] The sixth and seventh commandments appear in reverse order, and the Shema' begins with a phrase found in ⅁ but not in 𝔐.

(e) The *Geniza Fragments* (𝕮). The origin of these has been dis- 𝕮 cussed above (pp. 12f.). The extent of the treasure recovered from the Geniza is amazing. The number of fragments has been estimated at 200,000. Besides Biblical texts in Hebrew and in Aramaic and Arabic translations, there are also Midrash, Mishna, Talmud, liturgical texts, lists, letters, and much else. Of particular importance was the discovery of a nearly complete copy of the Wisdom of Jesus ben Sirach in Hebrew, previously known only in Greek; also a previously unknown writing in Hebrew was found, dating probably from the second or first century B.C., which was called the Zadokite Document, and has enjoyed a revival of interest in recent years because of its relation to the Manual of Discipline[55] discovered in 1947. The Biblical fragments alone from the Geniza, the earliest of which may date from the fifth century A.D., shed new light on the development of Masoretic work prior to the great Masoretes of Tiberias, enabling us to recognize the growth of the pointing system as we have described it above. Geniza fragments are now found in many librar-

50. M. H. Goshen-Gottstein, "The Psalms Scroll (11QPsᵃ); "A Problem of Canon and Text," *Textus* 5 (1966), pp. 22-33.

51. Y. Yadin has published a further fragment in *Textus* 5 (1966), pp. 1-11, to supplement the edition referred to in n. 46 above. Cf. also J. A. Sanders, *The Dead Sea Psalms Scroll* (1967).

52. First published by S. A. Cook in the *Proceedings of the Society of Biblical Archaeology* (1903), pp. 34-56.

53. *JBL* 56 (1937), pp. 145-176.

54. P. Kahle, *Die hebräischen Handschriften aus der Höhle* (1951), pp. 5f. For dating in the second half of the second century B.C., cf. N. Avigad, *Scripta Hierosolymitana* (1958; 1965²), p. 65.

55. Published in 2/2 of the edition mentioned in n. 46 above.

ies, most of them being in the Cambridge University Library and in the Bodleian Library at Oxford.[56]

(f) **Ben Asher Manuscripts.** For five or six generations, from the second half of the eighth century to the mid-tenth century, the Ben Asher family played a leading part in the Masoretic work at Tiberias. In the two surviving manuscripts that go back to the last two members of the family we find a faithful record of their scholarly achievements.

C   *Codex Cairensis* (C; pl. 20). This manuscript, containing the Former and Latter Prophets, was written and pointed by Moses ben Asher in A.D. 895. In one colophon (a note at the end of medieval manuscripts giving information about the scribe and other matters) he mentions the patron who commissioned the manuscript, and in a second colophon he names himself as the scribe. Further colophons record the fortunes of the manuscript. It was presented to the Karaite community in Jerusalem where it was seized as loot by the Crusaders. Later it was restored, coming into the possession of the Karaite community in Cairo, where it remains today. Lipschütz and others have demonstrated in an ingenious way that the codex is closer to the Ben Naphtali tradition than it is to the Ben Asher tradition.[57] This has led many to question its authenticity, e.g., Yalon, Teicher, Löwinger, Lipschütz; but contra cf. M. H. Goshen-Gottstein,[58] who insists that Ben Naphtali preserved the system of Moses ben Asher more faithfully than did his son Aaron (cf. p. 25 above).

The *Aleppo Codex* (pl. 21). This manuscript contains the complete Old Testament and dates from the first half of the tenth century. According to a colophon Aaron ben Moses ben Asher did not himself write the manuscript; he was responsible only for the pointing and the Masora. The pointing was done with special care, and it was regarded as a model codex: it was to be used liturgically only on the Feasts of Passover, Weeks, and Tabernacles, and otherwise used only for consultation by scholars to settle matters of doubt, and not for study. It was originally in Jerusalem, but came later to Cairo and finally to Aleppo. It was not available for use in BHK, as the editors explain on p. xxix. There was a report of its destruction during the anti-Jewish riots of 1947, but fortunately this proved false. It was saved, although with the loss of a quarter of its folios (i.e., Gen. 1–Deut. 28:26 at the beginning and from Cant. 3:12 to the end, including Ecclesiastes, Lamentation, Esther, Daniel, and

---

56. For basic information on the Geniza fragments, see M. H. Goshen-Gottstein, *Textus* 2 (1962), pp. 35-44.

57. L. Lipschütz, *Textus* 4 (1964), p. 6.

58. M. H. Goshen-Gottstein, "The Rise of the Tiberian Bible Text," *Studies and Texts* 1 (1963), p. 107.

Ezra),[59] and is now in Jerusalem. Now that it has been made available for scholarly examination it will be used as the base for a critical edition of the Bible to be published by the Hebrew University, Jerusalem.[60]

Codex Leningradensis (L; pl. 24). In view of the unavailability of L the oldest surviving manuscript of the complete Bible deriving from the last member of the Ben Asher family, the Codex Leningradensis, reproduced in BH, is of special importance as a witness to the Ben Asher text. According to its colophon it was copied in A.D. 1008 from exemplars written by Aaron ben Moses ben Asher. For a refutation of the earlier doubts of this colophon's authenticity, cf. BHK, p. xxix.[61]

(g) The *Petersburg Codex of the Prophets* (P).[62] This manuscript $V^P[V(ar)^P]$ contains Isaiah, Jeremiah, Ezekiel, and the Minor Prophets, with both the small and the large Masora. The codex was discovered by Firkowitsch in 1839, as he claims, in the synagogue of Chufutkaleh in the Crimea. Its significance derives not only from its age (dated A.D. 916), but also from the fact that its discovery finally made it possible to appreciate the nature of the Babylonian pointing system, the knowledge of which had been lost for centuries. Close examination and comparison with manuscripts discovered at the same time or later has shown, however, that while using the eastern signs the codex actually follows the western tradition in its consonantal text and its pointing. Thus it stands as an impressive symbol of the victory of the western tradition over the eastern (cf. pp. 14, 22f.). On several pages (212a, 221a) the Babylonian signs have been replaced by the Tiberian signs, and on folio 1b both systems stand side by side.

(h) The *Erfurt Codices* ([E1, 2, 3]). Three more codices are used in $[Var^{E\,1.2.3}]$

---

59. Subsequently the text of Deut. 4:38–6:3 was found in a photographic reproduction in the book *Travels through Northern Syria* by J. Segall (1910); cf. M. H. Goshen-Gottstein, *Textus* 5 (1966), pp. 53-59. In addition there are photographs of Gen. 26:37–27:30 in W. Wickes, *A Treatise on the Accentuation of the Old Testament* (1887); cf. M. H. Goshen-Gottstein, *Textus* 1 (1960), following p. 16.

60. Cf. the articles by Ben-Zvi, Goshen-Gottstein, Loewinger in *Textus* 1 (1960), pp. 1-111; on the Hebrew University Bible Project, see below, pp. 40f. See also pl. 21 and comments, p. 162.

61. P. Kahle, *Der hebräische Bibeltext seit Franz Delitzsch* (1961), p. 77, mentions that L shows many corrections, and he conjectures that these "represent the results of its collation with other Ben Asher codices." It is the judgment of Goshen-Gottstein, "The Rise of the Tiberian Bible Text," "that the Leningrad Codex was basically not a Ben Asher codex. It was secondarily brought into harmony with a Ben Asher Vorlage by endless erasures and changes" (pp. 101f.); this would require a check with the original. For Goshen-Gottstein the only actually known representative of the (Aaron) Ben Asher text is the Aleppo Codex. If he is correct in this very one-sided theory, it would then necessarily follow, for example, that after the loss of nearly a quarter of the Aleppo Codex we now in fact possess no Ben Asher text for nearly the whole of the Pentateuch. Will Goshen-Gottstein go this far? On his far-reaching hypotheses, cf. B. J. Roberts, *JTS* 15 (1964), pp. 253-264.

62. Published in a facsimile edition by H. L. Strack, *Prophetarum posteriorum Codex Babylonicus Petropolitanus* (1876).

BHK, known from their earlier location as Erfurtensis 1, 2, and 3. They belong to the former Prussian State Library in Berlin (Ms. Orient. 1210/11, 1212, 1213), now the State Library of Prussian Cultural Properties. They were used among others by Joh. Heinrich Michaelis for his edition in 1720 (cf. p. 38). They are noteworthy in that they (especially E3) are more or less related to the type of text earlier mistaken as the Ben Naphtali text (cf. pp. 24f.), though they mark a stage of transition to the later textus receptus.

E1, fourteenth century, contains the Hebrew Old Testament, Targums, and the large and small Masora.

E2, probably thirteenth century, contains the Hebrew Old Testament, Targum Onkelos, and the large and small Masora.

E3 is the most important of these manuscripts in both age and text; it is one of the oldest German manuscripts (Kahle dates it before A.D. 1100).[63] Contents: the Hebrew Old Testament, large and small Masora, and extracts from *Okhla weOkhla* (cf. p. 29). The consonantal text is by two scribes; the pointing is by four different hands, following in part the special tradition mentioned above (p. 25), and in part showing contacts with it.

(i) *Lost codices*. Finally, in some instances there are important codices cited which no longer exist but whose peculiar readings have been preserved. A number of these codices are referred to in BH.

Sev   *Codex Severi* (Sev). A medieval list found in manuscripts in Paris and in Prague enumerates thirty-two variant readings of a Pentateuch manuscript from the Severus synagogue in Rome. This manuscript was reputedly a part of the booty brought to Rome in A.D. 70, and presented by the Emperor Severus (222-235) to a synagogue he had built. If this tradition were correct, the manuscript would have been a scroll and not a codex (cf. pp. 9f.). Cf. BH apparatus at Gen. 18:21; 24:7; and BHK at Num. 4:3.[64]

Hill   *Codex Hillel* (Hill). Traditionally written by Rabbi Hillel ben Moshe ben Hillel about A.D. 600, this codex is said to have been very accurate and used for the revision of other manuscripts. Readings of this manuscript are cited repeatedly by medieval Masoretes and grammarians. Cf. BHK apparatus at Gen. 6:3; 19:6; and BHS also at Exod. 25:19; Lev. 26:9.

The medieval Masoretes also mention among others the following codices as standard, and cite readings from them:

---

63. E3 is probably of Italian origin according to J. Prijs, *ZAW* 69 (1957), pp. 172f.
64. Cf. also M. H. Segal, *JBL* 72 (1953), pp. 45-47, where all thirty-two variants are recorded; also J. P. Siegel, *The Severus Scroll and 1QIs*^{a}, *SBL Masoretic Studies* 2 (1975).

Codex Muga (cited in Ms. 4445, cf. p. 39, n. 73, and in the Petersburg Codex of the Prophets); cf. Lev. 23:13; 26:39. It is not certain whether Muga is the name of a scribe (Ginsburg), or if *muga* ("corrected") indicates a corrected text.

Codex Jericho, cf. BH apparatus at Gen. 31:36; Num. 24:23; and BHK at Num. 5:28.

Codex Jerushalmi, cf. BHK at Gen. 10:19.

Nothing more is known about these codices.

6. *PRINTED EDITIONS*

We can describe here only the most important of the large number of editions which have been printed.

(a) The *Second Rabbinic Bible* of *Jacob ben Chayyim*,[65] published by Daniel Bomberg in Venice, 1524/25, and known as Bombergiana (ℬ), is ℬ outstanding among the earliest printed Bibles in many respects. It was not the earliest,[66] yet it was the most important of its period, and it remained the standard printed text of the Hebrew Old Testament until the twentieth century. It is a Rabbinic Bible, which means that together with the Hebrew text is printed an Aramaic version (Targum) and comments by outstanding rabbis (Rashi, Ibn Ezra, Kimchi, etc.)—an extensive work of 925 leaves in four folio volumes. The special feature of the Bombergiana is that it also includes the large, the small, and the final Masora, which the editor had painstakingly assembled with tremendous labor from a number of manuscripts, mostly faulty and copied without any understanding of the Masoretic material, and that on the basis of this research his text was established. Also the variant readings of manuscripts which Jacob ben Chayyim collated are recorded. This text enjoyed an almost canonical authority up to our own time. Even in 1897 Ginsburg wrote that it represented the only Masoretic recension, and that any modern editor of the Hebrew text must show conclusive evidence for introducing any deviation from it. Kittel also reprinted it in the first two editions of his *Biblia Hebraica.* But by basing his work on late medieval manuscripts or on printed editions which reproduced them, Jacob ben Chayyim himself offers only the late medieval textus receptus. Nor should we expect the methodological standards of a sixteenth-century scholar's edition to meet

65. Jacob ben Chayyim was a Jewish refugee from Tunis who later became a Christian. He died before 1538.

66. Earlier editions included portions (all with Rabbinic commentary and to some extent with Targum), e.g., Psalms, 1477 (Bologna?), Prophets, 1485/86 (Soncino), Writings, 1486/87 (Naples), Pentateuch, 1491 (Lisbon), etc.; and complete Bibles, e.g., Soncino, 1488, Naples, 1491/93, Brescia, 1494. The first Rabbinic Bible was edited by Felix Pratensis and was also published by Daniel Bomberg in 1516/17, a considerable critical achievement which in large measure served as a basis for the second Rabbinic Bible of Jacob ben Chayyim (cf. P. Kahle, *WdO* 1, 1947/52, pp. 32-36). For further details see p. 172.

the requirements we would demand of a modern critical edition today, after several centuries of further scientific development. It is with full justification that from its third edition BH has replaced this text with an older one.

[V(ar)^M]   (b) The edition of *Johann Heinrich Michaelis* ([M]),[67] a Protestant theologian and orientalist at Halle and a prominent Pietist (1668-1738), follows mainly the text of Jablonski's 1699 edition, with an apparatus including the most important readings of the five Erfurt manuscripts (cf. pp. 35f.), and of a number of published editions. Many of these variants are only a matter of accents. Parallel passages are noted in the margin.

V^Ken 9   (c) *Benjamin Kennicott*, 1718-1783 (an Oxford theologian; librar-
[V(ar)^Ken] ian, 1767; and canon, 1770), published a compendious collection of variants still useful today: *Vetus Testamentum Hebraicum cum variis lectionibus*, 2 vol. (Oxford, 1776-1780) (V^Ken). Kennicott published the Masoretic text following the 1705 edition by E. van der Hooght, the Dutch scholar, and the Samaritan text following Walton's London Polyglot of 1753-1757. The copious apparatus notes the variants from the consonantal text in more than six hundred manuscripts and fifty-two editions of the Hebrew text, and in sixteen manuscripts of the Samaritan. Kennicott was able to undertake the massive task of collating all these manuscripts only with the aid of a staff of assistants, not all of whom were competent. Further, the manuscripts collated were comparatively late. The significance of this edition is discussed below.

(d) *J. B. de Rossi* did not publish an edition of the text, but only a collection of variants.[68] It contains a selection of the more important readings of 1,475 manuscripts and editions (p. xlv). The material surveyed is more extensive than that in Kennicott's apparatus, and also more accurately represented. De Rossi notes only variants of the consonantal text.

The actual value of both these editions for the recovery of the original text is very small. Apart from orthographic differences and simple scribal errors (such as haplography, dittography, inversion of consonants), the variants they record are concerned with the use of the plural or singular with collective nouns, the addition or omission of such words as כל or ו, the interchange of prepositions with similar meanings or of words with synonymous expressions (e.g., דבר for אמר), or of singular and plural

---

67. *Biblia Hebraica ex aliquot manuscriptis et compluribus impressis codicibus, item Masora tam edita, quam manuscripta aliisque hebraeorum criticis diligenter recensita etc.* (Halle, 1720).

68. *Variae Lectiones Veteris Testamenti, ex immensa MMS. Editorumq. Codicum Congerie haustae et ad Samar. Textum, ad vetustiss. versiones, ad accuratiores sacrae criticae fontes ac leges examinatae opera ac studio Johannis Bern. de Rossi*, 4 volumes (Parma, 1784/88). De Rossi issued a supplement in 1798: *Scholia critica in V. T. libros seu supplementa ad varias sacri textus lectiones.*

forms (e.g., דבריך and דברך). This certainly demonstrates the lack of any absolute uniformity in the transmission of the text, such as is assumed by the theory of a single archetype. But what is lacking is variants of any real significance for the meaning of the text, such as are found in New Testament manuscripts. These collections of variants provide scarcely any help in dealing with corrupt passages. The manuscripts they are based on have been so standardized in the Masoretic tradition that no startling results can be achieved by studying them. After our observations in discussing the history of the Masoretic text we can well understand these disappointing conclusions which in due course led to a decline in Masoretic studies.[69] The nineteenth and twentieth centuries have produced no comparable collections.

(e) *S. Baer* ([B]) collaborated with Franz Delitzsch from 1869 in   [V(ar)[B]] an attempt to produce the Masoretic text of the Old Testament (except for Exodus–Deuteronomy) in as exact a form as possible, basing their work on early editions and manuscripts.[70] "These editions contain much valuable material, but the arbitrary and unsystematic way Baer treated the Masora led him to reconstruct a text which never actually existed, so that his editions must be used with caution."[71]

(f) *Christian D. Ginsburg* ([G]) prepared an edition for the British   [V(ar)[G]] and Foreign Bible Society (1908ff.).[72] A new edition appeared in 1926. Ginsburg prints "substantially" the text of Jacob ben Chayyim's 1524/25 edition which he valued so highly, including in an apparatus the variant readings of more than seventy manuscripts and of nineteen editions published before 1524. These variants relate to orthography, vowel points, accents, and divisions of the text. The manuscripts he collated, mostly from the British Museum, are mainly from the thirteenth century and later.[73] Although this edition has a certain importance as a collection of Masoretic material, its value is lessened by the unevenness of the mate-

69. Cf. the opinion of E. F. C. Rosenmüller in discussing Kennicott's collection: "This whole congeries of variants, assembled at such an expense of time and money, leads only to one simple conclusion: that all the extant codices are very late in relation to the original . . . that they contain a wealth of scribal errors but a dearth of significant and useful readings, and that correspondingly little if any help may be anticipated from them for the corrupted passages in the Hebrew text" (*Handbuch der Literatur der biblischen Kritik und Exegese* 1, 1797, p. 247; cited in E. Preuschen, *ZAW* 9, 1889, p. 303).

70. *Textum Masoreticum accuratissime expressit e fontibus Masorae codicumque varie illustravit.*

71. P. Kahle in Bauer-Leander, *Historische Grammatik der hebräischen Sprache* (1922), p. 90; *idem, Der hebräische Bibeltext seit Franz Delitzsch, Delitzsch-Vorlesungen 1958* (1961), pp. 11-16.

72. *The Old Testament, diligently revised according to the Massorah and the early editions with the various readings from MSS and the ancient versions.*

73. But they also include the Pentateuch manuscript in the British Museum, Ms. Or. 4445, which Ginsburg dated about A.D. 820-850. This manuscript has no scribal colophon, as it has lost both its beginning and end. The way in which Ben Asher is cited suggests that it was written during his lifetime (pl. 22).

rial, which was gathered almost haphazardly, and the absence of any attempt to weigh or to group it. By far the majority of the variants are trivial, and do not affect the sense or the interpretation of the text. Variants in the early versions are very rarely noticed. The accuracy of the collations has also received occasional criticism, but this is due to the enormous size of the task Ginsburg undertook, which necessitated his reliance on a great number of assistants.[74]

(g) The British and Foreign Bible Society published a new edition in 1958, prepared by *Norman H. Snaith* (כתובים, נביאים, תורה). It is based primarily on British Museum Ms. Or. 2626-2628, which was written in Lisbon in 1482. Other manuscripts used include British Museum Ms. Or. 2375 (a Yemenite manuscript written in 1468-1480), and the Shem Tob Bible (a Spanish manuscript dated A.D. 1312) which was earlier in the library of David Sassoon. These manuscripts represent the Ben Asher tradition, making the text closely related to the third edition of BHK.[75] Following the practice of the Bible Society, the edition is without introduction and apparatus, although a list of the Haphtaroth (cf. p. 156 below) for the liturgical year is appended.[76]

(h) The *Hebrew University in Jerusalem* is preparing an edition of the Old Testament (The Hebrew University Bible Project), a *Sample Edition* of which was published in 1965 containing Isa. 2, 5, 11, and 51, and an extensive introduction, followed in 1975 by two fascicles containing Isa. 1:1–20:10.[77] This text is an exact reproduction of the Aleppo Codex (cf. pp. 34f.), including its large and small Masora. The special importance of this edition for scholarship lies not only in its making the text of this codex available for the first time, but also in the comprehensiveness of its four critical apparatus which reflect the history of the Old Testament text: the first gives the variants of the early versions; the second gives those of the scrolls from the Judean desert and the rabbinic literature; the third, the medieval manuscripts; and the fourth apparatus records peculiarities of script, pointing, and accents (of the Leningrad, Cairo, and other manuscripts). When this edition has been completed it will provide a more comprehensive basis for the study of the Old Testa-

---

74. On the Jerusalem edition of 1953: *Torah, Prophets and Scriptures, Jerusalem Edition. Corrected on the basis of the Masora of Ben Asher by Moshe David Cassuto;* cf. the critical review by P. Kahle, *VT* 3 (1953), pp. 416-420, and the response by L. Simon, *VT* 4 (1954), pp. 109f.

75. Cf. N. H. Snaith, *VT* 7 (1957), pp. 207f.; *idem, Textus* 2 (1962), pp. 8-13.

76. On the defects of this edition, cf. M. B. Cohen and D. B. Friedman, "The Snaith Bible: a critical examination of the Hebrew Bible published in 1958 by the British and Foreign Bible Society," *HUCA* 45 (1974), pp. 97-132.

77. M. H. Goshen-Gottstein, *The Book of Isaiah, Sample Edition with Introduction* (The Hebrew University Bible Project), Jerusalem, 1965; *idem, The Hebrew University Bible: The Book of Isaiah,* Pt. 1, 2, Jerusalem, 1975.

ment and its history than has ever before been available; its first two apparatus in particular promise a wealth of information, especially for rabbinic literature, which has always been very difficult of access. The achievement of this undertaking will doubtless require a very long time.

(i) Variants are also cited from the following:

[V(ar)^J] = Varia lectio codicis Jemenensis (a Yemenite manuscript [V(ar)^J] variant)[78] following R. Hoerning, *Description and Collation of Six Karaite Manuscripts of portions of the Hebrew Bible in Arabic Characters* (1889). These Karaite manuscripts are of the tenth and eleventh centuries with the Hebrew text transliterated into the Arabic script.

[V(ar)^O] = Varia lectio secundum Odonem (a variant cited by [V(ar)^O] Odo). In a Latin work by the medieval scholastic Odo, who is still unidentified, there are found seventy-eight quotations from the Hebrew Bible, four of which are pointed. This work, which is concerned with the conversion of the Jews, was compiled in the mid-twelfth century; the surviving copy (Trinity College, Cambridge) was written in the late twelfth or early thirteenth century. The Hebrew quotations, which together about equal in length the prophecies of Joel, are interesting for their deviations from the consonants of the Masoretic text, and also for their pointing, which is simpler than the Tiberian. Can these actually be examples of "early Masoretic or even non-Masoretic texts" as suggested by J. Fischer, their first editor?[79]

V(ar)^S = Varia lectio secundum Strack, a variant cited in Strack, V^S[V(ar)^S] *Grammatik des Biblisch-Aramäischen* (1921⁶). The readings of many unpublished manuscripts are included among the selections of Biblical Aramaic texts appended to the grammar.

[V(ar)^W] = Varia lectio secundum Wickes, a variant cited in [V(ar)^W] W. Wickes, *A Treatise on the Accentuation of the Three Poetical Books of the Old Testament* (1881), or *A Treatise on the Accentuation of the Twenty-one Prose Books of the Old Testament* (1887). This is a study of accent systems based on an extensive study of manuscripts.

---

78. Yemen, an area in southwest Arabia, had a considerable Jewish population. There are many Yemenite manuscripts in libraries in the United States and in Jerusalem. For information on these manuscripts, see Goshen-Gottstein, *Textus* 2 (1962), pp. 46-50; *idem, The Book of Isaiah*, Pt. 1-2, Isa. 1:1–22:10 (1975).
79. Cf. J. Fischer, *Bibl* 15 (1934), pp. 50-93; 25 (1944), pp. 167-195; *idem, BZAW* 66 (1936), pp. 198-206; but otherwise C. Peters, *Le Muséon* 51 (1938), pp. 137-149; R. J. Loewe, "Medieval Christian Hebraists of England," *Transactions of the Jewish Historical Society of England* 17 (1953), pp. 245f.

III
THE SAMARITAN PENTATEUCH (ய)

THE SEPARATION OF THE SAMARITANS FROM THE JEWS
was an important event in the history of post-exilic Judaism. We do not
know precisely when it was that the Samaritan community made the final
break from Jerusalem. According to an earlier view it occurred in the
course of the fourth century B.C. as the culmination of a long process.
But more recent research based on recent archeological studies and the
Qumran texts makes it probable that the separation did not occur until the
Hasmonean period, when Shechem was destroyed and the sanctuary on
Mount Gerizim was ravaged by John Hyrcanus.[1] The Samaritans took the
Pentateuch with them when they went into schism: thus we have the
Pentateuch in a second Hebrew recension, the Samaritan. As we re-
marked above (p. 6), the Samaritan Pentateuch was written in a special
script derived from an archaizing form of the Old Hebrew script of the
Hasmonean period (pl. 27).

When the Samaritan Pentateuch (cited as ய in BH) first became
known to the West through the discovery of a manuscript in Damascus in
1616, it aroused the most sanguine expectations. Some believed that it
brought them substantially closer to the original text of the Pentateuch.
Later its prestige waned, and as a result of Gesenius's verdict in 1815 it was
long regarded by many as practically worthless for the purposes of textual
criticism. Gesenius did not judge ய to be an independent witness to the
text, but rather a revision of ﬡﬠ, adapted in both its language and matter to
the views of the Samaritans. This inadequate appreciation was protested
in the nineteenth century by A. Geiger, and in the twentieth by P. Kahle.[2]

The problem of the Samaritan Pentateuch is that it differs from ﬡﬠ

---

1. J. D. Purvis, *The Samaritan Pentateuch and the Origin of the Samaritan Sect*,
Harvard Semitic Monographs 2 (1968); also H. G. Kippenberg, *Garizim und Synagogue*
(1971), and R. J. Coggins, *Samaritans and Jews* (1975).
2. *Theol. Studien und Kritiken* 88 (1915), pp. 399-439 (*Opera Minora*, 1956,
pp. 3-37).

in some six thousand instances. While it is true that a great number of these variants are merely orthographic (especially in its more frequent use of the plene forms), and many others are trivial and do not affect the meaning of the text, yet it is significant that in about 1,900 instances ᛉ agrees with ᛤ against ᛦ.[3] Some of the variants in ᛉ must be regarded as alterations introduced by the Samaritans in the interest of their own cult. This is true especially of the command inserted after Exod. 20:17 to build a sanctuary on Mount Gerizim, of Deut. 11:30 where שכם מול is added to מרה (מוֹאראַ), and of nineteen passages in Deuteronomy where the choice of the holy place is set in the past and the reference to Shechem is made clear (in the formula הַמָּקוֹם אֲשֶׁר יִבְחַר יְהוָה ᛉ reads בָּחַר for יִבְחַר).[4] But such obviously tendentious readings do not justify regarding all the other variants as intentional alterations, especially where ᛉ agrees with ᛤ.

The peculiar textual form of the Samaritan Pentateuch is far more probably explained as a popularizing revision of an original text which is naturally not to be identified with ᛦ (Kahle). Archaic forms were modernized, difficult sentence structures were simplified, and other adaptations were made to the style of popular texts (cf. pp. 16f.).[5] Such popularizations were useful only as long as it was necessary to make the Hebrew text as intelligible to the people as possible. They became unnecessary as soon as the next step was taken—the Hebrew text was translated into the popular language itself, Aramaic. This implies for ᛉ a very early date and makes it impossible to regard it as dependent on ᛦ. Instead, it is a very important witness to a form of the text that once enjoyed widespread use as shown by its agreements with the Qumran texts (cf. p. 16), the Septuagint, the New Testament, and some Jewish texts that escaped revision by official Judaism. These last provide a striking example in the chronologies of Gen. 5 and 11, where ᛉ is independent of both ᛦ and ᛤ. For the survival of the primitive text represented by ᛉ in medieval Masoretic manuscripts, see above (p. 20).

The Samaritans have preserved a pronunciation of the Hebrew text which is independent of the Tiberian Masoretic tradition and goes back to a very old tradition. Comparison with the Dead Sea Scrolls convinced Kahle that at times it reflects a pre-Christian usage, while a number of Samaritan manuscripts with vowel points prove that this pronunciation has not changed essentially in the last six hundred years. BHS

3. The New Testament agrees with ᛉ in some passages against ᛦ, as in Acts 7:4 and 7:32, and possibly also Heb. 9:3f. Presumably the New Testament depends upon a Greek Pentateuch which was similar to ᛉ at these points.

4. It would seem probable, on the other hand, that in Deut. 27:4 (ᛦ Ebal, ᛉ Gerizim) it was the Jewish text that was later altered. A final decision, however, is not possible; cf. the commentaries *ad loc.*

5. S. Talmon, "The Samaritan Pentateuch," *JJS* 2 (1951), pp. 144-150.

cites this Samaritan pronunciation in several chapters of Genesis with the
Samar siglum Samar.[6]
Manuscripts earlier than the thirteenth century are very rare. The
oldest known manuscript in codex format is in the Cambridge University
Library. "It contains a notice that it was sold A.H. 544 (A.D. 1149/50),
and it may have been written a long time before that. It certainly gives the
impression of being considerably older than the Samaritan Pentateuch
manuscripts written since A.D. 1200, of which we know a good many."[7]
The sacred scroll of the Samaritan community at Nablus (Shechem) is
quite famous: it is called the Abisha Scroll after its scribe. Actually it is a
compilation of many fragments. The older and more original part of the
Abisha Scroll comprises the main part of Num. 35–Deut. 34, and is
dated by its editor Pérez Castro in the eleventh century.[8]
The Samaritan Pentateuch was first printed in the Paris and London Polyglots (ɯ^W). A critical edition was edited by A. von Gall, *Der
hebräische Pentateuch der Samaritaner*, 1914-1918 (reprinted in Berlin,
1963): it offers an eclectic text based on late medieval manuscripts. A new
edition is being prepared by P. Castro.
For a Greek translation of the Samaritan Pentateuch, see p. 74;
for the Samaritan Targum, see pp. 79f.[9]

6. P. Kahle, *The Cairo Geniza* (1959²), Appendix II, pp. 318-335, cf. pp. 153-57;
idem, "Zur Aussprache des Hebräischen bei den Samaritanern," *Festschrift A. Bertholet*
(1950), pp. 281-286 (= *Opera Minora*, 1956, pp. 180-185).
7. P. Kahle, *The Cairo Geniza* (1959²), p. 67.
8. P. Kahle, *Studia Orientalia Ioanni Pedersen dicata* (1953), pp. 188-192. Edition: P. Castro, *Séfer Abiša'* (Madrid, 1959) (reviewed by E. Robertson, *VT* 12, 1962,
pp. 228-235). Cf. also P. Castro, *VTS* 7 (1960), pp. 52-60. A transcription of the Abisha Scroll
in Samaritan script, *Samaritan version of the Pentateuch, copied by hand* (Tel Aviv, 1959),
was published by Abraham Sadaka; a transcription in Hebrew square script by Abraham and
Ratson Sadaka, *Jewish Version, Samaritan Version of the Pentateuch, with particular stress
on the differences between both texts* (Tel Aviv and Holon, 1961-65), has the lacunae of the
Abisha Scroll supplied from the Abu al-Barakat Scroll, and shows the text of 𝔐 in a parallel
column with the differences distinguished typographically.
9. A comprehensive *Grammatik des samaritanischen Hebräisch* has been produced by R. Macuch, *Studia Samaritana* 1 (1969).

B
THE PRIMARY VERSIONS

IV

PRELIMINARY CONSIDERATIONS ON THE VERSIONS

THE HEBREW TEXT WHICH WE HAVE TODAY HAS BEEN altered from its original form by many circumstances, and undoubtedly contains many corruptions. Consequently the versions which enable us to reconstruct an older Old Testament text and to correct errors are very important. But we should also recognize that each of the versions comes with its own peculiar range of problems. For a long period the versions were approached rather naively and used directly for textual criticism on the uncritical assumption that the base from which they were translated could be readily determined. But the matter is not that simple. Anyone who translates also interprets: the translation is not simply a rendering of the underlying text but also an expression of the translator's understanding of it. And every translator is a child of his own time and of his own culture. Consequently every translation must be understood and appreciated as an intellectual achievement in its own right. This is especially true of the versions of the Bible which were produced to meet the pratical needs of a community.

Most versions of the Bible have been the work of anonymous translators (usually of many translators) who have given concrete expression in their work to the intellectual assumptions of their age and their culture, the religious and other opinions which they adhere to or respect, the prejudices and concerns which they adopt consciously or unconsciously, their education, their ability to express themselves, the conceptual range of the language they are translating into, and many other factors. We must therefore distinguish between what comes from the original text and what is added by the translator—a formidable task to accomplish before we can use the versions for purposes of textual criticism.

The history of most of the versions is beset by many problems which are yet unsolved and are perhaps insoluble, especially for their early period. In his discussion of the Syriac Peshitta, F. Rosenthal has wisely observed that of all the problems of literary criticism that of the Biblical versions is encumbered with such a variety of diverse matters that any hope for a scientifically conclusive solution is very slight. In almost every instance we find ourselves dealing basically not only with an unknown series of intermediate stages in the evolution of a translation, which stages have been lost to us and which we can never hope to trace with more than a bare degree of probability, but also with a wealth of oral tradition which could very well have developed for similar reasons along similar lines.[1]

The problems we have considered make for the fascination of versional studies and provide the incentive for further research, but they also show how far we are from any final solutions.

We will consider first the primary versions, which have a prior claim in textual criticism because they are based directly on the original language, and then the remaining versions, most of which are based on the Septuagint. Jerome's version, the Latin Vulgate, claims to have been translated from the Hebrew text, but as it is strongly influenced by the Greek versions and by the Old Latin versions which preceded it, we will consider it in the third section.

---

1. F. Rosenthal, *Die aramaistische Forschung* (1939), p. 206.

V

THE SEPTUAGINT (𝕾)

1. *INTRODUCTION*

IN ACCORDANCE WITH THE PURPOSE OF THIS BOOK 𝕾 IS considered here as a witness to the Old Testament text, but its great significance for the history of western thought deserves at least a brief mention. It was in 𝕾 that the Greek world first met the Old Testament revelation. "The most common attitude among Greeks who came into contact with the Old Testament was that this book and the cosmos are mutually related and must be understood together. Whatever they might think about the book, it appeared to be certain that it was a creation parallel to the world itself, equally great and comprehensive, and that both are the work of the same Creator. What other book in history has ever received a comparable verdict among thinking men?"[1]

For the early church 𝕾 was simply the standard form of the Old Testament. Augustine demanded that Jerome use this canonical form of the text and not the Hebrew original as the basis for his translation. It could well be said that the influence of the Old Testament upon the Christian world through the centuries, almost up to the present day, has been mediated linguistically and conceptually by the hellenistic forms it received in 𝕾. We must acknowledge with V. Ehrenberg that 𝕾 is a book of such critical significance that apart from it both Christendom and the western culture would be inconceivable.

2. *THE LETTER OF ARISTEAS*

We seem at first glance to be particularly well informed on the origins of

---

1. A. von Harnack, *Sitzungsberichte der Berliner Akademie* (1902), p. 509. A bibliography of the extensive literature has been compiled in Brock-Fritsch-Jellicoe, *A Classified Bibliography of the Septuagint, Arbeiten zur Literatur und Geschichte des hellenistischen Judentums*, 6 (1973).

Ⴒ, since we have in the Letter of Aristeas[2] an account which purports to have been compiled by one who was himself a participant in its preparation. It tells of how one day Demetrius of Phaleron, who is erroneously introduced as director of the famous library of Alexandria, reported to his royal master Ptolemy II Philadelphus (285-247 B.C.) that the Jewish Law (the Letter of Aristeas is concerned solely with the Pentateuch!) was worthy of a place in the royal library, but that it must first be translated into Greek. The king acted on this suggestion immediately. Envoys, with Aristeas among them, were sent to Eleazar the High Priest in Jerusalem with the request that he provide competent men for the work of translating. Eleazar responded by sending seventy-two men to Alexandria, six men from each of the twelve tribes, along with valuable Torah scrolls. After an impressive formal reception they provided the king with examples of Jewish wisdom in a series of profound sayings. Then they were taken to the island of Pharos, which is connected with Alexandria by a causeway, and there in quietness and seclusion they translated the Law in seventy-two days, with Demetrius writing down the text as they agreed on it. The completed translation was read first to the Jewish community (in Alexandria) who pronounced it beautiful, pious, and accurate. It was to be regarded as holy, with curses pronounced on anyone who would add anything to it, delete anything from it, or alter it in any way. Only after receiving the approval of the community did the translation come before the king who had commissioned its production. He marvelled at the spirit of the Lawgiver, and sent the translators back to their homes laden with valuable gifts.

This is the account in the Letter of Aristeas which was accepted and given further development by others, both Jews and Christians. Josephus (A.D. 37/38–*ca.* 100) preserves it with almost literal fidelity. *Philo* (*ca.* 25 B.C.–A.D. 40) makes the translation an act of divine inspiration, and the translators prophets: although they worked separately they produced a single text that was literally identical throughout. The Church Fathers followed Philo, extending the account from the Law, as in the Letter of Aristeas, to the *whole* of the Old Testament. Pseudo-Justin[3] in the third century even claims to have seen the remains of the cells where the translators did their work in strict isolation. This is obviously a pious legend which witnesses to the high esteem enjoyed by Ⴒ in the Christian church.

2. Text: *Aristeae Epistula*, ed. P. Wendland (1900); H. S. J. Thackeray in H. B. Swete, *Introduction to the Old Testament in Greek* (1914²). Translation: P. Wendland in E. Kautzsch, *Apokryphen und Pseudepigraphen des Alten Testaments* (1900); P. Riessler, *Altjüdisches Schrifttum ausserhalb der Bibel* (1928).

3. *Cohortatio ad gentiles XIII;* edited by J. K. T. von Otto, *Justini Opera* 3 (1879). Cf. the statements of Philo and the Church Fathers now in R. Hanhart, *VT* 12 (1962), pp. 146-49.

But even what the Letter of Aristeas itself relates is incredible in many respects. It was not written by a heathen courtier as it professes, but by a Jew who praises the wisdom and the Law of his people through the lips of a heathen king. The writer did not live in the days of Ptolemy Philadelphus, but more than a century later. Further, the Jewish Law was not translated to satisfy the curiosity of a royal patron of the arts, but because the Egyptian Jews no longer understood Hebrew and were in need of just such a translation. And finally, the translators were not Palestinian Jews, but members of the Alexandrian diaspora for whom Greek was the language of daily life.

The legendary character of the Letter of Aristeas has long been recognized.[4] And yet until quite recently it has influenced our view of $\mathfrak{G}$ in one important respect, namely in the assumption that $\mathfrak{G}$ represents a single version (of the *whole* Old Testament!), characterized by a clearly-established and authorized text from the first, and that for a long period it was the only Greek translation used by the Jews. We shall see this view has been seriously disputed in recent discussion.

3. THE ORIGIN AND HISTORY OF THE SEPTUAGINT TO THE SECOND CENTURY A.D.

We noticed that the Letter of Aristeas places the origin of the Pentateuch version in the first half of the third century B.C. In this it may very well be correct. It is also reliable in associating the version with the Jewish community in Alexandria, which was the most important in the Jewish diaspora. A Greek translation was needed there much as an Aramaic translation was needed in Palestine, and perhaps as with the Targums its beginnings may have been in the oral translations made for worship services. It is natural that the first part to be translated would be the most important part of the Old Testament for Jews, the Torah, and that the other books would follow in due course. The prologue to the Wisdom of Jesus ben Sirach (Ecclesiasticus) (*ca.* 116 B.C.) refers to a Greek version of the Law and also of "the Prophets and the other books." A long period must be allowed for the translation of the entire Old Testament. This

---

4. According to B. H. Stricker's interpretation of the Letter of Aristeas (*De brief van Aristeas: De hellenistische codificaties der praehelleense godsdiensten,* Amsterdam, 1956), the translation of the Pentateuch was ordered by Ptolemy Philadelphus in connection with his policy of hellenizing the Jews; but contra, cf. R. Hanhart, *VT* 12 (1962), pp. 141-43. L. Rost ("Vermutungen über den Anlass zur griechischen Uebersetzung der Tora," in *Wort-Gebot-Glaube, Eichrodt-Festschrift,* 1970, pp. 39-44) evaluates the data in the Letter of Aristeas in a more positive way: the translation of the Torah would provide a text guaranteed in its authenticity as an official version, authorized by the highest religious and political authority in Judaism, the High Priest in Jerusalem. This would have been a necessity for political reasons if it were to secure special rights for Jews in hellenistic cities in the future, and to protect these privileges.

precludes the possibility that it was the work of a single translator or group of translators. A close examination of the version's character yields the same conclusion. The translations of the individual books are not at all uniform, and the differences which occur even within single books have led Thackeray, as well as Herrmann and Baumgärtel, to suspect that Isaiah, Jeremiah, and the Minor Prophets were divided between two translators, while Ezekiel was the work of three.[5] Many books are translated almost literally, while others such as Job and Daniel are quite free. And yet, when the Greek Jeremiah lacks some 2,700 words that are found in the Hebrew, and the order of the text differs somewhat as well, it is evident that the difference is due not simply to the translator, but to his Hebrew exemplar, which must have differed from the Masoretic text we have today. In the texts from Qumran we find not only the longer text represented, but in a fragmentary Hebrew manuscript (4QJer[b]) we have the shorter text found hitherto only in Greek.[6]

We may say in summary that what we find in 𝔊 is not a single version but a collection of versions made by various writers who differed greatly in their methods, their knowledge of Hebrew, and in other ways. This diversity which makes it necessary to consider each book of the Bible individually is a large part of the problem posed by 𝔊, making it impossible to formulate the value of the version as a whole for textual criticism in any uniform way.

𝔊 made it possible for Jews living in the Greek diaspora to read their Holy Scriptures in their own familiar language. But it also provided an opportunity for non-Jews to study the Old Testament (cf. Acts 8:26f.). This was very important for the early church, because it gave wide currency to ideas with which the Christian message could be related. Furthermore, 𝔊 became *the* holy book of the Christians of the early centuries. This placed the Jewish community in a peculiar situation with regard to the version it had produced and held in honor. In disputes between Jews and Christians the Christians would often appeal to 𝔊, as in the discussion of Isa. 7:14. The Jews claimed that this passage refers to a young woman (νεᾶνις), not to a virgin (παρθένος). The Christians could

---

5. H. S. J. Thackeray, *The Septuagint and Jewish Worship* (1921); J. Herrmann and F. Baumgärtel, *Beiträge zur Entstehungsgeschichte der Septuaginta, BWAT* n.s. 5 (1923). While this thesis may hold for Jeremiah and Ezekiel, it has been contested for the other books; cf. J. Ziegler, *Die Einheit der Septuaginta zum Zwölfprophetenbuch. Vorlesungsverzeichnis Braunsberg* (1934); E. Tov, *The Septuagint Translation of Jeremiah and Baruch: a Discussion of an Early Revision of the LXX of Jeremiah 29–52 and Baruch 1:1–3:8, Harvard Semitic Monographs* 8 (1976). Tov explains the differences between Jer. 1–28 and 29–52 by the following hypothesis: the first part preserves the original Greek translation, while the second part represents a revision of the original Greek translation which has been lost for this part. Cf. also p. 182.

6. F. M. Cross, *ALQ*, p. 187.

respond by pointing out that even the version the Jews themselves had produced read παρθένος. In the course of time Christian insertions crept into the text, as in the ᴕ Ps. 13, Ps. 95, etc.[7] And then, when strict Jewish exegesis began to demand that a special meaning be ascribed to every letter of the text, the freedom of ᴕ with the text in some passages must have been offensive. Further, it was not based on the authoritative text of the second century A.D., but on an earlier text of the popularizing type. As a result it was almost inevitable that the Jews should eventually reject and condemn what they had once held to be indispensable and sacred.

4. *THE LATER GREEK VERSIONS*

Once ᴕ had been renounced, the Greek-speaking Jewish community faced the need for a version to replace it. Among the attempts to fill this need were a new version by Aquila and a revision by Theodotion. A new version was also made by Symmachus for the Ebionite (Jewish Christian) community.

(a) *Aquila* (α′ [A]) of Sinope in Pontus was a proselyte and a disciple of Rabbi Akiba,[8] according to Jewish tradition, in whose spirit he produced his slavishly literal translation. Although his vocabulary shows that he had a good knowledge of Greek, he was so absurdly devoted to the principle of literalism that the meaning of the text often suffered and his version sounded distinctly un-Greek. But it was exactly this bold literalism combined with an almost precious precision, especially in using words of similar sounds, that recommended his work to his Jewish contemporaries of about A.D. 130 and gave it considerable authority among them.[9] As late as A.D. 533 we find that in Emperor Justinian's conciliatory Codicil No. 146 this version is cited along with the inspired Septuagint as sanctioned for use in synagogues. Our knowledge of Aquila's version is based not only on quotations and Hexaplaric fragments (cf. pp. 55ff.), but also on the sixth-century palimpsests from the Cairo Geniza.[10]   α′ [A]

(b) *Symmachus* (σ′ [Σ]) produced a new version *ca.* A.D. 170   σ′ [Σ] designed not only for literal accuracy but also for good Greek idiom. According to Eusebius and Jerome, Symmachus was an Ebionite; accord

---

7. On the Christian insertions (additamenta christiana), cf. A. Rahlfs, *Psalmi cum Odis* (1931), pp. 30-32.

8. On Akiba's hermeneutics and his influence on Aquila, cf. now D. Barthélemy, *Les devanciers d'Aquila*, VTS 10 (1963), pp. 1-30.

9. For examples of Aquila's translation, cf. *Septuaginta*, edited by A. Rahlfs (1935) 1, pp. xxiv-xxvi; J. Rieder and N. Turner, *An Index to Aquila*, VTS 12 (1966).

10. Cf. F. C. Burkitt, *Fragments of the books of Kings according to the translation of Aquila* (1897); C. Taylor, *Hebrew-Greek Cairo Geniza palimpsests from the Taylor-Schechter Collection* (1900).

ing to Epiphanius he was a Samaritan converted to Judaism.[11] His version is found in only a few Hexapla fragments.

θ' [Θ]   (c) *Theodotion* (θ' [Θ]) was a proselyte at the end of the second century according to early church tradition.[12] He did not produce a new version, but revised an existing Greek version following the Hebrew text. Whether the version he used was the Septuagint (as Rahlfs affirms) is disputed.[13] The problem is posed by "Theodotionic" readings occurring in texts which are earlier than Theodotion (e.g., the New Testament, Barnabas, Clement, Hermas). F. G. Kenyon and P. Kahle assume that Theodotion revised an earlier text which is to be distinguished from the Septuagint, and which has survived in only a few early Christian quotations although it was once widely used. It has been commonly accepted that Theodotion's version of the book of Daniel supplanted that of the Septuagint in almost all manuscripts. This assumption should now be qualified, according to A. Schmitt's research,[14] by the recognition that the "θ" text in Daniel apparently cannot be ascribed to Theodotion.[15]

(οι) γ´(οι) λ'   In early manuscripts these three later versions are sometimes cited together as (οι) γ´ = οἱ τρεῖς (ἑρμηνευταί) or as (οι) λ´ = οἱ λοιποί (ἑρμηνευταί).[16] These sigla are also used in BHS.

In Origen's scholarly magnum opus (which we will discuss next) he made use not only of these three versions, which have in turn exercised a considerable influence on the transmission of the Septuagint, but also of yet other versions which are otherwise virtually unknown to us and which

---

11. H. J. Schoeps, "Aus frühchristlicher Zeit," *Religionsgeschichtliche Untersuchungen* (1950), pp. 82-119, finds traces of Ebionite theological terms, Greek education, and dependence on rabbinic exegesis in Symmachus. Thus there appears to be no doubt that he was an Ebionite Christian. Cf. also A. von Harnack, *Geschichte der altchristlichen Literatur* 2/2 (1904), pp. 164f.; and H. J. Schoeps, *Theol. und Gesch. des Judenchristentums* (1949), pp. 33-37.

12. D. Barthélemy, *Les devanciers d'Aquila* (1963), pp. 144f. (= *EHT*, 1978, pp. 72-85), suggests that Theodotion may be identified with Jonathan ben 'Uzziel, who lived in the first half of the first century A.D., and that he may have been a precursor of Aquila. Cf. also K. G. O'Connell, *The Theodotionic Revision of the Book of Exodus* (1972).

13. In some books there may be detected evidences of a Syrian-Mesopotamian milieu; cf. Klaus Koch, "Die Herkunft der Proto-Theodotion-Übersetzung des Danielbuches," *VT* 23 (1973), pp. 362-65.

14. A. Schmitt, *Stammt der sogenannte* "Θ"-*Text bei Daniel wirklich von Theodotion? NAG* 1/8. *Phil.-hist. Klasse*, 1966, no. 8.

15. The Greek text of the Minor Prophets found in 1952 (cf. pp. 180f.) contains many readings of Aquila, Symmachus, and Theodotion, although it is older than these. D. Barthélemy, *Les devanciers d'Aquila* (1963), wishes to see in it a common basis for Aquila and Symmachus which possibly goes back to Jonathan ben 'Uzziel (cf. n. 12), and to consider them as "surrecenseurs" of this early Palestinian recension. But it must not be forgotten that there were many other texts in which an assimilation to the Hebrew text was attempted. It is still too early to take a final stand on Barthélemy's thesis. Cf. also the following notes.

16. J. Ziegler, *Duodecim Prophetae* (1943), pp. 108, 72.

he called *Quinta* (ε' [E ̕]),[17] *Sexta*, and *Septima*. "The availability of so many different Greek versions of the Bible among the Jews of that time is incontrovertible proof of the great need for modern Greek translations, and of the inadequacy of the older versions made centuries earlier for the demands of the time."[18]

5. *ORIGEN'S HEXAPLA*

Orig
[Hex, hex]

The number of competing versions in addition to the original text was undoubtedly confusing, especially in discussions with the Jews. The Hexapla, a massive work compiled by the Alexandrian theologian Origen between A.D. 230 and 240, was an attempt to achieve some clarification. Origen stated that the chief purpose of the undertaking was to equip Christians for their discussions with Jews who made their appeal to the original text. It is not altogether certain whether he actually appreciated the textual problems of ൏ and was restrained in his comments because of its prestige in the church, as is so often asserted. He may himself have considered ൏ to be inspired.

Origen arranged the following texts in six parallel columns: (1) the Hebrew text (ο εβϱ' [ﬡ °]); (2) the Hebrew text transliterated into Greek;[19]   ο εβϱ' [ﬡ °] (3) Aquila; (4) Symmachus; (5) the Septuagint; (6) Theodotion. Eusebius reports that in the Psalms Origen added a fifth, sixth, and seventh version (see above). The Hebrew text stands in first place as the original, and the sequence of the versions corresponds to their relationship to the original, priority going to Aquila as the most literal. The primary interest of the Alexandrian scholar was to link ൏ to the original Hebrew text with the help of the other more literal versions.[20] To accomplish this he borrowed certain sigla designed by the great textual critic Aristarchus (217-145

17. D. Barthélemy, *RB* 60 (1953), p. 29 (= *QHBT*, 1975, p. 139; = *EHT*, 1978, p. 50), and *Les devanciers d'Aquila* (1963), pp. 215-220, wishes to identify this with the text which is attested in the leather scroll containing the Greek text of the Minor Prophets. Actually he can adduce some striking examples of agreement between the Greek Minor Prophets and the readings of Quinta cited by Jerome.

18. P. Kahle, *TLZ* 79 (1954), col. 90.

19. On the problem of the transliterated text, which Origen himself did not make but took from elsewhere, cf. P. Kahle, *JBL* 79 (1960), pp. 113-17; S. Jellicoe, *The Septuagint and Modern Study* (1978), pp. 106ff.

20. The tendency for such assimilations may be observed even before Origen; cf. Sanders-Schmidt, *The Minor Prophets in the Freer Collection and the Berlin Fragment of Genesis* (1927), pp. 25-29, 265; J. Ziegler, *Duodecim Prophetae* (1943), pp. 33f.; *idem, ZAW* 61 (1945/48), pp. 76-94 (see below, p. 182); P. Katz, "Frühe hebraisierende Rezensionen der LXX," *ZAW* 69 (1957), pp. 77-84. P. Kahle has stressed particularly that this tendency was already present in pre-Christian times, and that Origen "continued the work of the Jews of previous centuries, applying it to the Bible text of the Christians" (*TLZ* 79, 1954, col. 88). D. Barthélemy, *Les devanciers d'Aquila* (1963), p. ix (= *EHT*, 1978, p. 66), speaks of "a definite program for the translation and revision of the Greek Bible" which developed in Palestine under the influence of the Rabbinate in the first century A.D.

B.C.) which were in use in Alexandrian philological studies: the obelos
(−, ÷, ÷), the metobelos (/., ·/., ⟨) , and the asterisk (※). These were used
as follows:

c ob   (a) Words in 𝕾 which are lacking in the original text and which
strictly should be deleted are placed between an obelos and a metobelos,
e.g., ÷ εἰς Φαῦσιν τῆς γῆς⟨ Gen. 1:14.

c ast   (b) Words in the original text which are lacking in 𝕾 were borrowed from another version and inserted in the 𝕾 column placed between
an asterisk and a metobelos, e.g., ※ καὶ ἐγένετο οὕτως ⟨ Gen. 1:7.[21]

But Origen also interfered with the text of 𝕾 without indicating it,
so that the form of 𝕾 he gave in the fifth column is called the Hexaplaric
𝕾⁰[𝕾ʰ] recension (𝕾⁰ [𝕾ʰ]). This soon began to have a profound effect on
manuscripts. Jerome writes, "There is hardly a single book to be found
that does not have these (Hexaplaric additions)."[22]

The *Milan Fragments* (Codex rescriptus Bybliothecae Am-
brosianae O 39 sup.) discovered by Giovanni Mercati in 1895 show a clear
example of the format of the Hexapla. It is a palimpsest: the lower text is
an exegetical compilation (minuscule, ninth to eleventh century). First
there is the text of a Psalm in the columnar order of the Hexapla. This is
followed by the Septuagint text of the same Psalm and the catena written
in continuous lines (cf. p. 60). Some 150 verses of the Hexapla Psalter are
preserved in this way. The first column with the text in Hebrew is lacking,
and the sixth column does not give the text of Theodotion as we might
expect, but that of Quinta. The Septuagint column does not have the
Aristarchan sigla (cf. n. 21). The unique material in this palimpsest is of
great value not only for the study of the Greek versions, but also for the
history of the Hebrew language, because the transliteration of the Hebrew
text in the second column (the first column in this manuscript) reveals a
pronunciation of the Hebrew that antedates the Tiberian usage by centuries.[23]

---

21. P. Kahle (*JBL* 79, 1960, pp. 115f.) has recently deduced from the lack of
Aristarchan signs in the Milan Hexapla fragments that the Septuagint column did not contain
diacritical signs in either the Hexapla or the Tetrapla; instead, the Hexapla with its collection
of significant Jewish Biblical texts simply provided the basis for Origen's work in textual
criticism.
22. "Vix enim unus aut alter invenietur liber, qui ista (i.e., additamenta hexa-
plaria) non habeat."
23. Published as vol. 8 of *Codices ex ecclesiasticis Italiae bybliothecis delecti
phototypice expressi*, with the title: *Psalterii Hexapli Reliquiae: cura et studio Johannis
Card. Mercati editae*. The first volume appeared in 1958, with an introduction followed by
photographic plates and transcriptions of the fragments; in 1965 a further volume appeared
of *Osservazioni: Commento critico al Testo dei Frammenti Esaplari;* a volume with fragments of other manuscripts (indirect witnesses) is promised. H. J. Venetz, *Die Quinta des
Psalteriums: ein Beitrag zur Septuaginta- und Hexaplaforschung, Publications de l'Institut
de Recherche et d'Histoire des Textes, Collection Massorah*, Ser. 1, no. 2 (1974). Cf.
illustration, pl. 34.

Origen produced a second work besides the Hexapla, the *Tetrapla*, which contained only the four Greek versions. It is not certain whether the Tetrapla was a later abridgment of the Hexapla (the common view) or an earlier stage of its formation (Procksch).[24]

Both works were of enormous dimensions—the Hexapla comprised six thousand folios in fifty volumes—and could hardly have been copied often in their entirety. The original was in Caesarea in Palestine, and was probably destroyed in the Islamic conquest. Fortunately the Hexaplaric text of G was often copied; Pamphilus and Eusebius promoted its circulation. Although no authentic manuscript of the Hexaplaric Septuagint has survived, there are manuscripts which represent the text of Origen more or less closely. The relationships vary greatly from book to book. Among the important witnesses are *Codex Colberto-Sarravianus* (G; pl. 35) of the fourth or fifth century, which has the Aristarchan sigla, and several minuscules.[25] The Syriac translation of G^O [G^h] known as the *Syro-Hexapla* (Syh [S^h]) is of great value. It was prepared with meticulous care by Bishop Paul of Tella in A.D. 616-617 (pl. 37), and it also preserves the Aristarchan sigla. This version has survived in the ninth-century Milan *Codex Ambrosianus Syrohexaplaris*, which contains the Prophets and the Writings.[26] Besides these manuscripts of the Hexaplaric family there are also several belonging to other textual families which are significant for reconstructing Origen's text because of the Hexaplaric readings recorded in their margins. Among the uncials there are *Codex Coislinianus* (M) and *Codex Marchalianus* (Q; pl. 36). A survey of all the Hexaplaric material known in his time was compiled by *F. Field* in *Origenis Hexaplorum quae supersunt* (1875, reprinted 1964). An account of a recent find of Hexaplaric material for Isaiah is given by A. Möhle in *ZAW* n.s. 11 (1934), pp. 176-183.

Syh[S^h]

6. *OTHER RECENSIONS OF THE SEPTUAGINT*

Origen was not the only one to revise the Septuagint. Jerome mentions *three* recensions in his preface to Chronicles written about A.D. 400: "Alexandria and Egypt honor *Hesychius* as editor of the Septuagint; in Constantinople and as far as Antioch copies by the martyr *Lucian* are commended. The provinces between these two read the Palestinian

24. *ZAW* 53 (1935), pp. 240-269.
25. Cf. A. Schenker, *Hexaplarische Psalmenbruchstücke: Die hexaplarischen Psalmenfragmente der Handschriften Vaticanus graecus 752 und Canonicianus graecus 62* (1975).
26. Photographic edition by A. M. Ceriani, *Monumenta Sacra et Profana* 7 (1874). Other Syro-Hexaplaric texts have been published by P. A. de Lagarde, *Bibliothecae Syriacae . . .* (1892), and W. Baars, *New Syro-Hexaplaric Texts, edited, commented upon and compared with the Septuagint* (Leiden, 1968). The text of the Psalter in the Syro-Hexapla, however, is not Hexaplaric; cf. Rahlfs, *Psalmi cum Odis* (1931), p. 52.

codices prepared by *Origen* and promoted by Eusebius and Pamphilus. Thus the whole world is divided in competition by this three-fold variety." According to this statement the different provinces of the early church each had its own Biblical text. But we should not infer from Jerome's statement that these three were the only recensions, or that Hesychius and Lucian were regarded anywhere as absolutely authoritative.[27]

Lucian, a presbyter from Antioch, died a martyr in A.D. 312. Hesychius is perhaps to be identified with the bishop who was killed in the persecutions of Diocletian. While the Lucianic recension ($\mathfrak{G}^L$ [$\mathfrak{G}^{Luc}$]) is mentioned elsewhere, that of Hesychius is not. Our information about it is too vague to permit either description or dating.[28] There is no single principle which characterized the Lucianic recension. Ziegler describes it for Isaiah and the Minor Prophets in this way: "Lucian produced it from the Hexaplaric recension, but with no attempt to parallel the text of $\mathfrak{M}$ with any precision. The corrections based on $\mathfrak{M}$ (through the Hexaplaric recension, especially the later versions) are few in number and of little significance. More important for Lucian are the laws of Greek grammar and style, and it is in this area that most of his improvements are found."[29] Lucian's text is witnessed in the Biblical quotations of Chrysostom and Theodoret of Cyrrhus, as well as in numerous minuscules.[30] Beside the main body of Lucianic witnesses ($\mathfrak{G}^L$), two subgroups designated $\mathfrak{G}^{II}$ and $\mathfrak{G}^{III}$ may be identified in some manuscripts.[31]

The recensions mentioned above do not mark the final stage of the history of the Greek text. It continued to develop. The revised texts tended to mingle and influence one another, resulting in more or less mixed texts in all the surviving manuscripts. Because manuscripts could

(margin notes:)
$\mathfrak{G}^L$[$\mathfrak{G}^{Luc}$]

$\mathfrak{G}^{II}$; $\mathfrak{G}^{III}$

27. H. Dörrie, *ZNW* 39 (1940), p. 69.

28. J. Ziegler, *Isaias* (1939), p. 23; R. Hanhart, *Esther* (1966), pp. 98f. For discussion of the Hesychian recension, cf. S. Jellicoe, *The Septuagint and Modern Study* (1968), pp. 146-156, and J. W. Wevers, *ThR* 33 (1968), pp. 37f., who refers to "this shadowy form (*Schattengestalt*)" and "this dream figure (*Traumfigur*)."

29. J. Ziegler, *Duodecim Prophetae* (1943), p. 89.

30. P. Kahle, *TLZ* 79 (1954), col. 83-86, has indicated several older texts which contain Lucianic readings (e.g., John Rylands Papyrus Greek 458, Justin Martyr, Philo, Josephus), and reaches this conclusion: "Textual forms of the Greek Bible such as Lucian used for his revision must therefore have been widespread in the early centuries of our era" (col. 85). Indeed, the John Rylands Papyrus Greek 458 and the leather scroll found in 1952 containing the Greek text of the Minor Prophets "prove with certainty the existence of textual forms akin to Lucian . . . in the pre-Christian era" (col. 85). On the history of the Lucianic text which seems "to become ever more complex," cf. also J. W. Wevers, *ThR* n.s. 22 (1954), pp. 98-100. D. Barthélemy, *Les devanciers d'Aquila* (1963), p. 127 (= *EHT*, 1978, p. 71), is critical of the existence of a "Lucianic recension": it is rather the "Antiochene text," or essentially "the old Septuagint, more or less corrupted."

31. Cf. J. Ziegler, *Isaias* (1939), pp. 74ff.; *idem, Duodecim Prophetae* (1943), pp. 74ff.; *idem, Ezechiel* (1952), pp. 45f.

be copied from different exemplars, a single manuscript might follow
different revisions in its different parts, and on occasion this has misled
Septuagint scholarship. When Lagarde edited the Septuagint text of
Genesis to Ruth in 1883 (in BHK: 𝕲ᴸ),[32] he relied on manuscripts 19   [𝕲ᴸ]
108 on the assumption that because they are clearly Lucianic after
1 Samuel, they must also be Lucianic in the earlier books. Rahlfs was later
able to prove that these manuscripts are not Lucianic from Genesis to
Ruth 4:10, but represent here another textual type. "Thus even Lagarde's
supposedly Lucianic text is not Lucianic at all from Genesis to Ruth 4:10;
only the last twelve verses of Ruth (4:11-22) are actually Lucianic in
manuscripts 19 and 108, and consequently also in Lagarde's edition,
because of a shift in the text type of the exemplar they followed."[33]

7. LAGARDE'S PROGRAM

From what we have said it is evident that the history of the transmission
of the Septuagint is quite complex. None of the various surviving forms of
the text has preserved the original form of the version. Is it possible to
reach beyond the variety of the textual forms which exist today and find a
hypothetical unity underlying them—the original Septuagint? *Paul de
Lagarde* (1827-1891), who did so much for Septuagint research during the
last century, operated with a clearly defined program: "It has been my
intention through the years to reconstruct the three original recensions of
the Septuagint attested by Jerome, to have them printed in parallel columns, and to draw further conclusions from a comparison of these three
texts."[34] Thus Lagarde proposed the classification of Septuagint manuscripts, assigning them to the individual recensions with the help of patristic quotations and other criteria. After achieving this vantage the next step
could be taken toward the original text, which he assumed would be the
form farthest from the Masoretic text.

A great deal has been done to solve this problem, especially by
the Septuagint Project of the Göttinger Gesellschaft der Wissenschaften
under the distinguished leadership of *A. Rahlfs* (1865-1935). But the goal
proposed by Lagarde could not be attained. As we have noted, the
Hesychian recension cannot be recovered. And in other respects as well
the material itself demanded a modification of Lagarde's principles. The
problems in each book are different, as the two following examples show.

(a) In Rahlfs's edition of *Genesis* (Stuttgart, 1926), he has distin-

---

32. *Librorum Vet. Test. canonicorum pars prior graece* (1883).
33. A. Rahlfs, *Paul de Lagardes wissenschaftliches Lebenswerk im Rahmen
einer Geschichte seines Lebens dargestellt* (Mitt. d. Sept–Unternehmens d. Ges. d. Wiss. zu
Göttingen 4/1) (1928), p. 77.
34. P. de Lagarde. *Septuagintastudien* (Abhandl. d. Göttinger Ges. d. Wiss. 37)
(1891), p. 3.

$\mathfrak{G}^\text{C}$ guished between two larger groups (Origen and the Catena text[35]), six smaller groups, and a minuscule manuscript with a Lucianic text. Further, seven uncial manuscripts and several minuscules refused to conform to any group.

(b) In Ziegler's edition of *Isaiah* (Göttingen, 1939), the evidence is divided into four groups: (1) the Alexandrian text, represented by Alexandrinus, Marchalianus, minuscule manuscripts, Cyril of Alexandria,[36] and others. This group has preserved best the text of $\mathfrak{G}$, but has itself been influenced by secondary material, especially by the recensions (by $\mathfrak{G}^\text{O}$ [$\mathfrak{G}^\text{h}$] in particular); (2) the Hexaplaric recension, attested by Vaticanus, Venetus, the Syro-Hexaplar, some minuscules, and the Church Fathers Eusebius of Caesarea, Basil the Great, and Jerome; (3) the recension of Lucian, found in a main group of five minuscules and several subgroups, and in the commentaries of Theodoret and of (Pseudo-)Chrysostom, who defends the Lucianic text vigorously and explicitly against Palestinian attacks; and (4) the Catena group.

From these two examples it is apparent that the surviving evidence is much more varied than was suspected in Lagarde's program. Yet it is possible to distinguish certain groupings (although in Genesis even this requires further qualification), and while these groupings cannot be identified with the three classical recensions, yet their comparison can lead us back to an earlier form of the text. To this extent it may be said that Lagarde's proposals have been proven correct in their essentials, even though requiring some modification.[37]

8. *PAUL KAHLE'S THESIS*

But does the view of the origin and development of the Septuagint held by Lagarde and his followers actually correspond to the facts? Do they not attempt to treat a translation, where different principles apply, on the analogy of an original text? This question has been posed repeatedly, especially by P. Kahle in the Schweich Lectures for 1941, where he challenged Lagarde's thesis vigorously, with great thoroughness, mar-

---

35. Catena is the name given to "chain commentaries" made up of exegetical comments from various Church Fathers, in use from the sixth century (cf. pl. 38). The Catena manuscripts offer their own special late recension of the text, which is also taken over in other manuscripts with the omission of the Catena itself.

[$\mathfrak{G}^\text{Cyr}$]   36. Cyril, Patriarch of Alexandria (412-444), through his commentaries on a number of Old Testament books (cited as Cyr [$\mathfrak{G}^\text{Cyr}$]), is an important witness to the text used in Alexandria.

37. Cf. H. Dörrie, *ZNW* 39 (1940), pp. 57-110, and P. Katz, *ThZ* 5 (1949), pp. 1-24; *idem*, "Septuagintal studies in the mid-century. Their links with the past and their present tendencies," *Dodd-Festschrift* (1956), pp. 176-208.

shalling a wealth of evidence.[38] His statements there should be reviewed with careful attention, for they touch on a central problem of Septuagintal research, and if they are correct they suggest a completely new approach.

Kahle begins with a fresh interpretation of the Letter of Aristeas. He regards it, of course, as legendary, but the question remains as to why it was written. It is concerned with a translation of the Torah which was regarded as authoritative by the Jewish community in Alexandria. "There cannot be any doubt that the letter was written as propaganda for this standard translation."[39] The letter itself recognizes that this was not the first translation, for it mentions earlier unreliable ones (par. 314-16). Greek translations were as necessary for Jews living in the Greek-speaking diaspora as the Aramaic Targums were for their brothers in Palestine (cf. pp. 75f.). The first attempts may have been made as early as 300 B.C., and as they could hardly have been very satisfactory they were constantly subject to revision. This led to the desire and the need for a reliable standard Greek text, and one was produced by a commission on behalf of the Jewish community in Alexandria.[40] "It is this *revised* version with which the letter of Aristeas is dealing."[41] As the letter was written about 100 B.C., or perhaps a little earlier according to the modern view, it is this period to which the origins of the standard version (of the Torah alone!) must be assigned.

This standard text did not meet with immediate and exclusive acceptance any more than we should expect from parallel examples in the history of Bible translating. Other translations continued in use. We find traces of them in the Old Testament quotations of Philo, Josephus, the New Testament,[42] and in other texts, although the original form has sometimes been obscured by later corrections to agree with ᛌ. And even in the book of Judges, where Codex Alexandrinus and Codex Vaticanus differ so greatly that even Lagarde spoke of two different versions, the explanation is that we have here two forms of an Old Testament Targum.

Judaism made no attempt to produce a standard text beyond the Torah, as far as we know. And even this standard text, the Septuagint, was completely abandoned in the second century for new versions (cf. pp. 53ff.) which adhered closely to the officially-established Hebrew text.

38. P. Kahle, *The Cairo Geniza* (1947), pp. 132-179 (1959², pp. 209-264); a summary of the conclusions drawn there was published by Kahle in the *Festschrift O. Eissfeldt* (1947), pp. 161-180. The basic hypothesis is already found in *Theol. Stud. u. Krit.* 88 (1915), pp. 410-12 (= *Opera Minora*, 1956, pp. 10-12).

39. *The Cairo Geniza* (1947), p. 134 (1959², p. 211).

40. It seems probable that this commission met on the island of Pharos. Philo tells us (*de Vita Mosis* 2.5-7) that an annual festival was held there to commemorate the completion of the Septuagint.

41. *The Cairo Geniza* (1947), p. 137.

42. Particularly at variance with the text of ᛌ is the quotation of Isa. 42:1-4 in Matt. 12:18-20.

This Hebrew text was the final standard of authority for Judaism.

The Christian church, however, soon needed an authoritative *Greek* text of the Bible. This was achieved only after a transitional period in which different versions borrowed from the Jews were used side by side. Only one of these competitors survived while the others fell into disuse. To this text of the *entire* Old Testament, itself a collection of different versions with no impression of overall unity, the name "Septuagint" with all its attendant prestige was transferred in the second century. "The manuscripts handed down in the church lead us at best to a standard text used in the church—a text which was only gradually established, and did not itself stand at the beginning of the tradition."[43]

Thus in brief, Kahle may be said to view ⑥ on the analogy of the Aramaic Targums. The unity of the Targums was not in their origins, but something achieved over the centuries through the efforts of anonymous groups, and it was the same with ⑥, the Greek Targum. It is at this point that Kahle's program of Septuagint studies differs essentially from that of Lagarde and his followers: "The task set for scholarship here is not to reconstruct or even attempt a hypothetical reconstruction of the original text of the version, but to assemble and examine with the greatest care all the fragments and traces of the earliest forms of the Greek Bible we can discover. Only in this way will we be in a position to gain a realistic view of the Greek version of the Old Testament."[44] When the leather scroll containing the Greek text of the Minor Prophets was discovered (cf. pp. 180f.), Kahle reviewed the earlier evidence, primarily of Jewish origin, and concluded: "It would be wrong to construe these texts as authoritatively established Bible translations. They should be understood as forms of a Greek Targum which circulated (like the Aramaic Targums of the early period) in a great variety of drafts, each influencing the other in an attempt to approximate ever more closely the original Hebrew text. These relationships would appear with much greater clarity if we had more texts of the Greek Bible from Jewish sources."[45]

We cannot undertake an examination of the evidence marshalled by Kahle to determine the question whether in its entirety it demands or even permits the interpretation he has placed upon it. T. W. Manson, the editor of the Cambridge Septuagint, agreed with him;[46] P. Katz has opposed him vigorously.[47] More recent discoveries have not led to a solu-

---

43. P. Kahle, *Festschrift O. Eissfeldt* (1947), p. 177.
44. *Ibid.*, p. 180.
45. *TLZ* 79 (1954), col. 89f.
46. *Dominican Studies* 2 (1949), pp. 183-192.
47. *ThZ* 5 (1949), pp. 1-24; *idem, Philo's Bible: The Aberrant Text of Bible Quotations in Some Philonic Writings and Its Place in the Textual History of the Greek Bible* (1950). Whereas Kahle detects the remains of an old Jewish translation used by Philo himself in those Bible quotations which differ from the normal text of the Septuagint, Katz believed

tion. Thus P. Kahle regards the Greek scroll of the Minor Prophets discovered in 1952 as confirming his position (see above), while Barthélemy and Cross interpret it differently.[48] Eissfeldt has rightly pointed out the difficulty of a decision in view of the extent, the fragility, and the ambiguity of the evidence.[49] With reference to the Greek scroll of the Minor Prophets mentioned above, we are forced to agree with the majority of those who have examined it, that it cannot be considered as favoring Kahle's thesis. Thus J. W. Wevers has demonstrated for the text of Hab. 2:6, which has survived almost complete: "It is clear that the text represents a revision based upon the Hebrew text, because the changes tend toward a more literal translation . . . but it is equally clear that the reviser began from a Septuagint base."[50] His conclusion is perhaps too generalized: "Our text should bury Kahle's theory of 'multiple versions' once for all. This is an obviously Jewish text which is equally obviously a revision of the reputedly 'Christian' Septuagint text."[51] In theory there is much to be said for Kahle's admonition: "The editor of a Platonic *Dialogue* must attempt to produce the original text of Plato's autograph as nearly as possible. Can we speak, though, of such an original text for a version of the Bible?"[52] Kahle's thesis has yet to be verified in practice beyond reasonable doubt. Meanwhile his call to assemble and to examine thoroughly all the fragments and traces of the earlier forms of the Greek Bible still stands as a challenge.

9. *THE SEPTUAGINT AND THE HEBREW TEXT*

No other version has received as much attention for textual criticism as ⅏. Not only was it valued highly in antiquity, but in the nineteenth century many scholars practically preferred it over the Masoretic text. They believed that because of its pre-Christian origins it could assist in the recovery of an earlier, pre-Masoretic text that would be closer to the original than ℳ. But today we recognize that ⅏ neither was nor was

---

that these quotations may be traced to a late recension of the Septuagint influenced by Aquila, which has itself displaced the original Septuagint readings in some manuscripts of Philo's works. Cf. on this the review by G. D. Kilpatrick who concludes: "Thus while Dr. Katz has made an important contribution to the study of Philo's text he has not convinced us that the aberrant text is a recension of the LXX and not the remains of a distinct translation. The question remains open" (*JTS* n.s. 2, 1951, p. 89).

48. D. Barthélemy, *RB* 60 (1953), pp. 18-29 (= *QHBT*, 1975, pp. 127-139; = *EHT*, 1978, pp. 38-50); *idem, Les devanciers d'Aquila* (1963); F. M. Cross, *ALQ* (1961), pp. 170f.

49. *The Old Testament: An Introduction* (1965³), p. 709. Cf. also G. Zuntz, *ZAW* 68 (1956), p. 182, "The state of the problem is certainly different in different books; at least it is more or less complicated."

50. J. W. Wevers, *ThR* 33 (1968), p. 68.

51. *Ibid.*, pp. 67f.

52. P. Kahle, *Festschrift O. Eissfeldt* (1947), p. 162.

intended to be a precise scholarly translation. Many other factors and interests played a part in its formation. An uncritical use of it which ignores these factors can only lead to false conclusions. In the following paragraphs a few basic considerations are noted, with the reminder that 𝔊 differs so greatly from book to book that no generalization can be made without reservations.

(a) If we are tempted to prefer 𝔊 to 𝔐 as an older witness to the text, we should recall the unevenness of its own textual tradition. Whereas the consonantal text of 𝔐 has remained remarkably constant since the second century, the Septuagint manuscripts even centuries later have widely divergent texts. Lagarde was quite justified when he insisted from his own standpoint on establishing a consistent "original text" of 𝔊 before using the version for textual criticism. Kahle has now questioned this procedure fundamentally. Even those who disagree with Kahle must grant that today we are still far from having an "original text" of 𝔊 which can be compared with 𝔐 as a unified whole.

Even if such an "original text" were available, should it be preferred over 𝔐 simply because of its age? This raises the question of the Hebrew text underlying 𝔊. Is it necessarily better than 𝔐 because it is older? We have already noted that in hundreds of instances 𝔊 agrees with the Samaritan Pentateuch (cf. pp. 43f.). This and other observations suggest that the Hebrew text underlying 𝔊 was one of the popularizing texts mentioned earlier (pp. 16f.). This view held by Kahle is expressed most clearly by Nyberg in reference to the book of Hosea: " 𝔊 and 𝔖 are derived from early popular recensions in use among the Jews of the Diaspora, whereas 𝔐 offers a careful recension which is related to the Diaspora texts much as the classical texts of the great Alexandrian philologists are related to the popular texts of the classical authors which are now available to us from the Egyptian papyri."[53] The Qumran discoveries have shown that popular texts such as underlay 𝔊 were also in use in Palestine (cf. p. 52).

A word should be added here about the form of *script* used in the translation base of the Septuagint, because this is closely related to the concerns of textual criticism and has already led to far-reaching practical consequences. This question received considerable attention following 1923, when F. X. Wutz first proposed in an essay the thesis he later developed in more extensive studies:[54] that the translators of the Septuagint worked from a Hebrew text transliterated into Greek letters. This transliterated text was supposedly corrupted by scribal and other errors, or misconstrued by the translators. Working from these assumptions Wutz be-

53. H. S. Nyberg, *ZAW* 52 (1934), p. 254.

54. *ThBl* 2 (1923), col. 111ff.; later *Systematische Wege von der Septuaginta zum hebräischen Urtext* (1937), etc. Cf. P. Kahle, *Der hebräische Bibeltext seit Franz Delitzsch* (1961), pp. 31-41.

lieved he could recover the original Hebrew text. The fact that transliterated Hebrew texts existed cannot be denied, but so many factors argue against the assumption that ⅁ was translated solely from such a text that Wutz's thesis has not found acceptance. In a few instances it might well apply, but on the whole the Septuagint was apparently based on texts written in the new Aramaic script which in many forms already anticipated the square script.[55]

(b) How should ⅁ be assessed as a translation? What presuppositions did the translators bring to their work, what motives influenced them, and how accurately does their work reflect the original?[56] The answers to these questions are important for deciding how and to what extent ⅁ may serve as a useful witness in textual criticism. Here we can only indicate a few specific examples of characteristic features.

(i) The *language* of ⅁ is *Koine* Greek, the common Greek of the hellenistic period. Naturally in a Jewish translation from Hebrew there is no lack of Hebraisms and Aramaisms, but these are fewer than was imagined before the discoveries of Koine Greek papyri since the end of the nineteenth century.

Even where the translators tried to depart from the original text as little as possible, some degree of change was inevitable due to the nature of the Greek language. One example is the Greek preference for subordinate constructions over coordinate clauses, e.g., Gen. 24:28 מ

ותרץ הנערה ותגד לבית אמה ⅁ καὶ δραμοῦσα ἡ παῖς ἀπήγγειλεν εἰς τὸν οἶκον τῆς μητρός.

For a Hebrew word with as broad a range of meanings as דבר (ῥῆμα, λόγος, etc.) the translators could not always use the same Greek equivalent; they would have to find expressions appropriate to the context from the view of Greek idiom and thought. Thus for דבר we find Exod. 1:18 πρᾶγμα; 12:35 συντάσσειν; 18:16 ἀντιλογία; 18:22 κρίμα; 24:14 κρίσις; 8:8 ὁρισμός; 4:10 ἱκανός; 5:13, 19 καθῆκον; 16:4 τὸ (τῆς ἡμέρας); 18:11, 14 τοῦτο; 29:1 ταῦτα; 5:11 οὐδείς (with negative).[57] In these passages it would be unrealistic to imagine that the translators were dealing with different Hebrew words.

Often the Hebrew text demanded more lexical and grammatical knowledge of the early translators than they possessed. They were apparently unaware of the precise meaning of such a common word as דֶּבֶר ("pestilence"), for they rendered it either in the general meaning of θάνατος, or read it as דָּבָר (Hos. 13:14 δίκη; Hab. 3:5; Ps. 90:3 λόγος; Ps.

55. Cf. the various works of J. Fischer, e.g., *In welcher Schrift lag das Buch Isaias den LXX vor? BZAW* 56 (1930).

56. Cf. C. Rabin, "The Translation Process and the Character of the Septuagint," *Textus* 6 (1968), pp. 1-26.

57. G. Bertram, *ThR* n.s. 10 (1938), p. 153, where further examples may be found.

90:6 πρᾶγμα).[58] Ziegler's verdict on the translator of Isaiah is that "he was not scrupulously concerned to translate his original precisely, word for word. He does not hesitate to omit difficult or rare words if it does not disturb the meaning of a sentence, or to reconstrue the parts of a sentence if he has difficulty understanding the original. Sometimes he seems dominated by a particular idea which he permits to influence his translation of a passage. Thus in Isaiah we find a great number of examples of what we must strictly call 'free' translations."[59]

(ii) The differences between the Jews of the Greek diaspora and the people who wrote the Hebrew Old Testament were not restricted to matters of their language alone. They lived in a world of different social conditions, with different ways of thinking, and not least with differences of belief. Their environment affected them, "hellenized" them. They spoke more abstractly and philosophically about God than the "Hebrews," and they avoided the anthropomorphic and anthropopathic expressions which are so characteristic of the Hebrew Old Testament: Exod. 19:3, Moses does not ascend to God, but to the *mountain* of God; Exod. 24:10, the elders do not see God, but the place where God stands; Josh. 4:24, יד יהוה is translated δύναμις τοῦ κυρίου. The statement that "God repented" is avoided by circumlocution.[60]

Of particular significance is the expansion of the concept of God implied by the consistent translation of the divine name יהוה by κύριος: "The Bible whose God is Yahweh is a national Bible; the Bible whose God is κύριος is a universal Bible."[61]

In other instances the translators eliminated possible theological misunderstandings by avoiding literal translations. For example, they did not adopt the common Old Testament image of God as "the Rock" (צור), but substituted other expressions. Hellenistic religions saw in rocks and stones the symbols, abodes, and representations of divinity, so that "the use of this image in the Greek Old Testament, the Septuagint, which in contrast to the Hebrew text was always directed toward missionary, propaganda and apologetic purposes, could have led to serious misunderstandings, as though a rock were worshipped as the God of the Old Testament. So the image is sacrificed to the meaning. The Septuagint gives a new form to the text of the Old Testament, and in so doing preserves the spirit of the Old Testament revelation of God."[62]

58. *Ibid.,* pp. 155f.

59. J. Ziegler, *Untersuchungen zur Septuaginta des Buches Isaias* (1934), pp. 7f.

60. E. Stauffer, *TDNT* 3 (1965), p. 109 (*ThWNT* 3, 1938, p. 110), where further examples may be found. Cf. especially C. T. Fritsch, *The Anti-anthropomorphisms of the Greek Pentateuch* (1943), and the review by T. W. Manson, *JTS* 46 (1945), pp. 78f.; for a discussion of the problem, cf. J. W. Wevers, *ThR* n.s. 22 (1954), pp. 174-76.

61. A. Deissmann, *Neue Jahrbücher für das klassische Altertum* 11 (1903, 1), p. 174.

62. G. Bertram, *ZAW* 57 (1939), p. 101.

(iii) The efforts of the translators to make the Old Testament intelligible to their compatriots in Egypt led them to use terms native to their Egyptian and Alexandrian environment which were not the exact equivalents of Hebrew expressions. Thus the נגשׂים ("slave drivers") of Exod. 5:6, 10, 13 become the ἐργοδιῶκται ("overseers, foremen") familiar to us from the papyri of hellenistic Egypt.[63] For the particularly difficult list of fashion novelties in Isa. 31:18-24 which were strange to the translator, he simply supplied a list of comparable items from his own age and environment. "We cannot call his work here 'translation'; most of the expressions are substitutes rather than equivalents. Thus the Greek translation often refers to completely different objects, and is useless for determining the meaning of the Hebrew word."[64]

Finally we should note the attempt to make ancient words relevant to contemporary circumstances in Egyptian life. In Deut. 23:18 we read: "There shall be no cult prostitute (קדשׁה, Greek πόρνη) of the daughters of Israel, neither shall there be a cult prostitute (קדשׁ, Greek πορνεύων) of the sons of Israel." The choice of the terms πόρνη and πορνεύων for קדשׁ instead of ἱερόδουλος already alters the meaning of the passage. But even more significant is the addition: οὐκ ἔσται τελεσφόρος ἀπὸ θυγατέρων Ἰσραηλ, καὶ οὐκ ἔσται τελισκόμενος ἀπὸ υἱῶν Ἰσραηλ. The terms τελεσφόρος and τελισκόμενος refer to participation in the Mysteries. As cultic prostitution was a temptation to be resisted in ancient Israel, so the Mysteries were a temptation in hellenistic Egypt.[65] The Egyptian translators felt as justified as the Targumists in relating the text to their own times.

The influence of Jewish tradition as formulated in the Talmud and Midrash may also be observed in 𝔊. Thus behind a tradition in 𝔊 which departs from 𝔐 there may stand an interpretation which has its parallels in Jewish literature.[66]

In summary, the language and content of 𝔊 must be understood against the background of the particular doctrinal and religious situation which produced it and which it was intended to serve. This complicates its usefulness for textual criticism. Undoubtedly it is a most important and even indispensable witness to the text, assisting in the emendation of many corrupted passages. But it can be useful for textual criticism only after a careful appreciation of its nature, its various translation techniques, and its history. We must beware of attempting to reach the underlying Hebrew text through a simple and direct back-translation of the Greek text into Hebrew. Bertram's conclusion is sound: "The Septuagint belongs to the

---

63. Cf. J. L. Seeligmann, *Jaarbericht ex Oriente Lux* 2/6-8 (1939/42), p. 388.
64. J. Ziegler, *Untersuchungen zur Septuaginta des Buches Isaias* (1934), p. 208.
65. Cf. Seeligmann, *op. cit.,* p. 390d.
66. Cf. H. M. Orlinsky, *BA* 9 (1946), p. 24, and L. Prijs, *Jüdische Tradition in der Septuaginta* (1948).

history of Old Testament interpretation rather than to the history of the Old Testament text. It can be used as a textual witness only after its own understanding of the Old Testament text has been made clear."[67]

10. MANUSCRIPTS

The manuscript tradition of ᵷ is very extensive. Holmes and Parsons collected a total of 311 (actually 297) codices, including 21 uncials, for their edition (cf. p. 73). A. Rahlfs enumerated over 1,500 complete and fragmentary manuscripts (up to and including the sixteenth century) in his *Verzeichnis der griechischen Handschriften des Alten Testaments* (1914).[68] The minuscules are designated by arabic numerals in this list, ᵷ22.26.etc. and cited in BHS as ᵷ$^{22.26.etc.}$. In addition to these there are indirect witnesses, which include patristic quotations and versions in other languages which are based on ᵷ. Recent decades have also brought a valuable enrichment of evidence in the discovery of papyri which are earlier than any materials hitherto available.

(a) *Papyri*

(i) *Papyrus Greek 458 of the John Rylands Library* in Manchester dates from the middle of the second century B.C. and offers the *earliest* surviving text of the Greek Bible (pl. 28).[69] These six fragments retrieved from the wrapping of a mummy together with *Papyrus Fouad 266* (pl. 29), and a *leather scroll of the Minor Prophets* (pl. 30), constitute the few surviving fragments of the Greek Bible from the pre-Christian period whose Jewish origins are probable or certain.[70] They contain parts of Deut. 23:24–24:3; 25:1-3; 26:12, 17-19; 28:31-33, comprising a total of some fifteen verses and including a number of readings which are either peculiar to these fragments or find support in very few other witnesses.[71]

[ᵷ^{Beatty}]   (ii) The *Chester Beatty Papyri* ([ᵷ^{Beatty}]; pl. 31) are the most important of the papyri because of their extent and their age. When they were discovered they were described as the most important event for textual criticism since the discovery of Codex Sinaiticus. They comprise the remains of eleven codices, containing parts of nine Old Testament and fifteen New Testament books, the book of Enoch, and a homily by the Church Father Melito of Sardis. They date from the second to the fourth century A.D., and are probably the remains of a Christian library in the

---

67. G. Bertram, *BZAW* 66 (1936), p. 109. Cf. also *idem*, "Praeparatio evangelica in der Septuaginta," *VT* 7 (1957), pp. 225-249.

68. *Nachrichten von der K. Ges. d. Wiss. zu Göttingen, Phil.-hist. Kl.* (1914), Beiheft.

69. C. H. Roberts, *Two Biblical Papyri in the John Rylands Library* (1936).

70. Several fragments of the Greek Bible were also found at Qumran in Cave 4 (cf. P. W. Skehan, *VTS* 4, 1957, pp. 155-58 [= *QHBT*, 1975, pp. 219-222], and also P. Kahle, *The Cairo Geniza*, 1959², pp. 223-26), and in Cave 7 (cf. p. 31, n. 46).

Fayyum. The greater part of these manuscripts was acquired by the Englishman Chester Beatty in 1929 from the local inhabitants who had found them; other parts came into the possession of the University of Michigan and the American John H. Scheide; smaller fragments are in Vienna, in Italy, and in private collections,[72] and further extensive fragments of manuscript 967 are in the papyrus collections of Cologne (Ezekiel, Daniel, Esther) and Madrid (Ezekiel).[73] The Old Testament is represented in the Beatty papyri by considerable portions of Genesis, Numbers, and Deuteronomy, fragments of Isaiah and Jeremiah, parts of Ezekiel, Daniel, and Esther, and fragments of Sirach. The text of Daniel is especially noteworthy, because in Daniel another version had replaced that of 𝕾 in the manuscript tradition (cf. p. 54), so that until now the text of 𝕾 was known from only *one* eleventh-century manuscript.

(iii) The **Berlin fragments** of a Genesis manuscript (late third century, containing Gen. 1:16–35:8; pl. 32) should also be mentioned. These were published together with a late third-century codex of the Minor Prophets in 1927,[74] and the Papyrus Bodmer XXIV, containing Ps. 17–118 and also from the third century A.D.[75] From the fourth century there is the Antinoopolis papyrus, edited by C. H. Roberts in 1950, containing fragments of Proverbs. The papyrus book of the British Museum (𝕾^U [𝕾$^{Pap\ Lond}$]) is relatively late, from the seventh century; it was the first Biblical papyrus to be discovered and has been in the British Museum since 1836 (Papyrus 37). It comprises thirty-two folios of a Psalms codex containing the text of Ps. 10:2–18:6; 20:14–34:6, and represents the so-called Upper Egyptian text.

(b) **Manuscripts.** Among Greek manuscripts a distinction is observed between uncials or majuscules (in capital letters) and minuscules (in small letters). In antiquity only the capital letters were used for books, written in sequence but separately and without ligatures, although for common use (as in private letters) the letters were joined together in a cursive hand. From this cursive form the minuscule hand of the medieval period developed. Until the eighth century there were only uncials, in the ninth and tenth centuries uncials and minuscules were used side by side,

71. Cf. the thorough study by J. Hempel, *ZAW* 55 (1937), pp. 115-127.

72. Publications: F. G. Kenyon, *The Chester Beatty Papyri*, 7 vol. (1933-37; 1958); A. C. Johnson, H. S. Gehman, E. H. Kase, *The John H. Scheide Biblical Papyri: Ezekiel, Princeton University Studies in Papyrology* 3 (1938).

73. A. Geissen, *Der Septuaginta-Text des Buches Daniel Kap. 5–12 sowie Esther 1–2, 15* (1968); W. Hamm, *Der Septuaginta-Text des Buches Daniel Kap. 1–2, Papyrologische Texte und Abhandlungen* 10 (1969); M. Fernandez-Galliano, "Nuevas paginas del codice 967 del A.T. griego (Ez. 28, 19–43, 9)," *Studia Papyrologica* 10 (1971), pp. 1-79.

74. H. A. Sanders and C. Schmidt, *The Minor Prophets in the Freer Collection and the Berlin Fragment* (1927).

75. R. Kasser and M. Testuz, *Papyrus Bodmer XXIV* (1967).

and from the eleventh century only minuscules. Even though the minuscule manuscripts are later, they may be valuable as textual witnesses if they were copied from lost uncials containing a good text. For textual criticism it is important to recognize that until the eighth century texts were written with their letters in continuous sequence, without word division, accents, breathings, or punctuation.

As *sigla* to distinguish individual manuscripts Holmes and Parsons used roman numerals for the uncials (e.g., $\mathfrak{G}^{XI}$) and arabic numerals for the minuscules (e.g., $\mathfrak{G}^{62.147}$). Later Lagarde introduced capital Latin letters for the uncials, many of which have been widely adopted and are used also in BH. The following list of manuscripts cited in BH, either individually or under the siglum $\mathfrak{G}^{Ms(s)}$, is given in chronological order.[76]

$\mathfrak{G}^{62.147}$

$\mathfrak{G}^{Ms(s)}$

$\mathfrak{G}^B$ α) *Codex Vaticanus* (B). Fourth century. Vatican Library. Old Testament complete, but Gen. 1–46:28; Ps. 105:27–137:6 added in the fifteenth century. This manuscript enjoys very great authority. Rahlfs ascribed it to Lower Egypt on the basis of its content and text.

$\mathfrak{G}^S[\mathfrak{G}^{\aleph}]$ β) *Codex Sinaiticus* (S [ℵ]; pl. 33). Fourth century. Discovered by Tischendⵁf at St. Catherine's Monastery, Mt. Sinai, in 1844 and 1859. The main body of the manuscript is in the British Museum, London (since 1933, previously in Leningrad), but a small part is in Leipzig (Codex Frederico-Augustanus); place of origin possibly Palestine. Recent research attributes the manuscript to three scribes, two of whom were also correctors. Later correctors have also been identified and designated in

$\mathfrak{G}^{S1.2.3}$
[$\mathfrak{G}^{\aleph c.a,c.b,c.c}$]   BHS as $\mathfrak{G}^{S1.2.3}$, and in BHK as $\aleph^{c.a,c.b,c.c}$. The Old Testament text survives for Gen. 23:19–24:46; Num. 5:26–7:20 (both with lacunae); 1 Chr. 9:27–19:17; Ezra–Nehemiah (from Ezra 9:9), Esther, Tobit, Judith, 1 and 4 Maccabees, Isaiah, Jeremiah (to Lam. 2:20), Joel–Malachi (Greek order), Psalms, Proverbs, Ecclesiastes, Song of Solomon, Wisdom, Sirach, and Job.

$\mathfrak{G}^A$ γ) *Codex Alexandrinus* (A). Fifth century. British Museum, London. Gift to King Charles I of England in 1627, previously in the Patriarchal Library at Alexandria (hence its name). Old Testament lacks 1 Sam. 12:17–14:9; Ps. 49:20–79:11.

[$\mathfrak{G}^G$]   δ) *Codex Colberto-Sarravianus* ([G]; pl. 35). Fourth/fifth century. Main body of manuscript in Leyden, a smaller part in Paris, one folio in Leningrad. Contains Gen. 31:5–Judg. 21:12 in the Hexaplaric recension with Aristarchan sigla (cf. pp. 55f.).

$\mathfrak{G}^F$ ε) *Codex Ambrosianus* (F). Fifth century. Biblioteca Ambrosiana, Milan. Contains Gen. 31:15–Josh. 12:12 (with lacunae).

[$\mathfrak{G}^\Theta$]   ζ) *Codex Freer* ([Θ]). Fifth century. Acquired by Freer at Gizeh in

---

76. It is not possible here to go into questions of the textual characteristics and importance of the surviving papyri and manuscripts. For this see the introductions to the volumes of the Göttingen Septuagint.

1906, now in the Smithsonian Institution, Washington, D.C. Contains Deuteronomy (except 5:16–16:18) and Joshua (except 3:3–4:10).

η) *Codex Ephraemi Syri rescriptus* (C). Bibliothèque Nationale, Paris. 𝕾C A palimpsest, named for its upper writing, a thirteenth-century copy of the works of Ephraem Syrus. The lower writing is from the fifth century, containing fragments of Job, Proverbs, Ecclesiastes, Song of Solomon, Wisdom, Sirach, and the New Testament.

θ) *Codex Cottonianus* ([D]). Fifth/sixth century. British Museum, [𝕾D] London. 150 fragments of a manuscript destroyed by a fire in Ash- burnham House in 1731; there is an old collation made before the fire. Contains only Genesis.

ι) *Codex Marchalianus* (Q; pl. 36). Sixth century. Vatican Library. Contains Isaiah, Jeremiah, Ezekiel, Daniel, Minor Prophets. Hexaplaric notes in the margin enhance the value of this manuscript.

κ) *Codex Coislinianus* (M). Seventh century. Bibliothèque Nationale, 𝕾M Paris. Contains Genesis–1 Kgs. 8:40 (with lacunae), with scholia and Hexaplaric notes (cf. p. 57).

λ) *Codex Lipsiensis* ([K]). Seventh/eighth century. University Li- [𝕾K] brary, Leipzig; previously St. Saba Monastery, Jerusalem, acquired by Tischendorf in 1844. A palimpsest with upper writing in Arabic, A.D. 885-886; lower writing contains brief portions of Numbers–Judges. Also belonging to this manuscript are six folios in Leningrad containing frag- ments of Numbers–Judges.

μ) *Codex Basiliano-Vaticanus* (N). Eighth century. Vatican Library; 𝕾N previously belonged to the Basilians in Rome. Belongs with 𝕾V together with which it contains large sections of the Old Testament apart from the Psalms; lacking are Genesis–Lev. 13:59, and other parts.

ν) *Codex Venetus* (V). The second part of the above.   𝕾V

ξ) *Codex rescriptus Cryptoferratensis* ([Γ]). Grottaferrata in the Albian [𝕾Γ] Hills. Palimpsest, lower writing eighth century, upper writing thirteenth century. The lower writing contains fragments from several of the Minor Prophets, from Isaiah, Jeremiah, Ezekiel, and Daniel.

ο) *Codex Bodleianus Geneseos* ([E]). Ninth/tenth century. Bodleian [𝕾E] Library, Oxford. Contains Gen. 1–42:18 (with lacunae) written in uncials. To the same manuscript also belong folios containing Gen. 42:18–1 Kgs. 16:28 in a minuscule hand found in Cambridge (1f.), Leningrad (146ff.), and London (16ff.). The manuscript was discovered by Tischendorf and presumably came from the monastery on Mt. Sinai.

π) *Codex Atheniensis* ([W]). Thirteenth century. National Library, [𝕾W] Athens. Contains the historical books, Esther, Judith, and Tobit.

BHS also cites:

ρ) *Codex Veronensis* (R). Sixth century. A Greek-Old Latin Psalter in 𝕾R the Biblioteca Capitolare, Verona. The Septuagint text here represents the Western text according to Rahlfs. Cf. 𝔏ᴿ, p. 89.

𝔊ᵂ   σ) *A codex fragment* (W). Fourth century. Contains 1 Sam. 18:8-25.

11. *EDITIONS*

Theoretically there are two editorial methods possible in publishing an ancient text which has been preserved in a variety of forms in different manuscripts. (a) The text of a single manuscript can be printed, with the variant readings of the other manuscripts indicated in an apparatus. The use of such an edition requires working through all the assembled evidence and making one's own judgments. (b) A text can be reconstructed by selecting from the various available readings those which appear to be the earliest. Such an eclectic procedure produces a critical recension of the text which can be verified by the evidence provided in the apparatus. The first method has been followed in all the great scholarly editions of the past; the second is being tried for the first time in the Göttingen Septuagint. The method best suited to the Septuagint is still a matter of discussion. The principal editions are the following:

[𝔊ᶜ⁽ᵒᵐ⁾ᵖˡ]   (a) The *Complutensian Polyglot* (1514-1517; [𝔊ᶜ⁽ᵒᵐ⁾ᵖˡ]). The manuscripts on which this was based are now lost. J. Ziegler has shown that for the Minor Prophets it agrees frequently with the Lucianic text type,[77] with the third-century papyrus codex edited by Sanders (cf. p. 69), with the marginal notes of minuscule 86, and with the Coptic and Old Latin versions. From this we may infer that the Complutensian Greek text "was based on a text transmitting quite early readings which are not found in manuscripts known today."[78] Its text is therefore of particular value (pl. 47).

[𝔊ⱽⁿ]   (b) The *Aldine* edition (Venice, 1518; [𝔊ⱽⁿ]) offers a late text of little value. J. Ziegler has shown that for the Minor Prophets the Aldine text is based on a manuscript now lost, the larger part of which was derived from minuscule 68, and the remainder from minuscule 97.[79] "It is unfortunate that the editor of the Aldine edition relied on a manuscript transmitting a late text derived from the heavily Hexaplaric and Lucianic Catena group such as we find in minuscules 68 and 97."[80]

(c) The *Sixtine* edition (Rome, 1587) was an officially-sponsored edition commissioned by Pope Sixtus V. The text is essentially that of 𝔊ᴮ, with its lacunae supplied from several Vatican manuscripts, and with a wealth of variants appended. The use of 𝔊ᴮ marks significant progress,

---

77. *Bibl* 25 (1944), pp. 297-310.
78. *Ibid.,* p. 309.
79. *Bibl* 26 (1945), pp. 37-51.
80. *Ibid.,* p. 51.

although this is marred by dependence on the Aldine edition.[81] The Sixtine has served as normative for many editions into the nineteenth century, e.g., the London Polyglot (1654-1657), Holmes and Parsons (1798ff.), van Ess (1824 and later), the polyglot of Stier and Theile (1847-1855), Tischendorf (1850 and later), the Clarendon Press edition (Oxford, 1875) on which the concordance by Hatch and Redpath (1897ff.) is based.

(d) *Holmes and Parsons, Vetus Testamentum Graecum cum variis lectionibus* (1798-1827). The text is based on the Sixtine edition, with the addition of variants derived from three hundred manuscripts collated for this edition from patristic quotations and from daughter versions. These five large folio volumes contain a wealth of material that remains unsurpassed today. It is among the resources of BHK ($\mathfrak{G}^{\text{MSS(Holmes-)Parsons}} = $ manuscripts according to Holmes-Parsons). $\left[\mathfrak{G}^{\text{MSS}}_{\text{(Holmes-)}}\right.$ Parsons $\left.\right]$

(e) *H. B. Swete, The Old Testament in Greek* (3 vol., 1887-1891, and several later editions). A convenient popular edition which prints the text of $\mathfrak{G}^{\text{B}}$ (with lacunae supplied from A and S [א]), with an apparatus of readings from several important uncials.

(f) *Brooke-McLean-Thackeray-Manson, The Old Testament in Greek according to the Text of Codex Vaticanus, supplemented from other Uncial Manuscripts, with a critical Apparatus containing the Variants of the chief ancient Authorities for the Text of the Septuagint* (Cambridge, 1906ff.). The editors considered the time not yet ripe for preparing a critical edition, and offered the evidence quite objectively. The text is that of $\mathfrak{G}^{\text{B}}$,[82] with the correction of obvious errors and with lacunae supplied from A and S [א]. In the apparatus are noted all the uncials, some thirty selected minuscules, the daughter versions, Philo, Josephus, and early Christian writings. Published volumes include Genesis (1906) to Tobit (1940); no further volumes are planned.

(g) The alternative of presenting the text in a critical edition has been realized for the first time in the *Göttingen Septuagint: Septuaginta, Vetus Testamentum Graecum auctoritate Societatis Litterarum Göttingensis editum.* The text printed here is not that of a particular manuscript. At each point the reading is chosen which appears best in the light of the manuscript tradition as a whole, and with due reference to the Hebrew text. The apparatus, which offers a wealth of manuscript evidence arranged by textual groups (recensions), makes it possible for the reader to form his own judgment of the textual tradition independently of the editor. The goal is the best attainable text, which involves no claim that the

81. According to Lagarde and Rahlfs, with whom Ziegler agrees, the Sixtine represents an Aldine edition corrected from $\mathfrak{G}^{\text{B}}$ (and other manuscripts); cf. J. Ziegler, *Bibl* 26 (1945), pp. 49f.
82. From Exodus onward the text of the corrector of B (instead of the first hand) is adopted where it agrees with the main line of tradition.

original form has been recovered in every instance. The editions are furnished with valuable introductions. For the plan of this undertaking, which derives ultimately from Lagarde, and for criticism of it, see above (pp. 59f.). Already published are: *Psalmi cum Odis*, edited by Rahlfs (1931, revised 1967); *I Maccabees*, by Kappler (1952, revised 1967); *Isaias* (1939, revised 1967), *Duodecim Prophetae* (1943, revised 1967); *Ezechiel* (1952, revised 1977), *Susanna, Daniel, Bel et Draco* (1954), *Ieremias, Baruch, Threni, Epistula Ieremiae* (1957, revised 1976), by Ziegler; *II Maccabees* (1959, revised 1976), by Kappler-Hanhart; *III Maccabees* (1960), by Hanhart; *Sapientia Solomonis* (1962), *Sapientia Iesu Filii Sirach* (1965), by Ziegler; *Esther* (1966), *I Esdras* (1974), *Judith* (1978), by Hanhart; *Genesis* (1974), *Deuteronomy* (1977), by Wevers. Rahlfs published the books of *Ruth* (1922) and *Genesis* (1926) in a smaller format.

M. Margolis, *The Book of Joshua in Greek* (1931-1938) is modeled on the same principles as the Göttingen Septuagint.

(h) A critical manual edition of the entire Septuagint, designed for the use of students and ministers and at a modest price, was produced by *A. Rahlfs* in 1935 at the Württemberg Bible Society. It is based mainly on the three major manuscripts B, S [א], and A.

As an indispensable tool for research on 𝕲 we should mention *Hatch and Redpath*, *A Concordance to the Septuagint*, 2 vol. (1897), *Supplement* (1906).

12. *THE SAMARITICON*

The Samaritan Pentateuch was also translated into Greek. Origen often cites this translation as the *Samariticon*. Fragments have survived in a manuscript from the fourth century A.D. (cf. P. Glaue and A. Rahlfs, *Fragmente einer griechischen Übersetzung des samaritanischen Pentateuchs, Mitteilungen des Septuaginta-Unternehmens* 2, 1911). An inscription with the Greek text of the Blessing of Aaron (Num. 6:22-27), found in a Samaritan synagogue built in Thessalonica in the fourth century A.D., has been published by B. Lifshitz and J. Schiby in *RB* 75 (1968), pp. 368-378.

VI
THE ARAMAIC TARGUMS (ᵗ)[1]

ᵗ

1. *ORIGIN AND CHARACTER*

IT IS KNOWN THAT IN POST-EXILIC JUDAISM HEBREW
ceased to be spoken as the common language and was replaced by
Aramaic, which had become the official written language of the western
Persian empire. Hebrew was of course still understood and used in intellectual circles, especially among theologians. But for the larger part of the
Jewish community it became necessary to combine the usual Scripture lessons, which were read in Hebrew in the synagogue, with a translation into
Aramaic. The translating was called *targem*, the translator *turgeman(a)* or
meturgeman(a), and the translation *targum*. Since the need was felt at an
early date, the custom must be old and certainly pre-Christian. The
Jewish tradition associating it with Ezra (cf. Neh. 8:8) may well be
correct.

In the worship service the translation could be made only orally,
not read from a scroll; this was presumably to preserve its distinction
from the truly sacred text which was in Hebrew. The writing down of
Aramaic translations was not forbidden, and the existence of written
Targums by the beginning of the Christian era at the latest is no longer in
question. It is told of Rabbi Gamaliel, the teacher of Paul, that when a
Targum of Job was placed before him he spurned it and had it buried in a
wall. Targums were in use even at Qumran.[2] But with their development

1. On the problems of the Targums, cf. R. le Déaut, *Introduction à la littérature
Targumique* (1966), with full bibliographies; also J. Bowker, *The Targums and Rabbinic
Literature: An Introduction to Jewish Interpretations of Scripture* (1969); M. McNamara,
The New Testament and the Palestinian Targum to the Pentateuch (1966).
2. Thus a Targum of the book of Job was found at Qumran in Cave 11; cf. J. van der
Ploeg, *Le Targum de Job de la Grotte 11 de Qumran* (Amsterdam, 1962); A. S. van der
Woude, *Das Hiobtargum aus Qumran Höhle XI, VTS* 9 (1963), pp. 322-331; edition: *Le
Targum de Job de la Grotte XI de Qumran*, edited and translated by J. P. M. van der Ploeg
and A. S. van der Woude with the collaboration of B. Jongeling (1971). Otherwise to date
only the remains of a literal Aramaic version of Leviticus in Cave 4 have been found. The
so-called Genesis Apocryphon is not a Targum. Cf. J. T. Milik, *Ten Years of Discovery in
the Wilderness of Judaea* (1959), p. 31.

from oral translations it is only natural that the precise wording of the Targums should differ from place to place. While the Hebrew text and its normally accepted interpretation in Judaism remained authoritative, there remained the possibility of individual characteristics appearing in the form of words, extent of paraphrase, interpretation, representation, etc. Thus there was not at first a single original standard and authoritative Targum text, but rather a whole series of different Aramaic versions.

These different versions share in varying degrees certain characteristics which reflect their common practical purpose. The community was to be taught and edified; it was necessary to spell out clearly for them the message of the text. Consequently in no other versions of the Bible is the interpretive element as pronounced as in the Targums. They paraphrase, they add explanatory phrases, they reinterpret the text (sometimes quite boldly) according to the theological temper of their time, they relate the text to contemporary life and political circumstances, and so on. In particular they attempt to avoid anthropomorphic and anthropopathic statements about God. This approach to the text in the Targums, which occasionally almost ignores the meaning of the Hebrew text, reduces their value as textual witnesses, but makes them important documents for the history of Old Textament exegesis.[3]

2. THE VARIOUS TARGUMS

Of the varied profusion of the Aramaic versions that once existed only a small fraction has survived. Two basically different forms should be distinguished: those texts which represent the early Palestinian Targum, and those which were revised in Babylon—Onkelos for the Pentateuch and Jonathan for the Prophets. Most of the surviving Targums contain material from very different periods. Determining and dating the various strata is possible only with careful investigation—a process which is in many respects now only in its beginning stages.[4]

(a) The *Palestininan Targum* was never edited officially, and consequently it has never had a single authoritative form of text. All the manuscripts differ from each other to a greater or lesser extent. The characteristic traits of the older Targums just mentioned are especially pronounced in them.

Thanks to several fortunate discoveries in recent decades which have also advanced our knowledge of long-familiar texts, we are now able to see the Palestinian Targum in a clearer perspective. At first P. Kahle

3. A particularly bold reinterpretation was necessitated in Isa. 52:13–53:12 under the influence of anti-Christian polemics. The translation is now conveniently available in J. Jeremias, *TDNT* 5 (1967), pp. 693f. (*ThWNT* 5, 1952, pp. 691-93).

4. On the problem of dating the Targumic traditions: P. Wernberg-Møller, *VT* 12 (1962), pp. 312-330; cf. also G. Vermes, *Scripture and Tradition in Judaism* (1961).

recognized and edited the remains of an old Palestinian Pentateuch Targum which had survived in fragments of seven manuscripts from the Cairo Geniza, dating from the seventh to the ninth century (cited in BH as 𝔗ᵖ = 𝔗ᵖ Targum Palestinense).[5] These texts are not simple and literal translations of the Hebrew. Instead they have extensive explanatory insertions of a midrashic and homiletical nature. When the same passage has survived in several fragments, the differences between them are so great that there can be no question of a standard text. Further fragments have since been discovered, but most significant has been the discovery by A. Díez Macho in 1957 of a complete manuscript of the Palestinian Targum in *Ms. Neofiti I* of the Vatican Library comprising 450 parchment folios.[6] This manuscript, apparently written in Italy early in the sixteenth century,[7] is of the greatest importance for our knowledge of the Palestinian Targum and its related problems, especially in view of the fragmentary nature of the materials hitherto available. A. Díez Macho has already published *Neofiti I Targum Palestinense Ms de la Biblioteca Vaticana* 1, *Genesis* (1968); 2, *Exodus* (1970); 3, *Leviticus* (1971); 4, *Numbers* (1974); containing an introduction and the Aramaic text together with a critical apparatus and translations in Spanish, French (by R. le Déaut), and English (by M. McNamara and M. Maher).

These discoveries have made it possible to achieve a fresh historical understanding of long known and published Targums, and to prove their relationship to the Palestinian Targum. This is true of the so-called Fragment Targum and the Targum Pseudo-Jonathan. The **Fragment Targum,** also known as the *Targum Jerusalem II* (and cited in BH as 𝔗ᴶᴵᴵ), contains only the midrashic comments on individual verses, omitting the continuous translation of the text itself. We now recognize it "as a collection of midrashic material from the Palestinian Pentateuch Targum which was considered too valuable to ignore when the Onkelos Targum was introduced as the standard Targum for Palestine as well."[8] It was published by M. Ginsburger, *Das Fragmenten-Targum (Targum Jeruschalmi zum Pentateuch),* 1899. A new edition is being prepared by M. Black.

The Pentateuch **Targum Pseudo-Jonathan,** also called Jerusalem I (edited by M. Ginsburger from the British Museum Ms. Add. 27031, and

5. P. Kahle, *Masoreten des Westens* 2 (1930).

6. A. Díez Macho discusses some of the major problems of the Palestinian Targum in *VTS* 7 (1960), pp. 222-245, and includes a survey of the texts presently known (pp. 236f.). On Codex Neofiti 1, cf. A. Díez Macho, *Estudios Biblicos* 15 (1956), pp. 446f.; *idem, Christian News from Israel* 13/2 (July 1962), pp. 19-25; and M. Black, *TLZ* 82 (1957), col. 662-64. On the complex character of Neofiti 1, now cf. S. Lund and J. Foster, *Variant Versions of Targumic Traditions within Codex Neofiti 1; Aramaic Studies* 2 (1977).

7. M. F. Martin, "The Palaeological Character of Codex Neofiti I," *Textus* 3 (1963), pp. 1-35.

8. P. Kahle, *ZNW* 49 (1958), p. 110.

𝕮ᴶ   cited in BH as 𝕮ᴶ),[9] is peculiar in combining with the text of the official
Onkelos Targum (see below) midrashic material which was usually omitted from it. Earlier it was thought that the midrashic material had been
introduced into Targum Onkelos only after it was accepted as standard in
Palestine—the people were accustomed to it and missed it in the new
Targum. But recently Díez Macho has advocated a contrary explanation
with numerous evidences: Pseudo-Jonathan represents a Palestinian Targum more or less thoroughly revised from the Onkelos text.[10]

The foundations of the Palestinian Targum apparently go back to
pre-Christian times, and thus it is of great importance for our understanding of Judaism in the period of Christian beginnings. Its language is the
Aramaic spoken in Palestine, so that we can find here valuable material
for the study of Aramaic as it was spoken in the Palestine of Jesus' time.

[𝕮⁰]   (b) *Targum Onkelos* and *Targum Jonathan.* Targum Onkelos (𝕮⁰)
for the Pentateuch and Targum Jonathan for the Prophets are the best
known of the Targums, and are authoritative for Judaism. These are
quite distinct from the Palestinian Targums with their differing forms.
These are *official* Targums whose definitive wording was evidently established in Babylon in the fifth century after a long history of development.
They are based on older material that probably derives ultimately from
Palestine. Their names are probably derived (erroneously) from the Greek
translators Aquila (Onkelos) and Theodotion (Jonathan in Hebrew), who
were known for their literal versions of the Bible, faithful to Jewish
exegesis. Actually these two Targums can hardly have been the work of
single individuals. They were more probably produced by commissions
appointed to replace the various forms of the text then in circulation with
an official version conforming to orthodox Jewish interpretation, revised
according to the Hebrew text, and largely purged of midrashic elabora-
tions. Thus they mark a definitive point in the history of the Targums, and
only later came to establish themselves firmly in Palestine. Both Targums
attempt to reproduce the Hebrew text quite literally, so that as in the
earlier Greek versions of Aquila the language (a literary form of Aramaic
understood in all Aramaic-speaking lands) had to suffer.

Of these two the Targum Onkelos of the Pentateuch was naturally
accorded the greater authority, and like the original Hebrew text it was
also supplied with a Masora.[11] The text was edited by A. Berliner (1884-
1886) following the Editio Sabioneta of 1557.

The Targum Jonathan, which contains more haggadic material

9. For corrections cf. D. Rieder, "On the Ginsburger Edition of the 'Pseudo-
Jonathan' Targum of the Tora," *Leshonenu* 32 (1967/68), pp. 298-303.
10. A. Díez Macho, *VTS* 7 (1960), p. 239.
11. Edited by A. Berliner (Leipzig, 1877), and by S. Landauer (Amsterdam,
1896).

and in part goes back to pre-Christian times, was edited by P. de Lagarde
from Codex Reuchlinianus (*Prophetae Chaldaice: Paulus de Lagarde e
fide codicis reuchliniani edidit* (Lipsiae, 1872); cited in BH as 𝔗ᶠ[𝔗ᴸ]).   𝔗ᶠ[𝔗ᴸ]

The Targum for Joshua and Judges in the Yemenite tradition was
edited by Fr. Praetorius in 1899 and 1900 (cited in BHK as 𝔗ᴾʳ).   [𝔗ᴾʳ]

A new edition of the Targum has been published by Alexander
Sperber: *The Bible in Aramaic*, 1, *The Pentateuch according to Targum
Onkelos* (1959); 2, *The Former Prophets according to Targum Jonathan*
(1959); 3, *The Latter Prophets according to Targum Jonathan* (1962); 4-A,
The Hagiographa: Transition from Translation to Midrash (1968); 4-B,
The Targum and the Hebrew Bible (1973). In BHS volumes I-III are cited
and for the Hagiographa Lagarde's edition is cited (see below) as 𝔗.

(c) Besides the editions already mentioned, BH also refers to: the
Targum to the *Writings* edited by **P. de Lagarde** in 1873 (*Hagiographa
Chaldaice*, cited in BH as 𝔗ᶠ[𝔗ᴸ]; a selection of Targum texts edited in   𝔗ᶠ[𝔗ᴸ]
1888 by **A. Merx** with notes and a glossary, based on old manuscripts and
printed editions (Chrestomathia targumica, cited in BHK as 𝔗ᴹ); the   [𝔗ᴹ]
Targums of **Jacob ben Chayyim's** Rabbinic Bible of 1524/25 (cited in BHK
as 𝔗ᴮ); the Targums of **Buxtorf's** edition of Basel, 1618-1619 (𝔗ᴮᵘˣᵗ); and a   [𝔗ᴮ]𝔗ᴮᵘˣᵗ
wealth of material in **Brian Walton's** London Polyglot of 1654-1657 (cited
in BHK as 𝔗ᵂ). BHS also refers to the editio princeps of the Targum   [𝔗ᵂ]
published in Leiria, 1494.

3. *THE SAMARITAN TARGUM* (cited in BH as ᴴᴴᵀ)   ᴴᴴᵀ

Among the Samaritans also the sacred text, the Pentateuch, was translated into Aramaic, but there was never an official recension of it. Consequently almost every surviving manuscript has its own text. "We have
here an excellent example of a Targum in an earlier phase, through which
translations of the Bible usually pass before they reach their final text."[12]

Editions: The Paris (1645) and London Polyglots (1657); C.
Petermann, *Pentateuchus Samaritanus* (1872-1891; uncritical methodol-
ogy). P. Kahle has edited fragments with comments in *Zeitschrift für
Assyriologie* 16 (1901) and 17 (1902). A new edition of the Samaritan
Targum is being prepared by José Ramón Díaz on the basis of the best
manuscripts derived from an early text.[13]

---

12. P. Kahle, *The Cairo Geniza* (1959²), p. 52.
13. Cf. J. R. Díaz, "Ediciones del Targum samaritano," *Estudios Biblicos* 15
(1956), pp. 105-108; B. Grossfeld, *A Bibliography of Targum Literature* (1972), and its
critical review with supplementary material by W. Baars in *VT* 25 (1975), pp. 124-28.

VII

THE SYRIAC VERSION (Peshitta, ꕷ)

1. NAME AND LITERARY PROBLEM

AT A RATHER LATE DATE THE SYRIAC CHURCH DESIGNATED the version of the Old Testament in common use as the Peshitta (Jacobite pronunciation: Peshitto), i.e., "the simple or plain (scil. version)." It is not certain in what sense this was intended, whether to indicate it as the common (vulgaris) version, or one lacking in paraphrase, or perhaps to distinguish it as "simple" in contrast to the annotated Syro-Hexaplar text derived from the Hexapla (cf. p. 57).

The literary problem of the Peshitta is rather complex and suffers from the lack of a critical edition describing the manuscript tradition (but cf. p. 83). Syriac information on the origin of the Peshitta is largely of a legendary nature and of little value, e.g., one tradition dates the version in the reign of King Solomon, while another ascribes it to Christian sources.

The Peshitta has had a most varied history as revealed in its manuscript tradition and the differences from the standard text to be found in patristic quotations from the Bible. These relationships have been studied most thoroughly in the Pentateuch. The similarities between the Targums and the Peshitta observed over a century ago have led in recent decades to the theory that they are ultimately derived from an eastern Aramaic (Syriac) recasting of a western Aramaic Targum. After Baumstark, Kahle, and Peters (see literature) offered various evidences of contact between the Targums and the Peshitta, A. Vööbus demonstrated by a thorough examination of both the manuscript tradition and the patristic literature that in the Pentateuch there was an early stage so closely related to the Targums that the inference of direct dependence on an early Palestinian Targum is inescapable.[1] Delekat came to a similar conclusion for Isaiah.[2] This suggests immediate Jewish origins for the Peshitta, and historically this is easy to imagine. During the first century

---

1. A Vööbus, *Peschitta und Targumim des Pentateuchs* (1958); cf. however the critical review by J. Ziegler, *Theologische Revue* 58 (1962), pp. 304ff.
2. L. Delekat, *ZAW* 69 (1957), pp. 21-54; *Bibl* 38 (1957), pp. 185-199, 321-335.

the ruling house and leading circles of Adiabene (east of the Tigris) were won over to the Jewish faith for several decades (*ca.* A.D. 40-70). They needed a version of the Old Testament, especially of the Pentateuch, in their own language—Syriac. This places the beginnings of the Syriac version of the Old Testament in the middle of the first century A.D.[3]

According to other scholars the Peshitta is of Christian or Jewish Christian origin;[4] this is suggested by a certain laxness in the rendering of the Levitical Law as well as by the Syriac tradition itself, which, however, is not unanimous (see above). A conclusive answer cannot be given because so many questions about the early period remain unsolved.

The later history of the text is also complicated and only partially clear. It is clear from the manuscript tradition that the original Peshitta has undergone one or more drastic revisions, weakening considerably the traces of Targumic influence. But it was long before the revised text prevailed; Biblical manuscripts with little or no revision continued in circulation for a considerable time. On the whole, different forms of the text were in competition in Syria for centuries. Besides the revised text there were not only the archaic traditions, but also the Septuagint and the Syro-Hexaplar with readings of the late Greek versions in their margins, and even the Masoretic text (although to a lesser extent because Hebrew was little known), all of which were familiar and exercised their influence. The Septuagint was the most influential. This should be noted particularly when evaluating the Peshitta for textual criticism. Agreements with the Septuagint can be explained by the later intrusion of the Septuagint readings. In such instances the two witnesses are reduced in effect to one.

Thus the Peshitta has been shaped by many different hands, and in different books it is very uneven. Further research is necessary to establish its history and textual importance for *all* the books of the Old Testament. But already it may be affirmed that the Peshitta is an important witness to the Old Testament text, and must certainly be taken into account by the textual critic.[5]

3. Cf. P. Kahle, *The Cairo Geniza* (1959[2]), pp. 270-73.
4. Cf. A. Vööbus, "Syriac versions," *IDBS* (1976), p. 849.
5. M. D. Koster has presented an exhaustive study of the Peshitta text in the book of Exodus: *The Peshiṭta of Exodus: The Development of its Text in the Course of Fifteen Centuries, Studia Semitica Neerlandica* 19 (1977). On the basis of his examination of a large number of manuscripts from the fifth to the nineteenth century, including the "priceless" British Museum Ms. Add. 14,425 (cf. below and pl. 39), Koster draws the following picture: "This is the picture of a single translation of the Hebrew basic text into Syriac which in the course of time gradually moved further away from MT. . . . This development is characterized by a gradual extension of the text through the addition of complementary words and even (from 5b1 to BTR) a few explanatory sentences, which clearly mark the transition between the different stages. In as far as one can speak of a 'Targumisches Profil' in P, this is therefore to be found not at the beginning but at the end of the development of its text" (p. 212). Koster's important conclusions argue against the Targum and recension hypothesis: the extent of their relevance for the *whole* of the Old Testament remains to be demonstrated by further research.

2. MANUSCRIPTS AND EDITIONS

In the fifth century the Syriac church became divided into Nestorians and Jacobites, and accordingly the Nestorian (East Syriac) and Jacobite (West Syriac) traditions are to be distinguished. There is a series of early Peshitta manuscripts[6] beginning in the fifth century A.D., such as the British Museum Ms. Add. 14,425 from the year 464, containing Genesis, Exodus, Numbers, and Deuteronomy. The most important of these is the West Syriac *Codex Ambrosianus* in Milan, from the sixth or seventh century, containing the entire Old Testament; a photolithographic edition was published by A. M. Ceriani, *Translatio Pescitto Veteris Testamenti*, 1876 (S^A). Also cited in BHS are the London codex British Museum Add. 14,431 (S^B), the Leningrad codex Public Library No. 2 (S^C), and the London codex British Museum Add. 14,442 (S^D).

Also of importance are the Biblical quotations of the Syriac Church Fathers, such as Ephraem Syrus (d. 373) and Aphraates, who lived in the period before the division of the church. In BHK the readings of Aphraates, whose twenty-three treatises from the years 337-345 are the earliest surviving writings in the Syriac language, are cited as S^{Aphr}. BHS also cites readings from Jacob of Edessa, *ca.* 700, edited by Goshen-Gottstein ($S^{Jac\,edess}$), and from Bar Hebraeus, 1226-1286, edited by Sprengling-Graham ($S^{Bar\,Hebr}$).[7]

There has been to date no edition of the Peshitta that is completely satisfactory for critical purposes. The Paris Polyglot of 1645 became the standard text on which later editions were based, but it was itself dependent on a poor manuscript from the seventeenth century as its principal source. Although the deficiencies of this edition were recognized, it was reprinted in an even worse form by Walton in the London Polyglot of 1657 (S^W), with the readings of a few Syriac manuscripts appended in the sixth volume. All later editions were prepared for practical (missionary) purposes, for the use of the surviving Syriac communities in the mountains of Kurdistan, around Lake Urmia, and in northern Iran. Their textual value is slight. The edition of Lee (1823, cited in BH as S^L) is based mainly on the London Polyglot together with a few other manuscripts. The edition of Urmia (1852, reprinted 1854; cited as S^U) by the American Protestant Missionary Society, and that of the Dominicans of Mosul in 1887-1891 (reprinted 1951; cited in BHS as S^M) differ from the editions mentioned above by representing the East Syriac tradition.

Editions of individual books were prepared by W. E. Barnes and

Margin sigla: S^{Mss}, S^A, S^B S^C S^D, [S^{Aphr}], $S^{Jac\,edess}$, $S^{Bar\,Hebr}$, S^W, S^L, S^U, S^M

---

6. Cf. *List of Old Testament Peshitta Manuscripts,* edited by the Peshitta Institute, Leiden University (1961); Supplements *VT* 12 (1962), pp. 127f., 237f., 351; 18 (1968), pp. 128-143; 27 (1977), pp. 508-511.

7. M. H. Goshen-Gottstein, ed., "Neue Syrohexaplafragmente," *Bibl* 37 (1956), pp. 175-183; Sprengling-Graham, *Barhebraei Scholiae* 1 (1931).

others. In 1904 there appeared *The Peshitta Psalter according to the West Syrian Text edited with an Apparatus Criticus*, and in 1914 the *Pentateuchus Syriace post Samuelum Lee, recognovit, emendavit, edidit G. E. Barnes, adiuvantibus C. W. Mitchell, I. Pinkerton*, intended for practical use but drawing also upon manuscript studies.

　　A new edition of the Peshitta is in preparation under the direction of P. A. H. de Boer at the Peshitta Institute of the University of Leiden, sponsored by the International Organization for the Study of the Old Testament. Already published: *The Old Testament in Syriac according to the Peshitta Version, Sample Edition: Song of Songs, Tobit, 4 Ezra* (1966); *General Preface to the complete work* by P. A. H. de Boer and W. Baars (1972); 4/6 (contains several apocrypha and pseudepigrapha), edited by H. Schneider, W. Baars, J. C. H. Lebram (1972); 4/3, *Apocalypse of Baruch–4 Esdras* (1973); 2/4, *Kings,* edited by H. Gottlieb in collaboration with E. Hammershaimb (1976) 1/1, *Preface, Genesis*, prepared by the Peshitta Institute; *Exodus*, prepared by M. D. Koster (1977); 2/2, *Judges, Samuel*, edited by P. B. Dirksen and P. A. H. de Boer (1978).

C
THE OTHER VERSIONS

VIII
THE OLD LATIN (𝔏)

1. *ORIGIN AND PROBLEMS*

IN ROME ITSELF GREEK SUPPLANTED LATIN AS THE LAN-
guage of religion and philosophy until the third century A.D., when Latin
again became dominant; meanwhile in Southern Gaul and in North Africa
Latin always held its ground, and it is in these areas that we first find Latin
Biblical texts around A.D. 150. *Tertullian* (b. in Carthage *ca.* 160) appar- $𝔏^{Tert}$
ently used a written version of the Scriptures in a Latin quite different
from his own. The Latin version, like others, was produced to meet the
practical needs of public worship and private devotion. Presumably at
first the Lessons read in the worship service were translated orally for
those who were unacquainted with Greek. Then these translations were
written down and extended to include all the books of the Bible. It is
certain that *Cyprian* (d. 258) was dependent on the Old Latin text for his $𝔏^{CY}$
Bible quotations.

The *Old Latin* version, as distinct from the later version by Jerome,
was translated from the Septuagint, the text customarily used in the
Christian communities: it has been called "the Septuagint in Latin cloth-
ing."[1] The Old Latin is a particularly important witness to the Septuagint
text because it goes back to the period before the Septuagint recensions.
But there are great preliminary difficulties in the way of its use for textual
criticism, and these can only be overcome by research based on critical
editions of the manuscript tradition. The basic problem of Old Latin
research is the question whether there was originally a single version from
which the known forms are derived, or there were several independent
versions. Statements by the Church Fathers suggest a plurality of versions, as when Augustine distinguishes between Itala and several other
Latin versions. The problem is only made more difficult by the fact that if
there was an original version it was regarded as neither official nor

---

1. J. Ziegler, "Antike und moderne lateinische Psalmenübersetzungen," *SAM*
(1960), p. 5.

inviolate: independent alterations to improve its popular Latin idiom and bring it closer to its Greek base could well have produced such different forms of the text that their common origin would hardly be suspected. At all events an African text can now be distinguished from a European text which itself comprises several different subtypes. Thus Old Latin must be taken as a collective term rather than as designating a particular text. Considering the variety of the tradition which attests to continuous work on the texts, we cannot expect more than a fraction of the surviving manuscripts to have escaped the influence of the Septuagint recensions.

2. EDITIONS AND MANUSCRIPTS

As the Old Latin was superseded by the Vulgate in the early medieval period, interest in its manuscript tradition waned. Thus it has not survived in complete manuscripts in the way ග has. Instead, it has to be assembled from fragmentary manuscripts, liturgical books, and patristic quotations in commentaries, sermons, letters, etc. The Benedictine *Pierre Sabatier* (1682-1742) edited a collection of the material then known in *Bibliorum*
𝔏 *sacrorum latinae versiones etc.* (1739-1749; cited as 𝔏). Sabatier prints in one column the fullest continuous text he could find for a passage, and beside it the Vulgate, together with variants from other Old Latin sources in an apparatus. There are naturally many lacunae in the 𝔏 text.

S. Berger has brought together a series of unpublished Old Latin texts of the Old Testament in *Notices et Extraits des Manuscrits de la Bibliothèque National et autres Bibliothèques,* tome 34/2 (1893), pp.
[𝔏 (berger)] 119-152; cited in BHK as [𝔏(berger)].

A new edition following modern scholarly methods and including evidence discovered since Sabatier was undertaken in 1949: *Vetus Latina: Die Reste der altlateinischen Bibel nach Petrus Sabatier neu gesammelt und herausgegeben von der Erzabtei Beuron* (edited by Bonifatius Fischer). This large edition will include (1) all manuscripts and fragments of the Old Latin Bible, (2) all quotations in the writings of the Church Fathers to the period of Isidore of Seville (*ca.* 560-636), and of the more important later writers to the Carolingian period. Already published: 1, *Sigla* (1949); 2, *Genesis* (1951-1954); cited in BHS as 𝔏.

Besides the collections of Sabatier and Berger, BHK also refers to the following manuscripts.

(a) The **Constance Old Latin fragments of the Prophets,** edited by Alban Dold, with glosses together with the corresponding texts of the Prophets from Zürich and St. Gall, and published in *Konstanzer alt-lateinische Propheten- und Evangelienbruchstücke,* 1923 (pl. 40; cited
[𝔏D] in BHK as 𝔏D). This is a comprehensive edition and study of the frag-ments from a manuscript of the Prophets once in Constance which was probably written in northern Italy in the fifth century, and fragments of

which have been discovered since 1856 in the bindings of twenty-six parchment manuscripts. It includes fragments of Hosea, Amos, Micah, Joel, Jonah, Nahum, Ezekiel, and Daniel.

(b) The *Würzburg palimpsest codex* published by Ernst Ranke, *Par Palimpsestorum Wirceburgensium* (1871; cited as $\mathfrak{L}^h$). The lower writing [$\mathfrak{L}^h$] is from the fifth century (probably from central eastern France) and contains fragments of the Pentateuch and the Prophets.

(c) *Codex Lugdunensis* (pl. 41), in the Municipal Library of Lyons (cited as $\mathfrak{L}^L$). Edition: U. Robert, *Pentateuchi versio latina antiquissima e* [$\mathfrak{L}^L$] *codice Lugdunensi* (1881); *Heptateuchi partis posterioris versio latina antiquissimo e codice Lugdunensi* (1900). An uncial of the seventh century, probably written in Lyons; now mutilated, the manuscript contains parts of Gen. 16:9–Judg. 20:31.

(d) *Codex Gothicus Legionensis,* Léon, S. Isidoro (marginal readings cited in BH as $\mathfrak{L}^{Lg}$; BHS also distinguishes $\mathfrak{L}^{91}$, the codex; $\mathfrak{L}^{93}$, a $\quad\mathfrak{L}^{Lg}\;\mathfrak{L}^{91},$ transcript of the codex by C. Vercellone in Rome, 1864). A Vulgate text $\qquad\quad\mathfrak{L}^{93}$ from A.D. 690 with many Old Latin readings noted in the margin by the same hand for the Heptateuch and the books of Samuel, Kings, and Chronicles in the Old Testament.

(e) *Palimpsestus Vindobonensis* in the Biblioteca Nazionale of Naples since 1919 (BHK $\mathfrak{L}^{Vind}$). The lower writing is from the fifth century, [$\mathfrak{L}^{Vind}$] probably Italian. Contains parts of Genesis, Exodus, and Leviticus. The edition by Belsheim, *Palimpsestus Vindobonensis* (1885), is faulty (Dold, Fischer).

In BHS the following are also referred to.

(f) *Codex Parisinus Latinus bibliothecae nationalis 11947* (cited as $\mathfrak{L}^G$). An Old Latin Psalter of the fifth to sixth century, probably from the $\mathfrak{L}^G$ Benedictine Abbey of Corbie (France), now in the Bibliothèque Nationale, Paris.

(g) *Codex Veronensis* (cited as $\mathfrak{L}^R$). A Greek-Old Latin Psalter in $\quad\mathfrak{L}^R$ the Biblioteca Capitolare, Verona, from the sixth century. The following canticles are added to the Psalms: Exod: 15:1-21; Deut. 32:1-44 + 31:30; 1 Sam. 2:1-10; Isa. 5:1-9; Jonah 2:3-10; Hab. 3:2-19; Luke 1:46-55; Dan. 3:51-90 (cf. $\mathfrak{G}^R$, p. 71).

(h) *Fragmenta Sangallensia Prophetarum* (cited as $\mathfrak{L}^S$). These are $\quad\mathfrak{L}^S$ derived from a manuscript of the ninth to tenth century "whose leaves were found as endsheets in manuscripts bound at St. Gall" (Dold). Edited and published by A. Dold, *Neue St. Galler vorhieronymianische Propheten-Fragmente der St. Galler Sammelhandschrift 1398b zugehörig, Texte und Arbeiten* 31, 1940. Included are fragments of Ezekiel, Daniel, Hosea, Amos, Habakkuk, and Zephaniah; cf. (a) above for the publication of other fragments from the same source.

(i) Also cited in BHS are the following:

$\mathfrak{L}^{94}$ Readings from a lost tenth(?)-century manuscript inscribed in $\quad\mathfrak{L}^{94}$

the margin of Escorial, Biblioteca de S. Lorenzo, Incunabulum 54 (Venice, 1478).

𝕷¹¹⁵   𝕷¹¹⁵ Naples, Biblioteca Nazionale, Latin 1 (earlier Vindob. 17), fragments of 1 Samuel–2 Kings from a fifth-century manuscript.

𝕷¹¹⁶   𝕷¹¹⁶ Fragmenta Quedlinburgensia et Magdeburgensia, a fifth-century manuscript in the Preussische Staatsbibliothek, Berlin, containing 1 Samuel–2 Kings.

𝕷¹¹⁷   𝕷¹¹⁷ Fragmenta Vindobonensia, the endsheets of Vienna, Nationalbibliothek Codex Lat. 15479, containing fragments of 2 Samuel.

𝕷 ᵍˡ   𝕷 ᵍˡ A Latin Glossary, edited by D. de Bruyne, "Fragments d'anciennes versiones latines tirés d'un glossaire biblique," *Archivum Latinitatis Medii Aevi* 3 (Paris, 1927), pp. 113-120.

Often Old Latin Biblical quotations are preserved in the writings of Church Fathers, e.g., *Ambrose*, bishop of Milan (d. 397), who is cited in Ambr   BHS as Ambr.

IX

THE VULGATE (𝔳)

1. *JEROME'S VERSION*

WE HAVE SEEN THAT THE TEXT OF THE BIBLE CIRCULATED in a wide variety of forms in the Latin-speaking church. A uniform and reliable text was badly needed for theological discussion and liturgical use. Pope Damasus I (366-384) was accordingly moved to commission Jerome, a scholar eminently qualified by his knowledge of Latin, Greek, and Hebrew, to produce such a text. Jerome was born between 340 and 350 in Dalmatia, studied grammar and rhetoric in Rome, and then dedicated himself to an ascetic life and theological studies, living at various places in the western and eastern parts of the empire. As a hermit in the desert of Chalcis he had learned Hebrew from a Jewish Christian, and later   Hier [Hie] as a priest he had studied under Apollinarius of Laodicea and Gregory of Nazianzus. He was recalled to Rome in 382 and commissioned to work on the Latin Bible, which he began in Rome and continued as the head of a monastery near Bethlehem from the autumn of 386. His work there went far beyond the original plans. We can discuss only his work on the Old Testament here.

Various stages are to be distinguished:

(a) At first Jerome made a rapid *(cursim)* and partial revision of the Psalter according to the Septuagint, which enjoyed canonical authority at the time. This revision was introduced into the liturgy of the city of Rome, whence it received the name *Psalterium Romanum*. It is still in use today in the Office at St. Peter's, and in the Psalm texts of the Old Roman Mass.[1]

(b) Jerome undertook a second revision of the Psalter in Palestine, based on the Hexapla of Origen found at Caesarea in Palestine. This Psalter, which was first used liturgically in Gaul and is hence called the

---

1. Edition: R. Weber, *Le Psautier Romain et les autres anciens Psautiers Latins* (*Collectanea Biblica Latina* 10, 1953). De Bruyne's theory (*Revue Bénédictine* 42, 1930) that the Psalterium Romanum has nothing to do with this revision by Jerome has not been generally accepted.

Ga *Psalterium Gallicanum* (cited in BHS as Ga), was soon adopted elsewhere
and is still today a part of the official Roman edition of the Vulgate.[2] It is
essentially a revision of the Old Latin according to the fifth column of the
Hexapla. Apparently Jerome made similar revisions of the entire Old
Testament, but only the texts of Job and fragments of Proverbs, Song of
Solomon, and Ecclesiastes have survived.

    (c) The work which represents the real achievement of Jerome,
establishing his significance for the history of the text and exercising the
broadest influence for the history of western culture, is his *translation of
the Old Testament from the Hebrew text* which he accomplished in the years
390-405. He alone among the Christians in the West was capable of
making this translation from the original text, because of his knowledge of
Hebrew. Quite apart from the flood of criticism from those who regarded
him as a forger *(falsarius)*, we can appreciate how unprecedented, how
inconceivable his undertaking was if we consider that even Augustine
himself was disquieted at Jerome's setting aside the inspired, canonical
Septuagint to go back to a text which no one in the church but himself
could understand. Augustine feared that this would lead to a division
between the Greek and the Latin churches, and he never relinquished his
misgivings over the church's use of this version based on the Hebrew
text. This difference between Jerome and Augustine reflects different
appreciations of the Septuagint. Augustine regarded it as inspired
("Spiritus enim, qui in prophetis erat, quando illa dixerunt, idem ipse erat
etiam in septuaginta uiris, quando illa interpretati sunt," *De Civitate Dei*
18.43), while Jerome contested the inspiration of the Septuagint ("Aliud
est enim vatem, aliud esse interpretem: ibi Spiritus ventura praedicit, hic
eruditio et verborum copia ea quae intellegit transfert," *Praefatio in
Pentateuchum, Biblia Sacra iuxta Latinam Vulgatam Versionem* 1, 1926,
p. 67).[3]

    Jerome, however, was no iconoclast, and the independence of his
version should not be exaggerated, even though recent studies credit him
with a deeper knowledge of Hebrew than was earlier recognized.[4] As
there were no dictionaries or grammars in his day, his most important aids
were the Greek versions of the Septuagint, Aquila, Symmachus, and
Theodotion, and any information he could obtain from the Jewish side. As

---

2. Published as vol. 10 of the large Benedictine edition of the Vulgate (cf. p. 95):
Liber Psalmorum ex recensione Sancti Hieronymi (1953). It includes the *Epistula ad
Sunniam et Fretelam,* in which Jerome comments on particular passages in the Psalms and
on the method he observed. Cf. also J. Ziegler, *Antike und moderne lateinische
Psalmenübersetzungen* (1960).

3. Cf. also W. Schwarz, *Principles and Problems of Biblical Translation* (1955),
pp. 26-30.

4. Cf. B. Kedar-Kopfstein, *The Vulgate as a Translation,* Diss. Hebrew University, Jerusalem, 1968, pp. 50ff.; J. Barr, "St. Jerome's Appreciation of Hebrew," *BJRL* 49
(1966/67), pp. 281-302.

a result he kept very much along traditional lines, and the influences of the resources mentioned above are clearly observable in his work.[5] The distrust of his work shown by the majority of the theologians, as well as his own churchmanship, urged him to consider carefully the current Latin text.[6] He reinterpreted some passages in a quite Christian sense. On the other hand, the version does not hide the Greco-Roman education of its author, even if many particular traits may be attributed to later revisers. Thus the Rome edition of the Vulgate now in preparation (cf. p. 95) states that "the 'Ciceronianisms' of the Vulgate are largely from Alcuin. It is true that in many passages Jerome approaches classical Latin usage, yet he also retained more (real or supposed) 'vulgarisms' than the traditionally accepted text suggested."[7]

The work of Jerome thus presents a very complex image from the very beginning, and its later developments, which we can sketch only briefly in the next section, further increased this complexity. This seriously affects its value for textual criticism, for it is difficult to determine from the version without careful research precisely what Hebrew text Jerome had before him. In Stummer's words, "When Jerome agrees with the Septuagint or with the later translators against our present Masoretic text, I believe he should usually be disregarded. For at most it proves that in his day or at some later time this was the reading of the Septuagint; it cannot prove without further evidence that Jerome's Hebrew text differed from our own."[8]

2. THE HISTORY OF THE VULGATE[9]

It was only over a period of centuries that Jerome's version attained the general recognition that has been associated with the name "Vulgate" since the sixteenth century.[10] At the beginning of the seventh century it was on a par with the Old Latin in the esteem and usage of the church, but in the eighth and ninth centuries it won the lead. It was inevitable that when these two texts of the Latin Bible remained in use side by side they

5. The extent of Jerome's debt to the later Greek translators, especially Aquila and Symmachus, is shown by a wealth of evidence in the study by J. Ziegler, *Die jüngeren griechischen Übersetzungen als Vorlagen der Vulgata in den prophetischen Schriften (Vorl. Verzeichnis Braunsberg, Wintersemester, 1943/44)*.

6. G. Q. A. Meershoek, *Le Latin biblique d'après Saint Jérôme (Latinitas Christianorum Primaeva*, fasc. 20, 1966), p. 244, speaks of a "fidelité à la consuetudo." Meershoek suggests that as in the Gospels, so also in many books of the Old Testament Jerome's version deserves to be called a revision rather than a translation.

7. F. Stummer, *ZAW* 58 (1940/41), p. 258.

8. F. Stummer, *Einführung in die lateinische Bibel* (1928), p. 123.

9. Cf. R. Loewe, "The Medieval History of the Latin Vulgate," *CHB* 2 (1969), pp. 102-154.

10. On the history of the name "Vulgate," cf. E. F. Sutcliffe, *Bibl* 29 (1948), pp. 345-352; A. Allgeier, *ibid.*, pp. 353-390.

should influence one another. A revision of great importance was made by *Alcuin* (730/735-804), who was close to Charlemagne and from 796 was the Abbot of St. Martin in Tours. He made stylistic alterations in Jerome's version, as we have indicated. Through the scriptorium at Tours the text edited by Alcuin became "the standard text of France, (thus) bringing to its conclusion a process of development which finally assured, through centuries of struggle and vicissitudes, the sole and uncontested authority to the Vulgate text of St. Jerome."[11] About the year 1100 Abbot *Stephen Harding* produced an important scholarly edition for the Cistercian monasteries. In the later Middle Ages a newly revised standard text called the Paris Bible[12] became widely influential. It was in this recension that a division of the text into chapters devised by Stephen Langton, a teacher at Paris and later Archbishop of Canterbury (d. 1228), achieved general acceptance.

The decree of the Council of Trent on April 8, 1546, was of epoch-making significance for the later history of the Vulgate: it declared the Vulgate, in contrast to the burgeoning variety of new versions, to be the authentic Bible of the Catholic Church "i.e., authoritative in matters of faith and morals, without any implication of rejecting or forbidding either the Septuagint or the original Hebrew text, or in the New Testament the Greek text."[13]

This special recognition of the Vulgate necessitated an official edition of its text, but it was nearly a half-century before one was available. After a variety of attempts, a hastily prepared edition revised by Sixtus V himself (the *Sixtine* edition) appeared in 1589. This was withdrawn after his death and replaced by the edition of Clement VIII (the *Clementine* edition of 1592; the second and third editions of 1593 and 1598 included some improvements). Although even this edition cannot claim to have restored the text of Jerome, it has remained the official text until the present time. Worthy of note among the many modern editions of the Clementine text is *Biblia Sacra Vulgatae Editionis: Editio emendatissima apparatu critico instructa cura et studio Abbatiae Pontificiae S. Hieronymi in Urbe Ordinis S. Benedicti* (Turin, 1959). The apparatus compares the critical editions thus far published of Rome (Old Testament, see below) and Oxford (New Testament). The Psalms are printed in parallel columns representing the *Psalterium Gallicum*, the *Psalterium iuxta Hebraeos* (following the new critical edition by Dom H. de Sainte

11. B. Fischer, *Die Alkuin-Bibel (Aus der Geschichte der lateinischen Bibel* 1, 1957), p. 19.

12. The text which achieved wide distribution through the first Gutenberg Bible of 1452/55 and its successors in the fifteenth century was a very slightly revised form of this Paris Bible; cf. H. Schneider, *Der Text der Gutenbergbibel, Bonner Biblische Beiträge* 7, 1954.

13. F. Stummer, *Einführung in die lateinische Bibel* (1928), p. 172.

Marie, see below), and the *new version* prepared by the Pontifical Biblical Institute in 1945.

The Benedictine Order has been commissioned since 1907 with the preparation of a comprehensive edition, taking full account of the wealth of manuscript evidence (about eight thousand manuscripts), and designed to give a complete picture of the textual tradition. After exhaustive preliminary studies it began to appear in 1926 under the title: *Biblia Sacra iuxta latinam vulgatam versionem ad codicem fidem iussu Pii PP. XI cura et studio Monachorum Abbatiae Pontificiae S. Hieronymi in Urbe Ordinis S. Benedicti edita.* Already published volumes are: the Pentateuch, Joshua, Judges, Ruth, Samuel, Kings, Chronicles, Ezra, Nehemiah, Tobit, Judith, Esther, Job, Psalms, Proverbs, Ecclesiastes, Song of Solomon, Wisdom of Solomon, Sirach, Isaiah, and the Epistle of Baruch.[14]

A two-volume edition of the Vulgate has been published by the Württemberg Bible Society: *Biblia Sacra iuxta Vulgatam Versionem: Adiuvantibus B. Fischer OSB, J. Gribomont OSB, H. F. D. Sparks, W. Thiele; Recensuit et brevi apparatu instruxit R. Weber OSB*, 1969[1], 1975[2]. "Our text is a new text, established from the evidence of the manuscripts with the help of the two big modern editions" (p. xxii), i.e., for the Old Testament, the Benedictine edition mentioned above to the extent it has appeared. Its text has been accepted in this manual edition subject to careful verification and correction where necessary. For the Prophets and some other books a provisional text was printed (see the Foreword of the edition for a statement of its editorial principles). In the Psalter the *Psalmi iuxta Septuaginta emendati* (the Gallican Psalter) and the *Psalmi iuxta Hebraicum translati* are printed on facing pages.

A critical edition of Jerome's version of the Psalter from the Hebrew, which was not included in the Vulgate, has been produced by Henri de Sainte Marie, *Sancti Hieronymi Psalterium iuxta Hebraeos, Collectanea Biblica Latina* 11 (1954).

---

14. It must be added that several books contained in the Vulgate were not revised by Jerome because he did not regard them as canonical: Baruch (with the Letter of Jeremiah), Wisdom, Sirach, 1 and 2 Maccabees. These books appear, therefore, in the Old Latin version.

X

THE COPTIC VERSIONS (к)

COPTIC IS THE LANGUAGE OF THE NATIVE EGYPTIAN CHRIS-tians, and is written in an alphabet mainly derived from Greek (pl. 44). The Greek language was widely spoken in Egypt, but not among the native peasant population. As Christianity spread to these circles at an early date it had to use Coptic, the popular language, enriched by Greek loanwords. There are several dialects of Coptic, so that there are many quite different versions grouped together in BH under the term Coptic Sa[Sah] (к). The earliest was undoubtedly the *Sahidic* version of Upper Egypt,[1] translated from the Greek about the middle of the third century A.D., and probably undertaken at the official request of the church. This was followed by *Akhmimic,* which was based upon the Sahidic, and later in the Bo fourth century by the *Bohairic* (Lower Egyptian), which was translated from the Greek independently of the Sahidic.[2]

For textual criticism, especially for Septuagintal research, these versions are valuable for their antiquity. A great many complete and fragmentary manuscripts written before the end of the fifth century have survived, not a few of which date from the third or fourth century. On the basis of evidence presented by Grossouw and Ziegler for the Minor Prophets,[3] Kahle has suggested "that the basis for the Sahidic version was the Septuagint text as established by Origen for the fifth column of his Hexapla." "It is very probable that in the Sahidic version of the Minor Prophets we have evidence for the Septuagint text of Origen which was translated either within Origen's lifetime or at any rate very soon after his death, and which as early as the fourth century is supported by manu-

---

1. According to P. E. Kahle, Jr., *Bala'iza* (1954), Sahidic was the official dialect of the native population of Egypt and the official language of Alexandria long before the spread of Christianity.
2. On the history of the Coptic dialects and the Coptic versions of the Bible, cf. R. Kasser, "Les dialectes coptes et les versions coptes bibliques," *Bibl* 46 (1965), pp. 287-310.
3. W. Grossouw, *The Coptic Versions of the Minor Prophets: A Contribution to the Study of the Septuagint* (Rome, 1938); J. Ziegler, *Bibl* 25 (1944), pp. 105-142.

script evidence (Jonah in Budge, *Biblical Texts*),[4] evidence almost four hundred years older than the Syro-Hexaplaric version translated by Paul of Tella in the years 616 to 617, which up to now has been accepted as the main source for the Septuagint of Origen."[5] Ziegler himself is more cautious. He sees indications in this and related evidence "that even before Origen various passages had been corrected from the Hebrew text: we must beware of attributing agreements with 𝔐 too readily to Hexaplaric influence."[6]

4. Cf. pl. 44.
5. P. Kahle, *TLZ* 79 (1954), col. 94; *idem, The Cairo Geniza* (1959²), p. 261.
6. J. Ziegler, *Duodecim Prophetae* (1943), p. 34.

XI

ঀ

THE ETHIOPIC VERSION (ঀ)

ABOUT THE MIDDLE OF THE FOURTH CENTURY THE KING of Aksum in Ethiopia and his people were won over to Christianity. A translation of the Bible was probably begun shortly afterward, with the translators working from a variety of sources, even within single passages, possibly using the Syriac and Hebrew alongside the Greek.[1] But the completion of the version took a long while, possibly several centuries according to some. It is open to question how far the original version is represented in surviving manuscripts, the earliest of which is from the thirteenth century (pl. 45). In any event a considerable amount of later revision must be recognized, largely under Arabic influence. Ziegler has found that the Ethiopic version in the Minor Prophets is often associated with the Alexandrian group of Septuagint witnesses. "The Ethiopic frequently has a very free rendering. This is at times because the translator was not familiar with the Greek vocabulary, but at times due to his efforts to achieve a fluency of style and to render the difficult Greek original more readably."[2] (Cf. also p. 210.)

---

1. E. Ullendorf, *Ethiopia and the Bible* (1968), p. 56, suggests a "team of translators." He writes: "Work on one single linguistic *Vorlage* was, perhaps, the exception rather than the rule in the peculiar circumstances that obtained in the Aksumite kingdom of the fourth–sixth centuries."

2. J. Ziegler, *Duodecim Prophetae* (1943), p. 25.

XII
THE ARMENIAN VERSION (Arm)

AT THE BEGINNING OF THE FIFTH CENTURY, AFTER A PERIOD in which the national Armenian Church used Greek and Syriac for both literature and liturgy, the Armenian priest Mesrob (*ca.* 361-439) invented the Armenian alphabet and laid the basis for a national Armenian literature. At this time the Bible was translated. According to Armenian tradition, for which there is good evidence, this first version of the Bible (*ca.* A.D. 414) was based on the Syriac Peshitta and was very soon revised. The final official version which has come down to us was based on the Septuagint, but it also shows clearly the influence of the Peshitta. It may be that this official version was actually a revision of the first version which was made, at least in some books, with the aid of the Septuagint.[1]

1. Private communication from Professor A. Vööbus of Chicago. B. Johnson has called attention to the influence of Hexaplaric manuscripts on the Armenian version in *Die armenische Bibelübersetzung als hexaplarischer Zeuge im 1. Samuelbuch (Coniectanea Biblica, Old Testament Series 2, 1968).*

XIII

THE ARABIC VERSIONS (𝔄)

WITH THE VICTORY OF ISLAM THE USE OF ARABIC SPREAD
widely, and for Jews and Christians in the conquered lands it became the
language of daily life. This gave rise to the need for Arabic versions of the
Bible, which need was met by a number of versions, mainly independent
and concerned primarily for interpretation (pl. 46). The version by Saadia
Gaon[1] (of Egypt, and from 928 the head of the Jewish academy at Sura in
Babylonia), of which only a part has survived, was based on the Hebrew
text. It was also accepted by the Samaritans at first, but later subjected
continually to alterations, as is evident from the manuscripts. The textus
receptus of the Arabic version used today among the Samaritans is attributed to Abu Sa'id, who lived in the second half of the thirteenth
century.[2]

The value of the Arabic versions for textual criticism is slight. But
they make a contribution to the history of interpretation, and by shedding
light on the development of earlier versions they offer suggestions toward
the solution of their problems.[3]

Translation into Arabic were also made from the Septuagint, from
the Peshitta, and from other versions. The manuscripts and editions (especially the polyglots) contain for the most part translations of very diverse
origins. Thus it is in no sense a unified Arabic version that is represented
in BH by the sign 𝔄.

---

1. R. Ecker, *Die arabische Job-Übersetzung des Gaon Saadja ben Josef al-
Fajjumi, Studien z. AT u. NT* 4 (1962).
2. P. Kahle, *The Cairo Geniza* (1959²), pp. 53f.
3. Cf. R. Edelmann, *Studia Orientalia I. Pedersen dicata* (1953), p. 75.

D
TEXTUAL CRITICISM

XIV
THE AIMS OF TEXTUAL CRITICISM

THE HISTORY OF THE TEXT SHOWS CLEARLY THAT ALL OUR witnesses stand far removed from the original text both by time and by the processes of transmission. They contain, therefore, not only a great variety of scribal errors, such as occur inevitably in any form of manuscript transmission, but also some actual transformations of the original, both deliberate and accidental. Old Testament scholarship cannot rest content with such a situation. By means of textual criticism it attempts to ferret out all the alterations that have occurred and recover the earliest possible form of the text. This does not mean recovering the original wording of the sentences as they were first conceived, but the textual form of the Old Testament books when they attained their present shape and content and became canonical writings, i.e., in the fourth century B.C. or later, depending on the book. Even when the goal of textual criticism is defined in this way there should be no illusions about its attainability in detail. We should recognize that some corrupt passages will remain incapable of solution unless new discoveries open up new possibilities. But we should also recognize that only after the process of canonization was completed could such a mechanical attitude toward the text develop that an absolute literal accuracy could be expected of scribes. Before this occurred there was a period when apparently insignificant changes in wording aroused no objections unless the sense of the text were disturbed.[1]

The prehistory of our present Old Testament books lies beyond the province of textual criticism. Reconstructing the ipsissima verba of the prophets in their presumably original form, separating the various strands of the Pentateuch, investigating questions of literary integrity, and the like, are among the tasks properly entrusted to higher criticism,

---

1. Cf. the remarks on "popular texts" above (pp. 16f.), and G. Douglas Young, *Oudtestamentische Studiën* 8 (1950), p. 259, and earlier J. Wellhausen, *Der Text der Bücher Samuelis* (1871), pp. 16-21.

literary criticism, and exegesis. Although textual criticism, literary criticism, and exegesis frequently come into close contact and occasionally overlap in their practical application, yet in the interest of methodological clarity it is necessary to preserve in principle the distinction between these areas of research.

XV
CAUSES OF TEXTUAL CORRUPTION

1. *GENERAL REMARKS*

IF THE GOAL OF TEXTUAL CRITICISM CONSISTS IN REMOVing textual errors and restoring the original readings, the textual critic must have a clear idea of the kinds of errors he may expect to find. When copying out a text errors can occur in every conceivable way, as we well know from our own experience: sometimes we find it difficult to explain to ourselves later just how we came to make some particular error in writing down or transcribing a sentence. We can hardly expect at the outset to be able to correct and explain all the errors which eluded the attention of the early scribes, perhaps through sheer fatigue. A reading that appears doubtful or corrupt today may well have been caused by a lacuna in the copyist's exemplar due to a damaged writing surface, or a word or group of words that had become illegible. One error could easily give rise to several others and leave us no clue to how it happened. In many instances the assumption of a textual corruption which cannot be explained may be justified. But obviously such an assumption should be made as rarely as possible.

Besides those instances of textual corruption which cannot be explained because they depend on mere change, there is a whole series of errors which recur constantly whenever texts are copied out by hand. Where we can verify these typical errors we are on relatively safe grounds for restoring the text. A sound diagnosis is the first step toward a cure. Two major groups of typical errors may be distinguished: errors which are due to an unintentional, mechanical lapse on the part of the copyist (errors of reading and writing), and alterations which result from deliberation, leading to a departure from the copyist's exemplar (intentional alterations).

2. *ERRORS OF READING AND WRITING*[1]

These include all textual errors which arise from scribal misreading and miswriting (or even mishearing if transcribing from dictation). In order to prove that these errors are not the invention of modern textual critics but have actually occurred in manuscripts and can be expected in any manuscript, the following examples are taken primarily from a comparison of 𝔐 with the Isaiah scroll from Qumran (1QIsaᵃ). Because we are concerned here only with indicating a possible range of errors, the variants are simply listed without discussion.[2]

(a) *Confusion of similar letters* is the most frequent cause of errors of reading and writing. In the Hebrew square script the following are the most frequent confusions:

(i) ב and כ: Isa. 28:20 𝔐 כהתכנס, 1QIsaᵃ בהתכנס; Isa. 28:21 𝔐 בעמק, 1QIsaᵃ בהר, כעמק, כהר.

(ii) ד and ר: Isa. 9:8 𝔐 וידעו, 1QIsaᵃ וירעו; Isa. 14:4 𝔐 מדהבה, 1QIsaᵃ correctly מרהבה; Isa. 47:10 𝔐 ברעתך, 1QIsa² בדעתך; Isa. 33:8 𝔐 ערים, 1QIsaᵃ correctly עדים.

(iii) ה and ח: Isa. 30:33 𝔐 תפתה, 1QIsaᵃ תפתח; Isa. 42:16 𝔐 מחשך, 1QIsaᵃ מהשוכים; Isa. 47:13 𝔐 (K) הברו, 1QIsaᵃ חוברי, note also י for ו as in 𝔐 (Q); Isa. 51:9 𝔐 רהב, 1QIsaᵃ רחוב.

(iv) ה and ת: Isa. 42:25 𝔐 חמה אפו, 1QIsaᵃ correctly חמת אפו; Judg. 7:8 read צדת העם for צדה העם.

(v) ו and י: Isa. 5:29 𝔐 ושאג, 1QIsaᵃ ישאג as also 𝔐 (Q); Isa. 11:6 𝔐 ומריא, 1QIsaᵃ ימרו; Isa. 33:13 𝔐 ודעו, 1QIsaᵃ ידעו.

(vi) ע and צ: 2 Kgs. 20:4 𝔐 העיר, many manuscripts, Q, versions חצר (also confusion of ה and ח).

(vii) כ and נ: Isa. 33:1 𝔐 כנלתך, 1QIsaᵃ ככלותך.

For a large part of the Old Testament we must also consider the possibility of confusion occurring in the Old Hebrew script. Thus in Ps. 19:5 בהם may be derived from בים through a confusion of י with ה, which was quite similar in form. As the Lachish ostraca indicate, the letters א and ת, כ and נ, and ע and ד were quite similar in the Old Hebrew script, as were also ב and ר, ה and ח, and מ and נ (cf. pl. 48).

For assessing the readings of 𝔊 it is often important to remember the possible confusions of Greek uncial letters such as occur in the textual transmission of the New Testament.

---

1. F. Delitzsch, *Die Lese- und Schreibfehler im Alten Testament* (1920) provides a wealth of material; cf. also J. Kennedy, *An Aid to the Textual Amendment of the Old Testament*, edited by N. Levison (1928).

2. Numerous examples of scribal errors are given in J. Hempel, *Der textkritische Wert des Konsonantentextes von Kairener Genizafragmenten in Cambridge und Oxford zum Dt, NAG*, 1959, no. 10, pp. 220-234.

(b) *Transposition of letters* can occur most easily in an unpointed text, and it does occur frequently; Isa. 9:18 𝔐 נעתם, 1QIsaᵃ נתעם; Isa. 32:19 𝔐 העיר, 1QIsaᵃ היער; Isa. 28:1, 4 𝔐 גיא, 1QIsaᵃ גאי (as also proposed by L. Rost, *ZAW* n.s. 12, 1935, p. 292).

(c) *Haplography* (hpgr [haplogr]; "single writing") occurs when two identical or similar letters, groups of letters, or words are found together in an immediate sequence, and one of them is omitted by error.

    (i) *Omission of a single letter:* Isa. 5:8 𝔐 בית בבית, 1QIsaᵃ בית; Isa. 8:11 𝔐 בחזקת היד, 1QIsaᵃ כחזקת יד; Isa. 8:19 𝔐 בעד החיים, 1QIsaᵃ בעד חיים.

In the Lachish ostraca (3.9) the form חיהוה (= חי יהוה) is found; this suggests that two identical letters occurring together could sometimes be written once, even though they belonged to two different words. The reader had no difficulty in reading it correctly. It is tempting to view the many haplographies in the Old Testament in this light.[3]

    (ii) *Omission of two identical or similar words:* Isa. 26:3f. 𝔐 בך בטוח, 1QIsaᵃ בך בטחו; Isa. 38:11 𝔐 יה יה, 1QIsaᵃ יה.

(d) *Dittography* (dttg [dittogr]) is the accidental repetition of a letter, a group of letters, a word, or a group of words: Isa. 30:30 𝔐 השמיע השמיע, 1QIsaᵃ והשמיע; in Isa. 38:20 1QIsaᵃ repeats the whole of the preceding verse almost verbatim.

(e) *Omission by homoioteleuton* (homtel [homoeotel]; "similar ending") occurs when two words which are identical, are similar in form, or have identical endings are found close to each other, and the eye of the copyist moves from the first to the second, omitting the words that lie between them, e.g., Isa. 4:5f.: ברא יהוה . . . ענן [יומם ועשן ונגה אש להבה; יומם [לצל מהרב לילה כי על כל כבוד חפה וסכה תהיה. The words in brackets are lacking in 1QIsaᵃ; the scribe's eye passed from יומם in v. 5 to יומם in v. 6. For further examples in 1QIsaᵃ see Isa. 16:8f.; 23:15; 37:29; and perhaps also 40:7f. where the omitted words have been inserted. Omissions due to similarities in the beginnings of words are rarer (*homoioarcton,* homark [homoeoarct]).

(f) *Errors of joining and dividing words.* By contrast with Greek, which was written well into the medieval period without spacing or dividing signs between words (*scriptio continua*), there is no real proof of scriptio continua in Hebrew. A dividing sign is found regularly in the Siloam inscription and the Samarian ostraca, and frequently in the Lachish ostraca. As the recently-discovered manuscripts show, a space is found regularly between words in the square script, although it is admit-

---

3. On the principle of the double value of letters (whether single letters or groups of letters) which may be observed from the sixth century B.C. to the first century A.D., cf. now I. O. Lehman, "A Forgotten Principle of Biblical Textual Tradition Rediscovered," *JNES* 26 (1967), pp. 93-101.

tedly so small at times that it may be doubtful where one word ends and another begins. In such instances two words could be construed erroneously as one. The Lachish ostraca show examples of a scribe writing two words without an intervening space in order to fit the words into the space available (4.9; 5.10). And again, a single word could be divided between two lines. Both examples could easily lead to misunderstanding and a wrong construction of words and their divisions.

Erroneous joining of words is evident in Amos 6:12, where the generally adopted reading בבקר ים instead of בבקרים restores both parallelism and sense.

Erroneous word division is found in ℳ in Isa. 2:20 לחפר פרות, 1QIsaᵃ correctly לחפרפרים. In Jer. 2:21 the text has been made unintelligible by a wrong word division לי סורי הגפן; Duhm and many others read לסוריה גמן ("into a rotten vine").

(g) *Errors due to vowel letters.* Consonants were used as vowel signs at an early period, and as the recently-discovered manuscripts show, they were used quite freely for a time. If a vowel letter were later misconstrued as a consonant it would naturally lead to an error in the text. Thus from 1QIsaᵃ it appears that א was used as a vowel sign for *a* (e.g., Isa. 1:17, 23 יאתום for יתום, 1:4 עאון for עון, etc.). In Amos 2:7 a similar א is misconstrued as part of the root: read השפים for השאפים.

(h) G. R. Driver has demonstrated that *abbreviations* played a considerable role in the Hebrew text before the Septuagint, and that their misunderstanding led to garbled texts.[4] S. Talmon has also shown how many *double readings* have resulted from the insertion of synonymous expressions, etc.[5] Many obscure or corrupt passages can be restored when these sources of textual corruption are recognized.

3. *DELIBERATE ALTERATIONS*

Before the text of the Old Testament was officially established it was not regarded as unalterable. Accordingly we should expect to find that those who were concerned with the transmission of the text would occasionally make deliberate, fully intentional alterations in the text. In evaluating these alterations we must avoid thinking of them as "corruptions." They were made in good faith, with no intention of introducing a foreign element into the text, but rather with the aim of restoring the true text and (from the copyist's view) preventing misunderstandings. They must have

4. "Abbreviations in the Masoretic Text," *Textus* 1 (1960), pp. 112-131; 4 (1964), pp. 76-94; cf. M. Fishbane, "Abbreviations," *IDBS* (1976), pp. 3f.

5. "Double Readings in the Massoretic Text," *Textus* 1 (1960), pp. 144-184; cf. also *idem*, "Aspects of the Textual Transmission of the Bible in the Light of Qumran Manuscripts," *Textus* 4 (1964), pp. 95-132; *idem*, "Synonymous Readings," *Scripta Hierosolymitana* 8 (1961), pp. 335-383.

originated in a period when the letter of the text could still be changed in order to express its message more effectively for its readership and audience.

Many of these alterations we can recognize only with great difficulty if at all because the manuscript tradition of 𝔐 has preserved only a very few variant readings. Others are properly the province of higher criticism, whose borders are rather fluid at this point. Some examples should be given here.

There are certain small, common words which were easily inserted in the text, such as לאמר, שם, אשר, עתה, אחד, כל, ו. We have mentioned these in discussing the characteristics of the popular text, but this tendency is also represented in the manuscript tradition of 𝔐. "These words are almost always inserted to support an interpretation which is in itself quite possible. But it becomes significantly dangerous when they render obligatory an interpretation which would otherwise be no more than one possibility among others, especially when they have a bearing on the construction of whole sentences, determining their broader relationships."[6]

It is quite natural that a text which was not simply the object of scholarly study but intended to be read constantly by the whole of the Jewish community would be adapted to the linguistic needs of the community. Thus a rare word, or one used in an unusual sense, would give place to a more common word, e.g., in Isa. 39:1 𝔐 reads חזק in the sense of "get well, recuperate." The usual word for this is חיה, and 1QIsaᵃ actually replaces חזק with חיה in this passage. Other examples of adaptation to colloquial usage have been mentioned above (see pp. 16f.). The lack of early material for comparison makes it impossible to demonstrate these alterations in 𝔐 on a larger scale. But the parallel texts show that even 𝔐 was not immune to them. As a general rule, when the tradition offers variant readings with the alternatives lying between rare and common words, or involved and simple constructions, in each instance the former may be considered the original.

Since the wording of the text was subject to variation before it was officially established, it was also possible to substitute acceptable expressions for ones which were morally or religiously offensive. The treatment of the divine name בעל has been noted above (see p. 18). Another example is found in Job 1:5, 11; 2:5, 9 where we now read ברך "to bless" (with God as object), and should expect קלל "to curse." The scribes replaced the offensive expression "to curse God" with a euphemism.[7]

---

6. J. Wellhausen, *Der Text der Bücher Samuelis* (1871), p. 26.
7. Cf. A. Geiger, *Urschrift und Übersetzungen der Bibel* (1857; reprinted 1928), pp. 267ff.; this contains a great deal of material relevant to this subject.

gl [gloss]   ***Additions and glosses***[8] to the text should also be included among
deliberate alterations. Thus in 1 Kgs. 18:19 there are 400 prophets of
Astarte mentioned together with 450 prophets of Baal. They are absent,
however, from vv. 22 and 40, where they should have been included if they
had been a part of the original story. They are probably a later addition,
the result of a scholarly surmise. Occasionally an expression was given a
further explanation in the margin, and this gloss then found its way into
the text. Beside the early expression דביר הבית in 1 Kgs. 8:6 we find the
later and more usual expression קדש הקדשים. Such glosses can often be
recognized because they have not been inserted at the right place in the
text, and are awkward in the context; e.g., in Gen. 10:14 the marginal
note "from whom the Philistines are descended" is found before its ante-
cedent "the men of Caphtor" instead of after it, where it should be if it
were original.

The editorial activity which we glimpse in these deliberate alterations was in many respects official, and may be traced to an early
period.[9] This is a wide field which unfortunately has not yet been
examined as systematically as it deserves.

---

8. On the glosses, cf. the instructive essay by G. Fohrer, "Die Glossen im Buche
Ezechiel," *ZAW* 63 (1951), pp. 33-53.
9. P. Volz, *ZAW* 54 (1936), pp. 103f.

XVI
THE METHODS OF TEXTUAL CRITICISM[1]

1. *GENERAL REMARKS*

TEXTUAL CRITICISM, LIKE ANY OTHER SCIENCE, CANNOT achieve convincing results without a methodology which is appropriate to its subject matter and defined by it. An arbitrary procedure which hastily and unnecessarily dismisses the traditional text to rely on private conjecture can lead only to a subjective form of the text which is uncertain historically and without any claim to theological relevance. It is also likely to arouse a basic distrust of textual criticism itself, even where it is justifiable and necessary.

There is no precisely defined method for Old Testament textual criticism. It is questionable whether one is possible, because the tradition is so varied that an effective procedure for one problem would not be appropriate for another. But there are certain fundamental principles which are widely recognized, at least in theory if not in practice, and which are designed to keep textual criticism on a sound basis, avoiding the excesses of arbitrariness and subjectivity. These principles are not specifically theological, but have been developed from the application of the standard procedures of the science of textual criticism to the specific conditions of the Old Testament. Even the beginner should be familiar with them because they will not only provide him with some criteria for assessing the results of the various kinds of textual criticism he will constantly encounter in his exegetical work, but also give him guidance for his own further thought and practical application. We will therefore outline them briefly here.

2. *ESTABLISHING THE TRADITIONAL TEXT*

The starting point for any textual study must be the textual tradition itself.

---

1. A. Jepsen, "Von den Aufgaben der alttestamentlichen Textkritik," *VTS* 9 (1963), pp. 332-341.

Therefore it must first be decided which text is to be regarded as the traditional text. The various witnesses to the text should be examined, beginning with 𝔐, and continuing with the rest in roughly the order of their significance for textual criticism, e.g., ᵐ, 𝔊, α′, σ′, θ′, 𝔖, 𝔗, 𝔙, 𝔉, Sa, 𝔎, 𝔅, 𝔄, and Arm (for the justification of this order, see the discussion of the textual history of each of these witnesses). In this way the whole of the available manuscript evidence should be reviewed.[2]

A relatively simple picture can be given on the whole for 𝔐, whose manuscript variants are found in Kennicott, de Rossi, and Ginsburg, because real variants are rare. A preliminary sifting of the evidence may be made as it is collected by setting aside those readings which are scribal errors (misreadings, miswritings, omissions, dittographies, etc.), and those which are easily identified as deliberate (insertions of ו, כל, etc.). In order to have the most objective basis possible for evaluating the readings which survive this preliminary examination, it is necessary to ascertain the general character of the manuscripts in which they are found. The fewer errors a manuscript has, the more it commends itself as generally reliable and based on a good tradition. Further, in general, the older a particular reading is the more attention it deserves, provided it satisfies the criteria of language usage and sense in context: *manuscripta ponderantur, non numerantur* ("manuscripts are weighed, not counted"). The practice followed in BH of counting the manuscripts cited by Kennicott or de Rossi is inadequate because it does not indicate *which* manuscripts support a particular reading, and the manuscripts cited represent a wide variety in both age and value. On the whole the value, the special characteristics, and the interrelationships of the Hebrew manuscripts have not been examined adequately for the purposes of textual criticism.[3]

For the *versions*, especially for 𝔊, the manuscript tradition is

2. This means, of course, that for work in textual criticism the apparatus of BHK or BHS is not adequate by itself; it must be supplemented by the use of critical editions. Further, the apparatus is not altogether free of inaccuracies and errors (cf. J. Ziegler, "Studien zur Verwertung der Septuaginta im Zwölfprophetenbuch," *ZAW* 60, 1944, pp. 107-131, where the reliability of other editions [of the Septuagint] is also reviewed critically). Many criticisms have been raised in recent years, and most acutely by Orlinsky (cf., e.g., "The Textual Criticism of the Old Testament," in G. E. Wright, ed., *The Bible and the Ancient Near East,* 1961, pp. 113f.). Yet these criticisms are beside the point when they measure BHK by a standard that cannot be applied to an edition designed for students. J. Hempel rightly makes note of this with regard to Orlinsky (*ZAW* 71, 1959, p. 259).

3. This has been stressed again by many, including M. H. Goshen-Gottstein, *Bibl* 35 (1954), pp. 429-442 (= *Text and Language in Bible and Qumran*, 1960, pp. 51-64). J. Hempel has published a study of Deuteronomy (*ZAW* 52, 1934, pp. 254-274), and H. Gese one on the Minor Prophets (*ZAW* 69, 1957, pp. 55-69).

In connection with the HUBP edition of the Hebrew Bible an investigation has been undertaken for a large part of the Old Testament. In his essay "Hebrew Biblical Manuscripts," *Bibl* 48 (1967), pp. 243-290 (= *QHBT*, 1975, pp. 42-89), Goshen-Gottstein

much more complex. This must first be clarified before inferences may be drawn about the Hebrew text underlying it. For 𝔊, the editions of the Göttingen Septuagint provide a valuable guide through the mass of variants when used with discretion. Here also a preliminary sifting of the evidence should be made as it is collected. Variants within the 𝔊 tradition may be recognized and set aside immediately, e.g., corruptions of the Greek text (confusions of letters, etc.), or deliberate alterations (for a more idiomatic Greek usage). When assessing the variants in the manuscript tradition of any particular version, it should also be remembered that in many versions the text has been assimilated to 𝔐; thus if one reading agrees with 𝔐 while another reading differs, the former may be suspected of being a late assimilation to 𝔐. As with the Hebrew manuscripts, here also the principle holds that *"manuscripta ponderantur, non numerantur."*[4]

Obviously versions which are based upon or influenced by a particular version (usually 𝔊) may be accounted independent witnesses to the text only under certain conditions, such as when they appear likely or certain to have preserved an original reading of the version which has since been altered, perhaps by assimilation to 𝔐. Thus a reading which is attested by 𝔊 and 𝔏 is really attested only once, because 𝔏 is a daughter version of 𝔊.

3. *EXAMINATION OF THE TRADITIONAL TEXT*

After deciding which text is to be regarded as the traditional text—a task which we have seen is not merely a mechanical process of collecting the evidence but also involves a critical sifting of it—the real examination of the tradition can begin. For convenience we may divide this between the two aspects of linguistic form and subject matter. Our main interest centers on 𝔐. In every instance it deserves special attention because it is based on direct transmission in the original language, and it has been handed down with great care. The earlier tendency to undervalue 𝔐 in favor of the Greek version or even of modern conjectures has now been almost entirely abandoned, because 𝔐 has repeatedly been demonstrated to be the best witness to the text. Any deviation from it therefore requires justification. But this does not mean that we should cling to 𝔐 under all circumstances, because it also has its undeniable faults which can be

---

comes to a very negative judgment on the results achieved: "Among all the MSS and fragments known so far there is not even one the deviations of which can be significantly connected with any non-Massoretic tradition. We possess no medieval manuscript which, on the strength of its readings, may be termed 'valuable' or be worthy of our attention more than any other" (p. 277; = *QHBT*, p. 76). Cf. also above, pp. 38f.

4. It has often been noted with criticism that in the apparatus of BHK the versions, and 𝔊 in particular, are cited far too extensively, uncritically, and indiscriminately. BHS has done well in exercising a far greater discretion in this regard.

corrected to some extent with the help of the other witnesses. It is clear from the history of the text that vocalization of מֿ does not have the same significance as the consonantal text, and that alterations in the pointing do not qualify properly as emendations (cf. pp. 21ff.).

As a general rule מֿ is to be preferred over all other traditions whenever it cannot be faulted either linguistically or for its material content, unless in particular instances there is good reason for favoring another tradition. The question whether מֿ can be faulted either linguistically or materially is to be decided at times only after intensive investigations. Specifically, if a reading of מֿ is rejected, every possible interpretation of it must first have been fully examined. It is unscholarly to oppose a reading of מֿ merely for its lack of agreement with an interpreter's viewpoint. When such a conflict arises, it is the theory that should defer to the textual tradition, and not the reverse.

The *linguistic* examination is concerned first with grammatical and lexical possibilities. Research in these fields is still continuing, so that we must often look for new interpretations which have not yet been incorporated in the standard grammars and lexicons. The possible range of meanings for a word can often be detected only by using a concordance[5] and checking all the occurrences of a word in the Old Testament. Not infrequently such an "internal interpretation" suggests a possible construction of a text that has not been noted before and which makes good sense of the traditional Hebrew text. Especially useful are instances of *parallelismus membrorum*. This approach has shown many widely accepted emendations to be unnecessary. Another useful tool for linguistic interpretation is the study of *related Semitic languages*. These often shed a new light on words whose meaning in the Old Testament is still obscure. In addition to Arabic, which has long been in use, we are now indebted also to Akkadian, Old South Arabic, and Ugaritic among others, as well as to Egyptian, a mixed Semitic-Hamitic language which is important for loanwords in the Old Testament. This is a rapidly developing field, with excavations constantly increasing our resources (cf. recently the texts from Ugarit and Mari). Many useful results may be expected. As an example may be cited Hab. 3:6b-7a, where the unintelligible phrase לֹו

---

5. Useful tools include S. Mandelkern, *Veteris Testamenti Concordantiae Hebraicae atque Chaldaicae* (1937²; reprinted 1955), and G. Lisowsky, *Konkordanz zum hebräischen AT* (1966²). The references in the *Handwörterbuch* of Gesenius-Buhl (1915¹⁷; latest reprint 1962), L. Köhler-W. Baumgartner, *Lexicon in Veteris Testamenti Libros* (1958², 1969³), and F. Brown, S. R. Driver, and C. A. Briggs, *Hebrew and English Lexicon of the Old Testament* (Oxford, 1907; corrected ed. 1952), take the place of a concordance for many words.

תחת און is the Ugaritic word תחתאון "destruction" with the preposition ל.[6]

Finally in this connection it should be noticed whether or not a text appears genuine on the basis of stylistic, material, form critical, or other grounds. Irregularities detected in this way often lead to the recognition of insertions, glosses, displacements, and other disturbances in the original text. As our knowledge in many of these fields (e.g., meter) is still quite limited and open to discussion, and subjective judgments are particularly easy to make, a greater degree of critical reserve than is commonly observed is in order.

In examining the *subject matter* we are concerned with determining whether or not a topic, an idea, or an expression is an original part of the text in the light of what is known from other parts of the Old Testament world. This approach leads to the recognition of later alterations and the elimination of later insertions. Textual criticism comes into close contact at this point with literary criticism and exegesis. Therefore for methodological integrity it is very important to be quite clear whether a text is contested on the grounds of textual criticism, literary criticism, or exegesis. The limits of textual criticism as defined above (pp. 103f.) should be recalled explicitly in this context. Finally, in examining the subject matter we should remember how fragmentary our knowledge of the Old Testament world remains. We should recognize the possibility that we may not understand a particular text because our knowledge is limited. As it grows—and it does grow with every excavation—we have greater grounds for confidence that we may yet learn the meaning of passages that are still obscure. It is essential for the Old Testament scholar to follow closely every new discovery in the world of the Old Testament, and be prepared to reconsider earlier solutions in the light of new knowledge.

Not only 𝔐, but the versions also must be subjected to intensive examination, for it is conceivable that even when 𝔐 reads an acceptable or possible text, a version which differs from it may preserve the original text. When evaluating an early version for textual criticism it is particularly important that it not be treated piecemeal, i.e., considering only isolated readings without regard for the whole character of the version, its translation method, its bias, its intellectual background, etc. The information in the apparatus of BH should be regarded only as suggestions to be followed up by intensive research in the versions themselves. Only those

---

6. Cf. K. Elliger in *Das Alte Testament Deutsch, ad loc.*; the suggestion goes back to Albright. For further material cf. G. R. Driver, "L'interpretation du texte masorétique à la lumière de la lexicographie hebraïque," *ALBO*, Sér. 2/18 (1950); J. Barr, *Comparative Philology and the Text of the Old Testament* (1968).

variant readings which cannot be construed as translational errors, over-sights, or due to the language, spirit, bias, or translation method of the version should be (back-translated and) placed beside 𝔐 as genuine variants.

4. *THE DECISION*

After the evidence of the tradition has been collected and examined, the decision must be made as to which text is to be regarded as the original or the nearest approximation to it. When the various textual witnesses are reviewed the following patterns are generally found.

(a) 𝔐 and all other witnesses offer a text which is unobjection-able, which makes sense, and has been preserved without a variant. Here we may naturally assume that the original text has been preserved by the tradition, and that it should be accepted implicitly. It may seem strange that this point requires statement here, because it seems so obvious. But anyone acquainted with the history of Old Testament scholarship will not consider it unnecessary.

(b) When 𝔐 and all or some of the other witnesses are found on careful examination to differ from each other so that there are real var-iants, the following possibilities may occur.

(i) 𝔐 preserves a reading which is either probably or certainly original, while the variants supported by the other witnesses are secon-dary (misreadings, misunderstandings, intentional or unconscious correc-tions); here 𝔐 is to be followed.

(ii) 𝔐 and the other witnesses support different but apparently equally possible or plausible readings, none of which is either clearly or even probably secondary. Generally 𝔐 would be given preference here as a matter of basic principle, but other factors must also be considered. The rule may apply of preferring the reading which is more difficult from the viewpoint of language and subject matter *(lectio difficilior)*—or the alter-nate rule that of two readings the one which best explains the develop-ment of the other is to be preferred. Often in such instances the verdict *non liquet* ("unsolved") must be accepted.

(iii) The text of 𝔐 is doubtful or impossible on linguistic or contextual grounds, while other witnesses offer a satisfactory reading. If evidence for the originality of the latter is available, and especially if the reading of 𝔐 is demonstrably a corruption of it, then the text of 𝔐 should certainly be corrected by it. The objection that 𝔐 offers the lectio dif-ficilior in this instance is not valid because the contrast is not between an easier and a harder reading but between a satisfactory reading and one that is meaningless or corrupt. But again, if the satisfactory reading in a version seems to be a translator's attempt to cope with a Hebrew text which was already corrupt, then the version offers nothing more than a very early conjecture, and the verdict must be that the original text of the tradition has not been preserved.

(c) In such an instance, and similarly when 𝔐 and the other witnesses fail to provide a reading that is linguistically or contextually [conj] probable or even possible, an emendation may be attempted by conjecture or the problem may be regarded as beyond solution *(crux interpretum)*. A conjecture may be justified if textual corruption has entered the tradition so early that it antedates the earliest versions. But if a text is to be emended by conjecture, this should be done with as close a dependence as possible on the existing textual tradition, and with due regard for the causes of textual corruption sketched above in chapter XV (cf. for example the conjecture at Jer. 2:21, p. 108). And further, the tentativeness of any text established in this way should also be acknowledged.

5. *PSYCHOLOGICAL CONSIDERATIONS*

Finally, we should underscore once again the importance of giving due attention to the psychological aspect present in all textual critical work. Namely, whenever an error is suspected, the conditions that could have given rise to such an error should be considered. The various possible causes of textual corruption listed in chapter XV may be useful as suggestions, but they are by no means exhaustive. If the cause of an error can be discovered, the first step has been taken toward recovering the original text with some degree of certainty. It is precisely the careful consideration of this psychological aspect that assures to textual criticism the certainty it needs, that makes proposed emendations more convincing, and provides a proper finish to the work. If it does no more than place a restraint on too drastic a treatment of the text, this is no small achievement.

No book in the literature of the world has been so often copied, printed, translated, read, and studied as the Bible. It stands uniquely as the object of so much effort devoted to preserving it faithfully, to understanding it, and to making it understandable to others. We may remember the scribes and Masoretes with their strict regulations and subtle studies, the translators, the medieval monks tracing the text out letter by letter in their quiet cells, the exegetes, and especially Luther, who devoted the greater part of his exegetical work to the Old Testament.

What was the real motive for all this concern about the Bible? Certainly not merely an interest in a venerable relic which deserved preservation because of its antiquity. Literatures as old or older than the Old and New Testaments have disappeared, leaving only some scant allusions and an occasional fortunate discovery of fragmentary remains to remind us that they once existed. It is something else that has made people devote themselves to the Bible and ensure its preservation for their own and later generations: the recognition of its meaning for all generations, the knowledge that here flows the fountain of life, because God himself speaks in it.

It is this same motivation which inspires our work on the Bible today. It would be wrong to regard the present account of the vicissitudes of the Old Testament text in its transmission as though it were written solely as a matter of academic interest in things past, or even as an attempt to expose the imperfections of the text incurred in its transmission by men. Even this has its serious theological significance if we think of the servant form of the Word of God as finding expression also in the transmission of the text. Yet we are not so much concerned with discovering imperfections and errors as with overcoming them. We are concerned primarily with the original form of the Old Testament record, as we are with the message of the Bible as a whole, because we want to be confronted with this original Word itself, and not with an interpretation made of it by fallible scribes in the course of its transmission. The history of the text, as well as the textual criticism which is based on it, are inseparably a part of any Old Testament scholarship that is consciously theological. "Without textual criticism there can be no real understanding of Old Testament religion, no real Old Testament theology. Anyone who penetrates more deeply into textual criticism knows that theology and textual criticism are not two separate fields, but that at this deepest level they are interdependent."[7]

But does concentration on the letter of the text, many people tend to ask, actually lead to confrontation with the message of the Bible? Is this not precisely the wrong approach? This attitude probably appeals to such statements of Luther as: "No one can understand even one iota of the Scriptures unless he has the Spirit of God."[8] But this reveals a misunderstanding, for we must remember that it was the same Luther who insisted so strongly on the "Word" in opposition to the "Spirit" of the religious enthusiasts, and who repeatedly pointed out that God "never gives anyone the Spirit or faith without the outward sign or word in which he has enshrined it."[9] What Luther means by these apparently contradictory statements is that God has linked his Spirit to the written and spoken word; but he controls the working of his Spirit in the Word by his own unlimited sovereign will.[10] "Literal understanding and spiritual under-

7. P. Volz, *ZAW* 54 (1936), p. 113.
8. *De servo arbitrio*, Weimar ed. (1883ff.) 18, p. 609.
9. *Idem*, p. 136.
10. H. Bornkamm, *Das Wort Gottes bei Luther* (1933), p. 12.

standing are therefore not to be separated. We cannot acquire the one without also having the other."[11] Because this is so, the concern for the letter of the text which this book seeks to promote has genuine theological relevance.

11. K. Holl, *Gesammelte Aufsätze* 1 (1948[7]), p. 558.

1. AN INSCRIBED BOWL FROM LACHISH

Cf. p. 5. Illustration from O. Tufnell, *et al., Lachish IV (Tell ed-Duweir): The Bronze Age* (1958).

The bowl found in 1935 is now ascribed by D. Diringer to the thirteenth century B.C. (*Writing,* 1962, p. 240; in *Lachish IV,* p. 129, Diringer proposed the second quarter of the fourteenth century). The inscription is an example of proto-Canaanite writing, written with a brush dipped in white chalk. Seven of the eleven signs are well preserved. The inscription should be read from right to left.

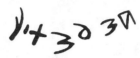

Most scholars identify the first five signs with the letters *b š l š t*, i.e., a form of the number "three" with the prepositional prefix *b*. Other readings have been proposed for the first letter; the inscription has also been considered to read from left to right (cf. the review by Diringer in *Lachish IV,* p. 129).

The sixth sign is probably a division mark, and the seventh the beginning of another word now illegible.

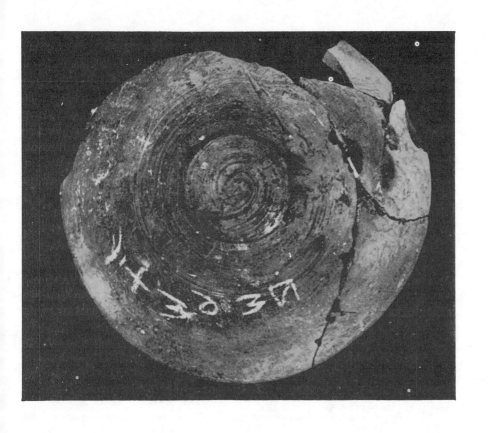

2. *THE STELE OF MESHA, KING OF MOAB*

Cf. p. 4. Illustration from K. M. Kenyon, *Bible and Archaeology* (1949²).

In 1868 F. A. Klein, a missionary, discovered this victory inscription on black basalt in Dhiban (the ancient Dibon, capital of Mesha), north of the river Arnon (Wadi al-Mawjib) in Jordan. The stone was later broken up by bedouin, but a paper squeeze made earlier enabled the text to be reassembled and restored. The monument is 1 m. high, 0.6 m. across, and is now at the Louvre in Paris.

Of the thirty-four lines in Phoenician-Old Hebrew script (cf. pp. 4, 217), twenty-seven are preserved entirely. They celebrate the victory of Moab over Israel after a period of Moabite submission (cf. 2 Kgs. 3:4-27), and record Mesha's program of building cities.

"This stele of Mesha' king of Moab is of great importance as the sole historical monument of the Moabite kingdom and a record of historical relations between Moab and Israel which are glossed over or omitted from the Old Testament. It further reveals Moabite as a Semitic dialect almost identical with Hebrew and proves the advanced stage of writing in a petty kingdom lying off the main historical routes in the 9th century B.C." (G. R. Driver, *Semitic Writing,* 1976³, p. 109).

The script is remarkably developed, with a tendency toward cursive and simplified forms. It is noteworthy that both words and sentences are divided, the words by dots and the sentences by strokes.

Text with translation and commentary: H. Donner and W. Röllig, *Kanaanäische und Aramäische Inschriften* (1962-1964), no. 181; J. C. L. Gibson, *Textbook of Syrian Semitic Inscriptions* 1 (1971), pp. 71-84.

Translation: H. Gressmann, *Altorientalische Texte zum Alten Testament* (1926²), pp. 440-42; W. F. Albright in *ANET*, pp. 320f.; E. Ullendorf in *DOTT* (1961), pp. 195-99; K. Galling, *Textbuch zur Geschichte Israels* (1968²), pp. 51-53.

3. THE SILOAM INSCRIPTION FROM JERUSALEM (ca. 700 B.C.)

Cf. p. 4. Illustration from D. Diringer, *The Alphabet* (1948).

In 1880 an inscription in Old Hebrew letters was found on the rock facing at the opening of a rock tunnel leading from the Gihon spring (now Mary's Well) to the Pool of Siloam (cf. p. 4). It records the successful completion of the tunnel. The original was later removed and is now at the Museum of the Ancient Orient in Istanbul.

Although the account gives neither names nor date, it most probably refers to the cutting of a tunnel by Hezekiah (725-697 B.C.; cf. 2 Kgs. 20:20 and 2 Chr. 32:30), which suggests a date around 700 B.C. This is confirmed by palaeographical evidence. "The writing may fairly be assigned to the same general stage of development as that represented by the Moabite Stone but is lighter and more flowing, while some of the letters have considerably altered their shape" (Driver, *Semitic Writing,* 1976[3], p. 119).

The text of six lines is 38 cm. high and 72 cm. wide. An area of about 70 cm. square was prepared and the inscription occupies the lower half. Was the upper half intended for a pictorial representation (Gressmann), or has the first half of the inscription been lost (Albright)?

Text with translation and commentary: H. Donner and W. Röllig, *Kanaanäische und Aramäische Inschriften* (1962-1964), no. 189; J. C. L. Gibson, *Textbook of Syrian Semitic Inscriptions* 1 (1971), pp. 71-84.

Translations: H. Gressmann, *Altorientalische Texte zum Alten Testament* (1926[2]), p. 445; W. F. Albright in *ANET,* p. 321 (with bibliography); N. H. Snaith in *DOTT* (1961), pp. 209-211; K. Galling, *Textbuch zur Geschichte Israels* (1968[2]), p. 59.

4. LACHISH LETTER NO. 4

Cf. p. 4. Illustration from H. Torczyner, *et al., Lachish I (Tell ed-Duweir): The Lachish Letters* (1938).

During the excavation of a room under the city gate-tower of Tell ed-Duweir, the site of the Biblical Lachish, eighteen ostraca inscribed in the Old Hebrew script were found in 1935, and another three in 1938 (cf. p. 6). They were found in a burned stratum, apparently from the destruction of the city by the Babylonians when the kingdom of Judah was defeated in 588-587 B.C.; thus they represent the last days of the Southern Kingdom. Their contents comprise mostly a military correspondence revealing the distressed state of Judah during the Babylonian invasion.

"As in other countries where potsherds were used for messages, the writer begins his letter on the outside of the sherd and continues only when necessary on the less smooth inner surface. The scribes of the Lachish letters used a reed pen, and wrote in an iron-carbide ink, as the chemical analysis has shown" (H. Torczyner, *Lachish I,* 1938, p. 204).

The hand is a beautiful cursive, the product of a literary tradition centuries old. The use of word dividers is irregular; for the writing of חיהוה in 3.9, cf. p. 107. The language is Biblical Hebrew, especially reminiscent of Jeremiah and Deuteronomy. It confirms the fact that the language of the Biblical books preserved in מ is predominantly that of pre-exilic Judah. The ostraca are of great philological, palaeographical, and historical value as the only known group of documents in classical Hebrew. They are now in Jerusalem and London.

Transliteration in square character (selections): K. Galling, *Textbuch zur Geschichte Israels* (1950), pp. 63-65.

Translations: J. Hempel in *ZAW* 56 (1938), pp. 126-139; W. F. Albright in *ANET,* pp. 321f.; D. W. Thomas in *DOTT* (1961), pp. 216f.

Complete edition: H. Torczyner, תעודות לכיש, *Library of Palestinology of the Jewish Palestine Exploration Society* 15/17 (1940), not available to the author.

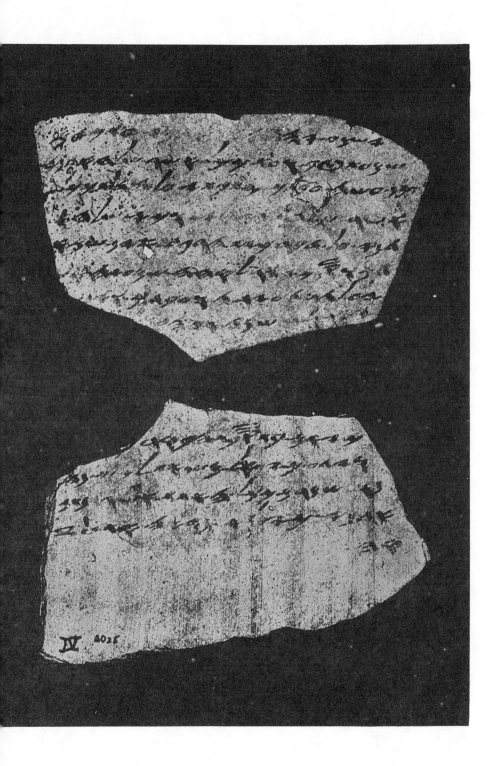

5. THE ELEPHANTINE PAPYRUS

Cf. pp. 3f. Illustration from E. Sachau, *Aramäische Papyrus und Ostraka aus einer jüdischen Militär-Kolonie zu Elephantine* (1911), pl. 1. Contents: Letter to Bagoas, lines 1-17.

Numerous papyri in the Aramaic language and script were among the documents discovered by the Berlin Papyrus Commission during excavations undertaken in 1907 and 1908 on the island of Elephantine in the Nile opposite Aswan. These papyri date from the fifth century B.C., and include letters, legal documents, parts of the Story of Ahikar, fragments of the Darius inscription of Behistun in an Aramaic translation, and other items. From these we have learned about the existence of a "Jewish military colony" in Elephantine[1] with a temple in which Yahu (Yahweh) was worshipped together with a goddess Anathbethel and another god (אשמביתאל, pronunciation unknown; cf. M. Noth, *Geschichte Israels*, 1963[5], pp. 266f.).

These papyri attest how widely the Aramaic language and script were used in the Persian empire (cf. p. 4). After the Phoenician-Old Hebrew script, the Aramaic script represents a second branch of the north Semitic alphabet from which developed not only the square script, but the Nabatean, Palmyrene, and Syrian (Estangela) scripts as well. Its earliest examples are ninth-century B.C. inscriptions from the area of Aleppo. "The Aramaic script gradually assumed a distinctive character which is marked by the following main tendencies: (1) the opening of the tops and the sides of a few letters (the *beth*, the *daleth* and *resh*, and *'ayin*) is a prominent feature; (2) the endeavor to reduce the number of separate strokes, in the *ḥeth* and *ṭeth*, for instance, is also noticeable; (3) angles become rounded and ligatures develop. These tendencies were pronounced during the Persian period. By the fifth century B.C. the transformation is complete, as we can gather . . . especially from the cursive Aramaic writing on papyrus used in Egypt between 500 and 200 B.C." (D. Diringer, *The Alphabet*, I [1968[3]], p. 200).

Cf. A. E. Cowley, *Aramaic Papyri of the Fifth Century B.C.* (1923); *idem, Jewish Documents of the Time of Ezra* (1919); H. H. Rowley in *DOTT* (1961), pp. 260-65. Also E. G. Kraeling, ed., *The Brooklyn Museum Aramaic Papyri* (1953).

1. On the military colony of Elephantine cf. E. G. Kraeling, ed., *Die Religion in Geschichte und Gegenwart* (1958[3]) 2, col. 415-18 (with bibliography); B. Porten, *Archives from Elephantine. The Life of an Ancient Jewish Military Colony* (1968).

7. THE ENTRANCE TO QUMRAN CAVE 1

Cf. p. 13. Illustration from E. L. Sukenik, אוצר המגילות הגנוזות (1954).

In the spring of 1947 in Jerusalem the now famous manuscripts found in a cave near the Dead Sea first came to light. The war in Palestine prevented searching for the cave itself until the beginning of 1949, when it was examined under the direction of G. L. Harding and R. de Vaux, but no further texts of any considerable extent were discovered. The cave is in a particularly dry area of Palestine, 12 km. south of Jericho, 1 km. north of Khirbet Qumran, 150 m. up a precipice difficult to scale. It was discovered accidentally by a herdsman searching for a lost goat. Later investigation revealed about thirty caves in the area which showed traces of use in antiquity. In ten of them further manuscripts were found hidden, some of which were of considerable length (Caves 2-11).

All of these caves are very closely associated with the ancient settlement of Khirbet Qumran. From the excavations carried out from 1951 to 1956 we learn that Qumran was founded under John Hyrcanus (135-104 B.C.) or Alexander Jannaeus (103-76 B.C.).[1] It was "the administrative center, the place of assembly, and the burial ground of a community that lived scattered about the area" (de Vaux), until it was destroyed by Roman troops in A.D. 68 during the first Jewish War (A.D. 66-70). Most probably the scrolls found since 1947 were hidden in the caves because of these military events. Later, Qumran appears to have served as a Roman military post, and finally as a stronghold for the Jewish rebels of the second Jewish War.[2]

The evidence of the excavations and many details in the writings discovered argue for the identification of Qumran with the site in the Judean desert "above Engedi" described by Pliny the Elder as the center of a community of pious Jews who lived in solitude as celibates—the Essenes.[3]

---

1. A first settlement in the later Jewish monarchy (eighth to seventh/sixth century B.C.), apparently identified with 'Ir-hammelach (City of Salt, Josh. 15:62), ended in complete destruction.

2. On the excavations of Khirbet Qumran, cf. R. de Vaux, *Archaeology and the Dead Sea Scrolls*, Schweich Lectures 1959 (1973²).

3. Objections to this identification have been raised by K. H. Rengstorf, *Hirbet Qumran und die Bibliothek vom Toten Meer*, Studia Delitzschiana 5 (1960), who prefers to identify the library with a library of the Jerusalem temple.

8. *TWO JARS FROM CAVE 1*

Cf. p. 8. Illustration from E. L. Sukenik, מגילות גנוזות 2 (1950).

The undamaged jars illustrated here were taken by the bedouin when they first discovered the cave, and later bought by Professor Sukenik of Jerusalem. Their height (without lids) is 65.7 cm. and 47.5 cm., and their width is 25 cm. and 26.5 cm. respectively. They were designed to protect the scrolls from damage.

Fragments of about fifty more jars of the same or similar pattern were found in an archaeological examination of the cave. If each contained three or more scrolls, Cave 1 could once have accommodated a library of 150 to 200 scrolls. But "the only solid evidence for the possible quantity is the number of different books which can be identified, and these amount to about seventy-five. How or where so many of these documents were removed or damaged is a question which is at present unanswerable."[1] As for the possible removal of manuscripts centuries ago, we may remember a letter from the Nestorian Patriarch Timothy I of Seleucia (727-823), which tells of an Arab hunter who was led by his dog to a cave where he found a large number of books. "The hunter went to Jerusalem and reported it to the Jews. They came in crowds and found the books of the Old (Testament) and others in Hebrew script."[2] But nothing definite can be asserted about this.

Jars of the same or a similar pattern have also been found in nearby caves and in Khirbet Qumran itself. These are very important for establishing dates. "All this pottery belongs to the Hellenistic and Roman period, and there is nothing from later periods. When we reflect that the manuscripts are numerous and the pottery plentiful, that the manuscripts constitute a homogeneous group, and that the pottery belongs to a single period, it is difficult to resist the conclusion that the manuscripts were deposited or abandoned in the caves at the same time as the pottery."[3]

1. G. L. Harding, *Qumran Cave I, Discoveries in the Judaean Desert* 1 (1955), p. 3.

2. The letter was reported by O. Eissfeldt, *TLZ* 74 (1949), col. 597f.

3. R. de Vaux, *Archaeology and the Dead Sea Scrolls*, Schweich Lectures 1959 (1973²), p. 102.

9a. *A SAMUEL FRAGMENT FROM CAVE 4* (4QSam^b)

9a. *A SAMUEL FRAGMENT FROM CAVE 4* (4QSam^b)

Illustrations 9a and 9b from J. T. Milik, *Ten Years of Discovery in the Wilderness of Judaea* (1959). Text: 1 Sam. 23:9-13.

The fragments of 4QSam^b are among the oldest Biblical texts from Qumran, and are ascribed by Cross (*JBL* 74, 1955, pp. 147-172) to the period about 200 B.C. or somewhat earlier.

9b. *A FRAGMENT OF THE SONG OF MOSES* (4QDeut.^q)

The fragments of the Song of Moses written in stichs, of which P. Skehan published Deut. 32:8, 37-43 in 1954 (*BASOR* 136, pp. 12-15), are of particular importance for preserving (with ⑤) a text more original than ﬨﬧ, which reads a shortened and "demythologized" version.[1] V. 43 is illustrated here:

4 Q	ﬨﬧ
הרנינו שמים עמו	הרנינו גוים עמו
והשתחוו לו כל אלהים	
כי דם בניו יקום	כי דם־עבדיו יקום
ונקם ישיב לצריו	ונקם ישיב לצריו
ולמשנאיו ישלם	
ויכפר אדמת עמו	וכפר אדמתו עמו

Rejoice, you heavens, with him;	Praise, O nations, his people;
And bow before him, all you gods.	
For he avenges the blood of his sons	For he avenges the blood of his servants
And takes vengeance upon his adversaries.	And takes vengeance upon his adversaries.
He repays those who hate him	
And atones for the land of his people.	And atones for his land, his people.

1. According to R. Meyer who has reviewed the fragment at length in *Verbannung und Heimkehr, Rudolph-Festschrift* (1961), pp. 197-209.

10. THE FIRST ISAIAH SCROLL (1QIsaᵃ = ᗯᵃ)

Cf. pp. 8, 32. Illustration from E. L. Sukenik, מגילות גנוזות 2 (1950).

The first Isaiah scroll is shown opened to col. 32 and 33 (Isa. 38:8–40:20). It can clearly be seen that the scroll is composed of separate sheets of leather. Its use is also clear: the beginning of the scroll is to the right, and the end is to the left. For convenience in using and preserving Torah scrolls a rod (roller) was attached at each end to roll it on; for other books a rod at the beginning was adequate. At the end one sheet was usually left blank to serve as a protective covering for the scroll.

Now that the place where the scrolls were discovered has been identified and investigated (cf. pp. 134, 136), it may be accepted as certain that they are ancient and genuine. Doubts about their age and authenticity such as S. Zeitlin raised repeatedly in the *Jewish Quarterly Review* (1949-1950) can be regarded as settled on the basis of evidence. Even in the matter of dating there has been definite progress. The destruction of Khirbet Qumran, which occurred in A.D. 68 (cf. p. 134), provides a terminus ante quem for the writing of the scrolls, for they are very closely associated with that settlement. But when the scrolls were deposited in the cave they could already have been considerably aged; in fact they show unmistakable signs of long and heavy use (cf. the back of the scroll in the illustration). Now it is significant that the wealth of documents from the caves in the Judean desert has given a fresh impetus to the study of Hebrew palaeography. The researches of Albright, Sukenik, Trever, Birnbaum, Cross, and others have made it possible to trace the development of the script from the third century B.C. to the second century A.D.,[1] and to determine the place of individual documents in this sequence. This does not mean, of course, that a specific year can be assigned to each document. The first Isaiah scroll is in the script of the earliest scrolls from Cave 1, and can be dated in the second century B.C.; it lacks final forms for kaph, pe, and tsade.

1. Cf. the progress report on the research by N. Avigad, *Scripta Hierosolymitana* 4 (1958), pp. 56ff., and especially F. M. Cross, in Wright, *Bible and the Ancient Near East* (1961), pp. 133-202.

11. *THE FIRST ISAIAH SCROLL* (1QIsaᵃ = 𝔔ᵃ)

Cf. p. 32. Illustration (Isa. 40:6-20; slightly enlarged) from the edition by M. Burrows, *et al.;* cf. p. 31.

The illustration shows that the original text of the Isaiah scroll in vv. 7f. lacked the words כי רוח יהוה אשבה בו אכן חציר העם יבש חציר נבל ציץ which are present in 𝔐. A later hand has added them in an awkward script between the lines and down the left margin. It is obvious that the omission could have been caused by homoioteleuton. The scribe's eye skipped from נבל ציץ in v. 7 to the identical words in v. 8. But it is striking that the same omission is found in 𝔊, and that the words are marked with an asterisk by Origen (cf. p. 56). It is conceivable that the agreement between the original text of the Isaiah scroll and 𝔊 is sheer coincidence: the omission in both instances could have been due to homoioteleuton. But it is also possible that the text of 𝔐 is the result of a later expansion which was lacking in the exemplar of 𝔊 and the Isaiah scroll. The phrase אכן חציר העם has frequently aroused suspicions.

In the added phrase the name of God is represented by four dots. Did the scribe stand in such awe of the divine name that he dared not write it? It is more probable that the space was reserved in this way for the addition of the name later—in a different script. In other texts the name Yahweh is frequently written in Old Hebrew script (cf. pp. 5, 146f.).

In v. 8 the word ודבד has a dot under each letter, probably to indicate that this word would be deleted.

In 40:14-16 (from the second וילמדהו to the end of the verse) the hand is different from that of the surrounding text. But there is no suggestion that an original omission in the manuscript is being supplied. "Either another scribe has spelled his colleague for a brief moment, or the scribe has simple sharpened his pen or changed to a different pen" (M. Burrows, *BASOR* 113, 1949, p. 32).

Two of the many variants in this excerpt are of special importance: in 40:6 ואומרה (𝔐 ואמר) confirms the commonly proposed emendation *wa'omar* (𝔊 𝔙), and in 40:17 וכאפס (𝔐 מאפס) supports the conjecture כאפס (cf. BHK second apparatus and BHS apparatus).

12. *THE SECOND ISAIAH SCROLL* (1QIsa^b=𝔔^b)

Cf. p. 32. Illustration from E. L. Sukenik, מגילות גנוזות 2 (1950).

The second Isaiah scroll, as the illustration shows (col. 1, Isa. 48:17–49:7; col. 2, Isa. 50:7–51:8), is in poor condition. The leather has disintegrated in part, with lacunae in each column. Opening the scroll was particularly difficult because in many places the leather had become glued together. The surviving portions are from 2 Isaiah, with only fragments remaining from 1 Isaiah.

The script is relatively small, but it is beautiful and clear. In comparison with the first Isaiah scroll the agreement of the second Isaiah scroll with 𝔐 is striking. To an extent the vowel letters are used even more sparingly than in 𝔐: שלמך (𝔐 שלומך) 48:18; צר (צור) 48:21; כלתי (כליתי) 49:4. But it also uses vowel letters where they are lacking in 𝔐: יוצרי (יצרי) 49:5; גאל (גואל) and קדש (קדוש) 49:7.

Variants from 𝔐: 48:17 מדרכיך (מדריכך); 49:4 אכן אך (אכן); 49:6 הנקל (נקל) and הארץ (ארץ); 49:7 with the first Isaiah scroll אדני יהוה (אדני); יקומו (וקמו); 50:11 ומאזרי (מאזרי). The second Isaiah scroll exhibits significantly fewer variants from 𝔐 than the first, and these do not go beyond the range of variants observed in medieval manuscripts. This fact led Kahle to infer than IQIsa^b had been assimilated to the standard consonantal text, and therefore could not have been written before this standard text was available.[1] But since the scroll cannot be dated later than the 60's of the first century A.D. on archaeological grounds, and on the basis of palaeographical evidence it should apparently be assigned several decades earlier and could itself very well transmit the text of an even earlier exemplar, it has been taken by some as evidence for the existence of the type of text we identify as Masoretic long before the Masoretic period.[2] Although the text of this scroll presents very few problems in itself, it poses for us the basic and still unsolved problem of the age of the Masoretic text.

1. Kahle, *Die hebräischen Handschriften aus der Höhle* (1951), p. 81.
2. Cf. especially B. J. Roberts, *BJRL* 42 (1959/60), p. 144, who refers to the "likely existence of a pre-Massoretic 'Massoretic' text"; cf. also p. 16.

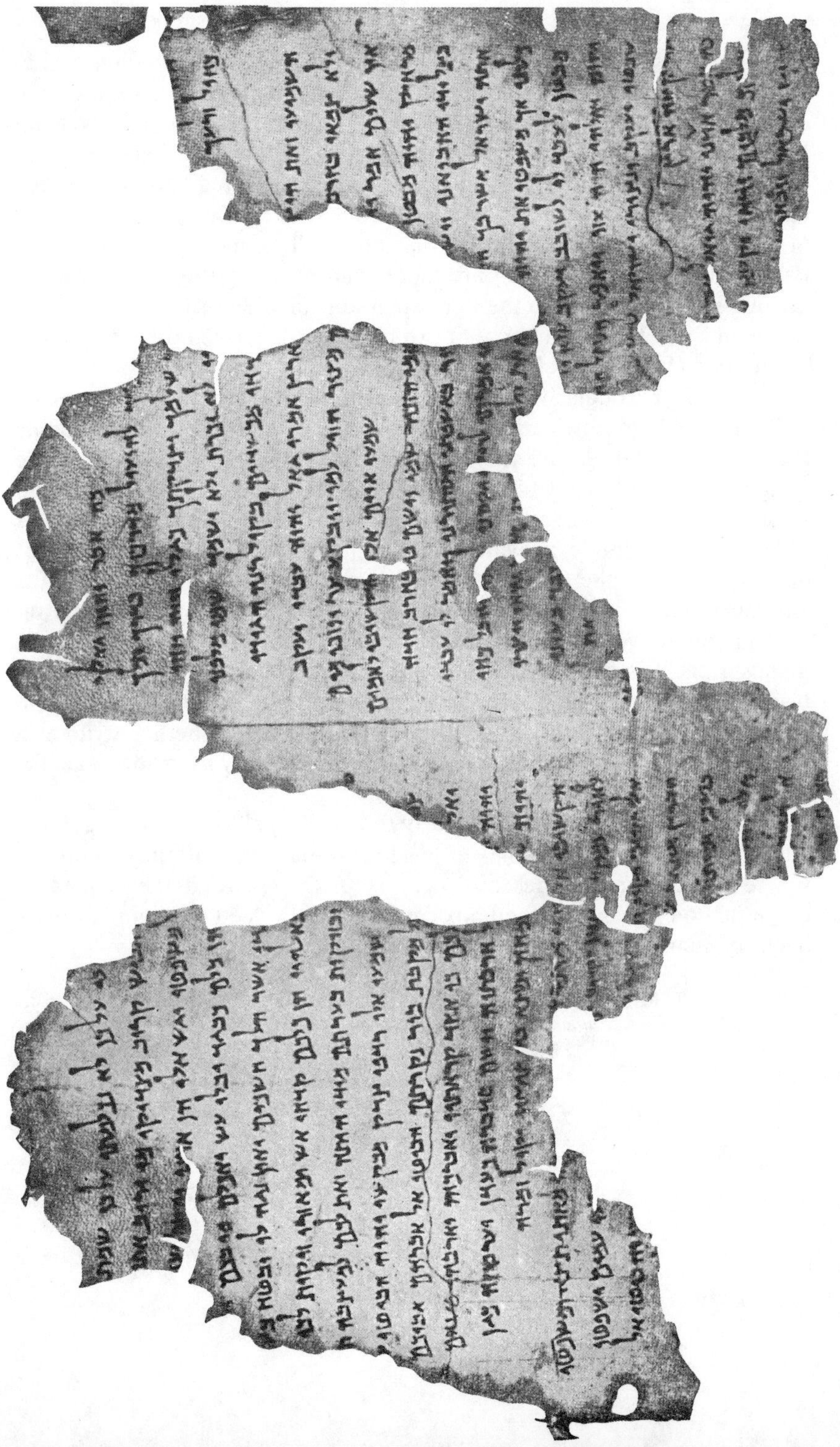

13. *THE HABAKKUK COMMENTARY*

Cf. p. 32. Illustration (col. 9 and 10, Hab. 2:7-14) from the edition cited on p. 31, n. 46.

This scroll is of special religious and historical significance be-cause, like the Manual of Discipline and other Qumran texts, it is a source of new information about a religious movement in pre-Christian Judaism. It is important for the history and criticism of the Old Testament text because the prophetic words of Hab. 1 and 2 are cited and commented upon sentence by sentence. The text cited in the scroll differs from that of 𝔐 in a way reminiscent of the first Isaiah scroll. Some sixty examples of its deviations from 𝔐 which are more than purely orthographical (e.g., scriptio plena) are cited in the third apparatus of BHK. In some instances the lemma and the comment on it exhibit discrepancies in their citation of the text of Habakkuk (cf. 1:8, 11; 2:16).

It is particularly noteworthy that the divine name Yahweh is written in Old Hebrew script (cf. col. 10, lines 7 and 14). In other scrolls the words אל and אלי are treated similarly. This peculiar writing of the divine name is referred to by Origen and also a Jewish tradition. And again, among the fragments found in the Cairo Geniza are some examples of the Aquila version in which the divine name in Old Hebrew script occurs written in the Greek text. This would imply that such a practice was once very common. In the text of the commentary itself the tetra-grammaton is avoided and אל is used in its place. In the period of these manuscripts it is evident that '*adonai* was read for the tetragrammaton because the first Isaiah scroll, for example, reads אדני where 𝔐 has יהוה (3:17), and conversely (6:11; 7:14; 9:7; 21:16; 28:2). Whether written in Old Hebrew or in the square script, יהוה served merely as an ideogram for אדני.[1]

The illustration shows clearly the horizontal lines from which the letters are suspended, and the vertical lines which mark off the columns of the text. Scholars of the third century A.D. regarded these lines as essential components of the book format. They traced the lining of texts back to Adam, regarding the practice as of extreme antiquity.[2]

1. Cf. Eissfeldt, *TLZ* 74 (1949), col. 225; also Kahle, *Handschriften*, pp. 63ff.
2. L. Blau, *Studien zum althebräischen Buchwesen* (1902), pp. 142ff.

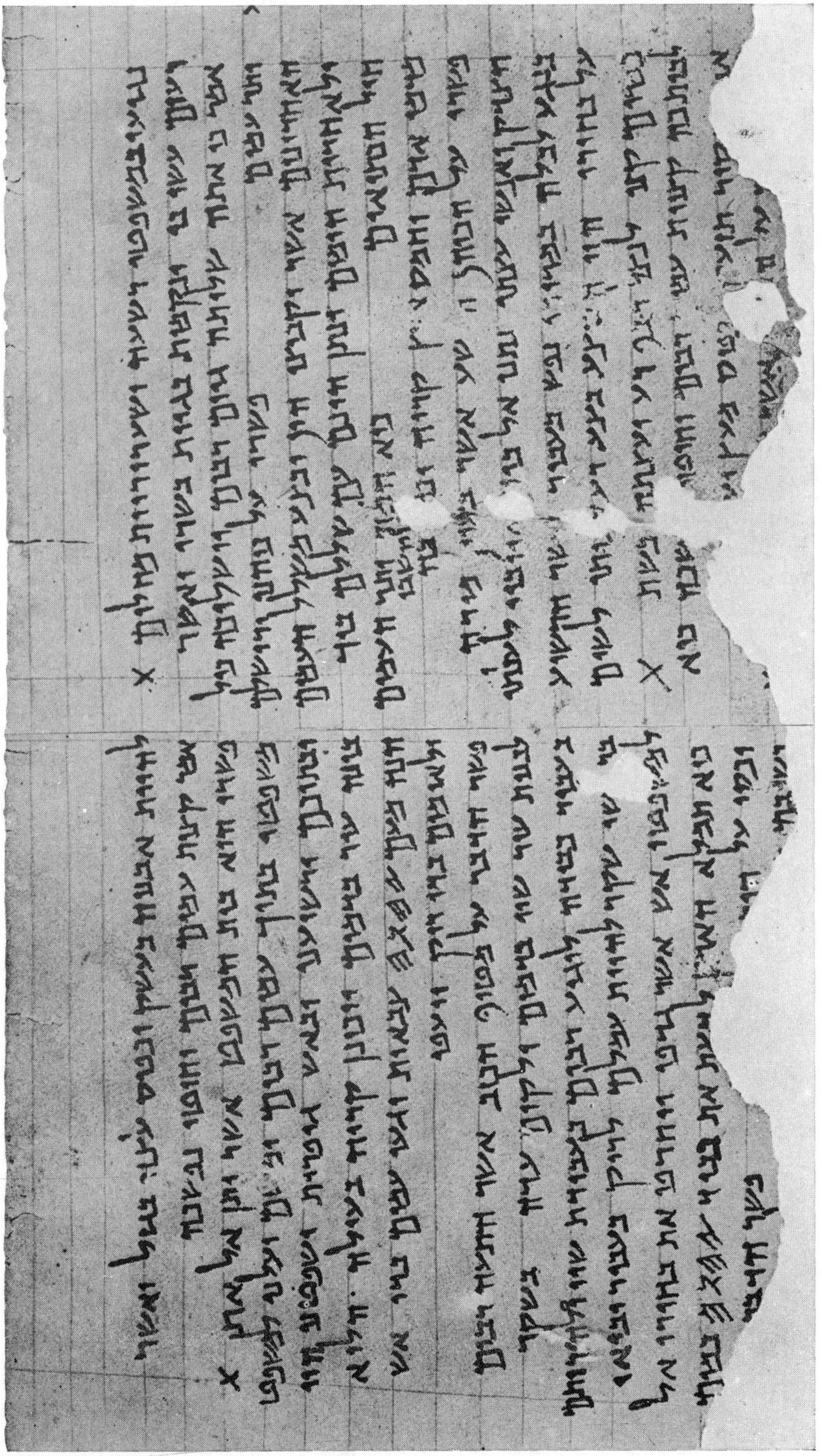

14. FRAGMENTS OF LEVITICUS IN OLD HEBREW SCRIPT

Cf. p. 5. Illustration with transcription from E. L. Sukenik, מגילות גנוזות 2 (1950).

The texts illustrated contain parts of Lev. 19:31-34; 20:20-23; 21:24–22:3, 4, 5. They were brought to light during the investigation of Cave 1 directed by Roland de Vaux and G. Lankester Harding in February 1949. These fragments are the earliest examples of the Old Hebrew script written on leather. A dot is also used here as a word divider. One variant from גו is found in 20:21: היא replaces the Masoretic הוא with Qere perpetuum.

The conjecture that the fragment is of Samaritan origin derives its probability from the known Samaritan practice of using the Old Hebrew script for the Torah. But Kahle has pointed out that the fragment follows the Jewish text where the Jewish and Samaritan traditions differ in Lev. 20:22. Dating the fragment posed great difficulties at first because comparable material was lacking; suggestions ranged from the fifth to the first century B.C. The use of the Old Hebrew script has in itself little bearing on the age of the document because there were still scrolls written in this script in the first Christian centuries (cf. pp. 5f.). Qumran experts are agreed today that the texts in the Old Hebrew script come from the same period as the texts in the square script. It is possible that this script which was preserved from the pre-exilic period enjoyed a renaissance in the Maccabean period with its surge of nationalism (cf. Cross, *ALQ*, p. 34). Just as the Samaritan text found its parallels in Qumran, so did the script which the Samaritans preserved and used.

אלהיכם . מפנ[י]

מאלהיך . אני . יהו[ה]

את[ו] כאזרח . מכם

ישאו

[א]חיו . נדה . היא . [ער]ות

[ושמרת]ם . את . כל . חקתי . ואת . כל .

אתכם . הארץ . אשר . אני .

תלכו

אל[ה]

ישראל

. בניו .

. אשר .

[לדרתיכ]ם . כל . איש . אשר .

[א]שר . י[קדישו] . בני .

[מלפ]ני . [א]ג[ני]

נפ[ש]

בכל . ש[רץ]

15a. A FRAGMENT WITH PARTS OF DEUT. 29:14-18 AND 30:20–31:5

Illustration from G. L. Harding, *Palestine Exploration Quarterly* (1949), pl. 20.

The fragment was acquired from "outside sources" (Harding). Its text of Deut. 31:1 is sensational! This verse reads:

𝔐   וילך משה וידבר את[1] הדברים

Fragment   ויכל משה לדבר את כל

𝔊   καὶ συνετέλεσεν Μωυσῆς λαλῶν πάντας τοὺς λόϳους τούτους.

𝔊 and the fragment are in agreement against 𝔐. "Thus for the first time in the history of the Bible we are confronted with a Hebrew scroll of Deuteronomy which actually supports the Septuagint text of an entire verse."[2] This confirms the conjecture that in this passage 𝔊 is based on a Hebrew exemplar that differed from 𝔐. Bertholet, Marti, and Steuernagel had already emended 𝔐 on the basis of 𝔊, while König defended the originality of 𝔐 (cf. the commentaries). The variants arose because of a transposition of the letters in the first word. The d ·fense of the reading in 𝔐 rests on its being the lectio difficilior, but against it is the fact that its idiom is strained. The latter argument weighs so heavily that in my opinion the reading of 𝔐 must be rejected.

1. Twenty-eight Hebrew manuscripts add כל.
2. J. Leveen, *The Listener* (August 25, 1949), p. 323.

15b. PART OF AN UNOPENED SCROLL

From the 1949 excavations. Illustration from G. L. Harding, *Palestine Exploration Quarterly* (1949), pl. 21.

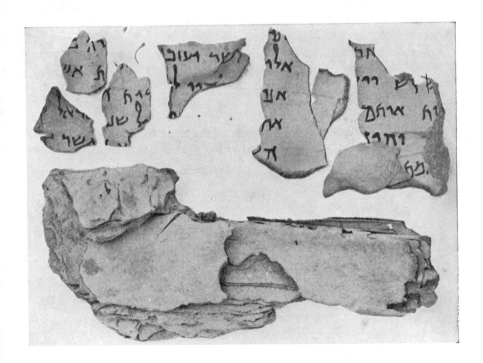

16. *THE MINOR PROPHETS SCROLL, MURABBA'AT 88*

Illustration (Amos 8:11–9:15) from P. Benoit, J. T. Milik, R. de Vaux, *Les Grottes de Murabba'ât, Discoveries in the Judaean Desert* 2 (1961).

In the fall of 1951 four caves were discovered by bedouin in the deep recesses of Wadi Murabba'at in the Judean desert, 17 km. to the south of Qumran and quite unrelated to it. In the spring of 1952 they were investigated carefully by G. L. Harding and R. de Vaux. It was evident from the objects discovered that the caves had been inhabited repeatedly from 4,000 B.C. to the Arabian period. A papyrus palimpsest in the Old Hebrew script, the oldest manuscript from Palestine, is from the eighth-century B.C. settlement (cf. pp. 7f.). A great number of documents including two letters from Simon ben Kosiba (Bar Kochba) attest that these caves served during the second Jewish revolt (A.D. 132-135) as a refuge for a group of Jewish insurgents.

The Minor Prophets scroll (col. 8 is shown here) was found by bedouin in 1955 in a fifth cave which was used as a grave. It dates from the second century A.D. The scribal hand is more developed and exhibits a greater consistency in the Murabba'at texts than in the Qumran texts. There are even striking similarities to the script of medieval manuscripts (Milik, *op. cit.*, p. 71).

The text is in almost complete agreement with 𝔐, suggesting that an authoritative standard text already existed in the first half of the second century A.D.

Note in the illustration: Amos 8:11 (line 1) the three words והשלחתי רעב בארץ have been added above the line; 9:5 (line 15) has ואבל כל יושב instead of the plural as in 𝔐; 9:8 (line 22) a י has been added to השמיד.

To mark the end of the book of Amos a space of three lines at the end of the column and of two lines at the beginning of the next column has been left blank. Single blank lines indicate the end of a paragraph (lines 6, 18, 22); cf. the use of ס after 8:14 and פ after 9:12 in BH. The beginning of a new paragraph after 9:6 is not observed in 𝔐.

17. A PAGE WITH BABYLONIAN POINTING

Cf. pp. 22f. Illustration (Job 37:17–38:15; Berlin Ms. or. qu. 680 = Ec 1) from P. Kahle, *Masoreten des Ostens* (1913).

The ninety-four parchment folios now in Berlin are the remains of a once complete manuscript of the Writings; seven more folios are in the Glaser collection in New York. Originally the pointing was purely Babylonian. This was later revised by a Yemenite hand. "In the reproduction the original pointing is often very difficult to read, while the revised pointing stands out clearly" (Kahle). The Masora parva has been written for the most part in the text and over the word it refers to. The Masora magna is in the lower margin: it cannot be seen in the illustration because it has been destroyed by mildew. For a detailed discussion see P. Kahle, *Der masoretische Text des Alten Testaments nach der Überlieferung der babylonischen Juden* (1902); cf. also *Masoreten des Ostens* (1913), p. 140.

18. A HAPHTARAH FRAGMENT WITH BABYLONIAN POINTING

Cf. pp. 22f. Illustration (Isa. 62:8f., and Hos. 14:2f., with Targum; Cambridge B 15¹ = Kb 7,1) from P. Kahle, *Masoreten des Ostens* (1913).

Selections from the Prophets were read in the Jewish worship service immediately after the Law. Such a selection was called a Haphtarah (plural, Haphtaroth). The name (from the Hebrew הפטיר "to conclude") is evidently to be explained from the fact that the reading from the Prophets concluded the reading of the Scriptures (I. Elbogen, *Geschichte des jüdischen Gottesdienst*, 1962⁴, pp. 174-184). From an early time the Haphtaroth were collected in special scrolls or books.

The page illustrated contains verses from the Haphtarah for the Sabbath before the New Year celebration and from the Haphtarah for the Sabbath after the New Year. According to Kahle it derives from a sumptuous manuscript like the Petersburg codex of the Prophets, and is an example of the most developed form of the Eastern system of pointing.

As was customary, each Hebrew verse is followed by its Targum. In the margin Isa. 63:7-16 has been written by a later hand, also with each verse followed by its Targum.

אֲשֶׁר בְּגָדֶיךָ חַמִּים
תַּרְקִיעַ עִמּוֹ לִשְׁחָקִים
הוֹדִיעֵנוּ מַה נֹּאמַר לוֹ
הַיְסֻפַּר לוֹ כִּי אֲדַבֵּר
וְעַתָּה לֹא רָאוּ אוֹר בָּהִיר הוּא בַּשְּׁחָקִים
מִצָּפוֹן זָהָב יֶאֱתֶה
שַׁדַּי לֹא מְצָאנֻהוּ
וּמִשְׁפָּט וְרֹב צְדָקָה
לָכֵן יְרֵאוּהוּ אֲנָשִׁים

וַיַּעַן יְהוָה אֶת אִיּוֹב מִן הַסְּעָרָה וַיֹּאמַר
מִי זֶה מַחְשִׁיךְ עֵצָה בְמִלִּין
אֱזָר נָא כְגֶבֶר חֲלָצֶיךָ
אֵיפֹה הָיִיתָ בְּיָסְדִי אָרֶץ
מִי שָׂם מְמַדֶּיהָ כִּי תֵדָע אוֹ מִי נָטָה עָלֶיהָ קָּו
בְּרָן יַחַד כּוֹכְבֵי בֹקֶר
וַיָּסֶךְ בִּדְלָתַיִם יָם
מִשּׂוּמִי עָנָן לְבֻשׁוֹ
וָאֶשְׁבֹּר עָלָיו חֻקִּי
וָאֹמַר עַד פֹּה תָבוֹא וְלֹא תֹסִיף
הֲמִיָּמֶיךָ צִוִּיתָ בֹּקֶר
לֶאֱחֹז בְּכַנְפוֹת הָאָרֶץ
תִּתְהַפֵּךְ כְּחֹמֶר חוֹתָם

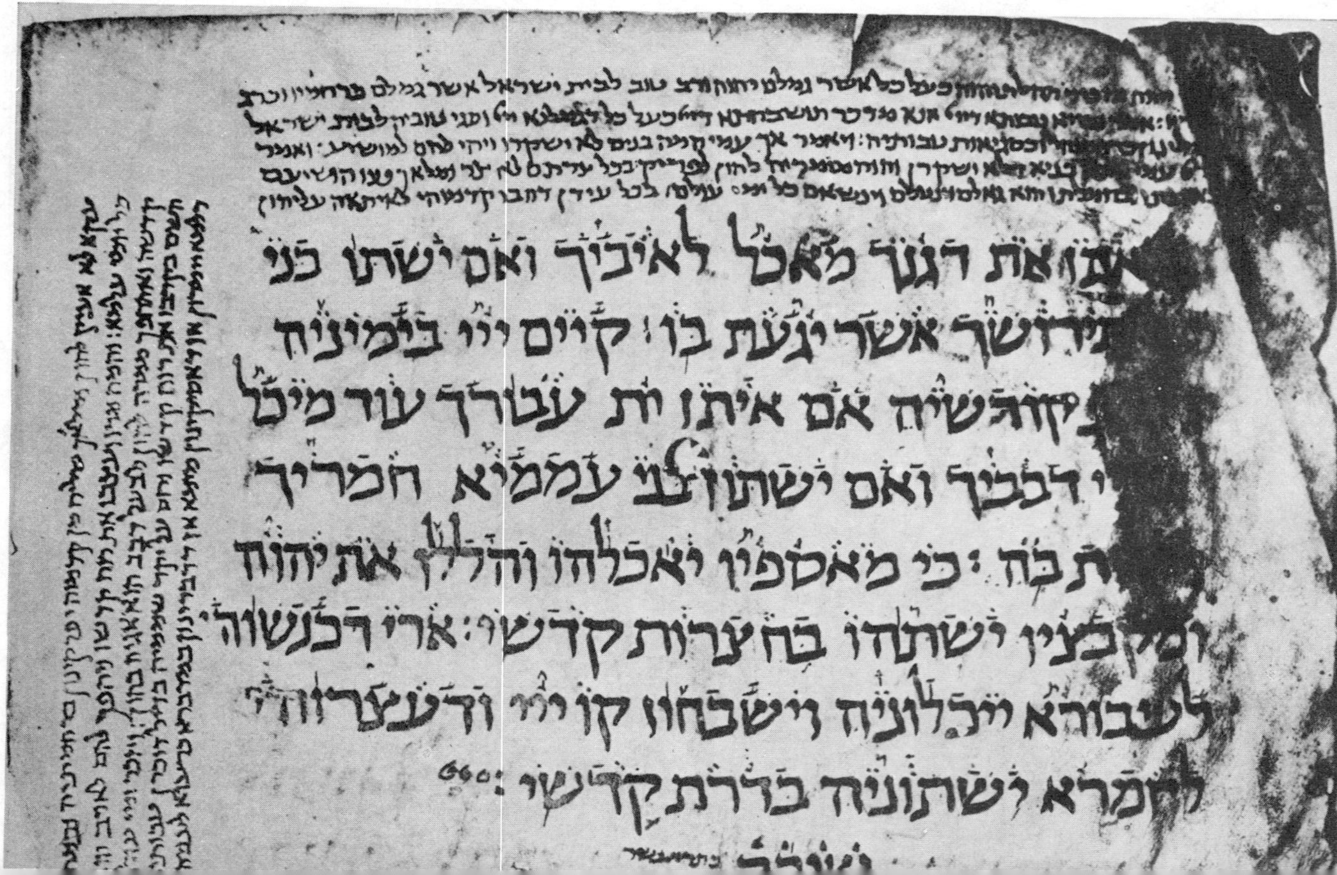

שובה ישראל עד יהוה אלהיך כי כשלת בעונך
תוב ישראל לדחלתא דיוי אלהך ארי
איתקילתא בחובך: קחו עמכם דברים
ושובו אל יהוה אמרו אליו כל תשא עון וקח
טוב ונשלמה פרים שפתינו : קריבו
עמכון פיתגמין דאוריתא

19. *A FRAGMENT WITH PALESTINIAN POINTING*

Cf. p. 23. Illustration (Isa. 7:11–9:8) from P. Kahle, *Masoreten des Westens* 2 (1930).

The rediscovery of the Palestinian system of pointing at the end of the last century was due to this fragment (Oxford Ms. Heb e 30, fol. 48b) and a few other folios which together comprise the remains of a manuscript of the Prophets (cf. P. Kahle, *ZAW* 21, 1901, pp. 273-317).

This manuscript is also remarkable for presenting the Hebrew text in an *abbreviated* form. Only the first word of each verse is written in full, and each of the following words is represented by a single (not always the first) letter together with vowel point and accent. These abbreviated forms are already referred to in the Talmud by the term סירוגין. They were probably designed as memory aids for synagogue lectors and school students.

Whereas words are abbreviated consistently in this text, Biblical manuscripts had long made occasional use of abbreviations for certain words that occur frequently. When these abbreviations were not recognized in copying, they would naturally lead to textual corruption. F. Perles in particular has sought to prove that abbreviations were the cause of corruption in the pre-Masoretic text of the Bible in numerous passages.[1]

---

1. *Analekten zur Textkritik* (1895; n.s., 1922); cf. now also G. R. Driver, "Abbreviations in the Massoretic Text," *Textus* 1 (1960), pp. 112-131; 4 (1964), pp. 76-94.

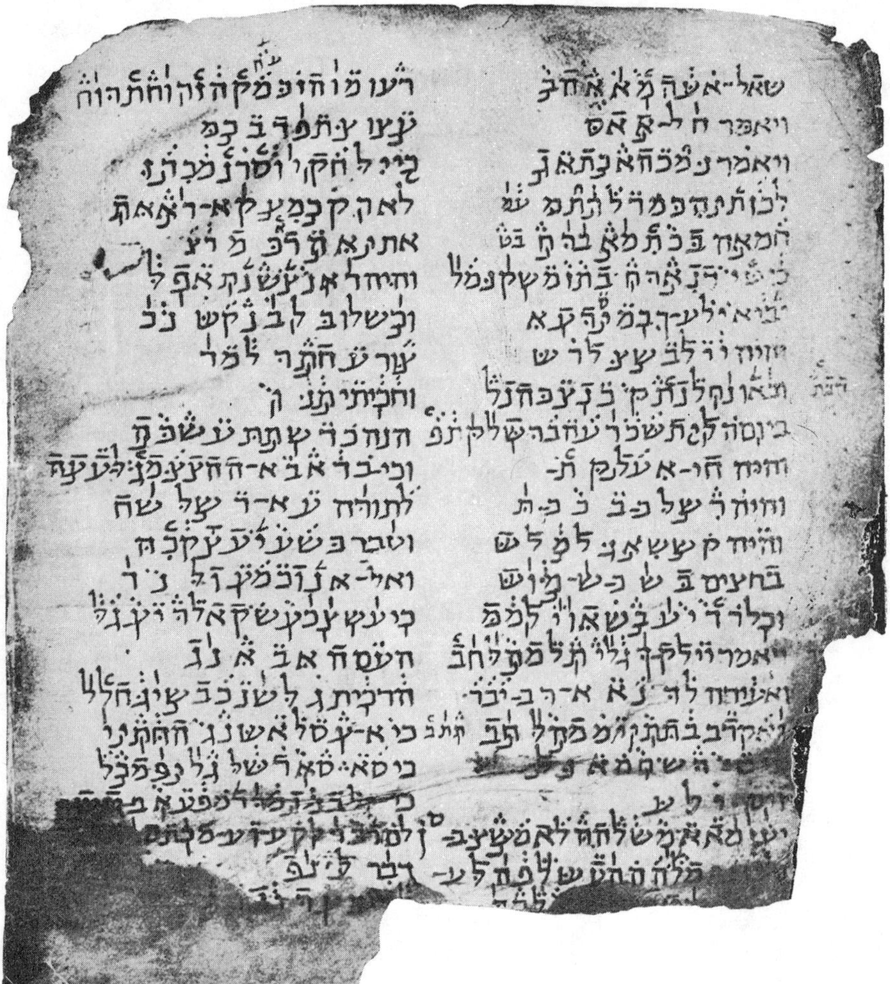

20. *CODEX CAIRENSIS*

Cf. p. 34. Illustration (Jer. 2:16-33) from a photograph kindly provided by P. Kahle.

An excerpt from the second colophon at the end of the manuscript:

I, Moshe ben Asher, have written this Codex *(maḥzor)* of the Scripture according to my judgment 'as the good hand of my God was upon me' (Neh. ii, 8), 'very clearly' (Deut. xxvii, 8), in the city of Ma'azya-Ṭabarīya, 'the renowned city' (Ezek. xxvi, 17) . . .

It was written in the year 827 after the destruction of the Second Temple [= A.D. 895] . . .

[by another hand] Whoever alters a word of this Maḥzor or this writing or erases one letter or tears off one leaf—unless he understands and knows that there is a word in it in which we have erred in the writing or in the punctuation or in the Masora or in defective or in plene—may he have neither pardon nor forgiveness, neither 'let him behold the beauty of the Lord' (Ps. xxvii, 4) nor let him see the good that is reserved for those who fear Him (Jer. xxix, 32). He shall be like a woman in impurity and like a leprous man who has to be locked up so that his limbs may be crushed, the pride of his power be broken, his flesh be consumed away that it cannot be seen and his bones that were covered made bare (Job xxxiii, 21). Amen!

Whoever reads shall hear; whoever hears shall understand; whoever sees shall perceive. Peace! (Kahle, *The Cairo Geniza*, 1959², p. 96).

For the complete text of the colophons with English translation see Kahle, *op. cit.*, pp. 92-97; German translation in *Masoreten des Westens* 1 (1927), pp. 15f.

קר יקר יהל יוא אאת ג
תעשה לך עכל אות
יחזק זא לה רך בעת מי
מלך כ דרך ועשו
מה לך ודרך מצרים
לשתו תמ שחר וכמ ור ך
לדרך אשור לשתות
מי נזר יתי סכך דר רעך
ומש מוך ך יתם סך
ורעי דרא י כ יר ע עמר
עבך את יחזה אלהך
ולא פך יר דלא ארך פ אם
ארע יהוה צבאות כי
מעלם שבר יתי עלך
נתקתי מוס חרתיך
ואמר כי לא אעבד
כי ער גבעה גבהה
ותהת כל עים רענו
את צעה וה יחה ואנף
נתע עך סוך כלה
קרע אמת ואף והמ
ל סרי רחם נבוקה
כפה תכב סי כנרי

ורא פנעס ובעת רעתם
אמרו סוזה וחוש יעעו
ואיה אלהך אשר
עשית לך יקו מואם
ושיעוך בעת רעתך
מ מספר עריך חיו
אלהיך יהודה
הוי מה תריבו אל
כלם פישע תם בי נאכ
יחיה דשוא הכיתי
את בניכם מוסר לא
לקחו אכלה חרבכם
נביאכם כ אריה משחת
הדור אתם ראו רבה
יהוה המדבר הייתי
לישראל אם ארץ
ואם ל ה נקוזי ואמרו
עמי רזנו לא גבא
עוד אליך יתהשבח
בתאה עריה כלה
ומ שריה ועב עו שחוו
ימים אין כ מ פר ה
תטום ורזך ובקש

ותרבי ר ים יתם נתתם
עתך ד פמיגאם ארו
יהוה איך ותאמר לא
נכ וט לת אחר יהמעט
לא וחל שתר אי רזך
בא ר עד מה עשית
בכרה קל משרסת
רוכ כ זה פר חו למד
מד בר רבאות נפש
שא פל רוח חה אצ עתה
מי ושבת מ ל מ בקשו
לא וי צא ב חר שות
ימ צא ואן ימני וגר
מש ף ת זר גמ למעמה
וטא מרו נט ש לאכר
את לב תזו רס ומחר יהם
אלך בכשר ה גבל בני
יהוה ישכ לם בת
ישראל ה זה מל כ יהמ
שר וזט ו כהוכ מ ה דיג
ל כ מאים ה אום ר יסה לך
א בלו אתו ולא על כ אות
יה זו עלי דס פנו אל ארף

21. *THE ALEPPO CODEX*

Cf. pp. 34f. Illustration (Deut. 31:28–32:14) with the kind permission of the Hebrew University Bible Project.

The Aleppo Codex (A), which has probably been in Aleppo since the end of the fourteenth century and has been kept in Israel for the past several years, is described in a dedication inscription as written by Shelomo ben Buya'a, the scribe of the manuscript dated A.D. 930 and shown in pl. 23, and provided with pointing and Masora by Aaron ben Asher. Recent research has proved it to be a particularly valuable witness to the Ben Asher tradition. A report (apparently accurate) that can be traced back to the fifteenth century identifies it with the "model codex" of Maimonides, who wrote: ". . . and the book we rely on in these matters (scil. the correct transcription of the open and closed parashoth of the Torah, and the format of the Psalms) is the book recognized in Old Cairo (מצרים) which contains all twenty-four books and was earlier in Jerusalem where it was employed for the correction of other books. Everyone has relied upon this book because Ben Asher corrected it (לפי שהגיהו) and established the details of its text (ודקדק בו) over a period of many years, correcting it many times as it has been transmitted; I have relied upon it in the Torah book which I have transcribed in accordance with his prescriptions" (from P. Kahle's translation in *Masoreten des Westens* 1, 1927, pp. 11f.; on its identification cf. now the exhaustive study by Goshen-Gottstein, *Textus* 1, 1960, pp. 17-58, and "The Aleppo Codex and Ben Buya'a the Scribe," *Tarbiz* 33, 1963/64, pp. 149-156).[1]

The page illustrated departs from the usual format of the codex (of three columns a page) in accordance with the Masoretic rules for the Song of Moses which are mentioned by Maimonides. The six lines before the Song are to begin with particular words; signs resembling letters are used to fill out the lines as necessary. According to Maimonides the Song itself should be written in sixty-seven lines, the precise number in A (others stipulate seventy lines). There were also rules for the five lines following the Song.

1. A. Dotan, "Was the Aleppo Codex actually vocalized by Aharon ben Asher?" *Tarbiz* 34 (1964/65), pp. 136-155 (cf. *IZBG* 33, 1966/67, p. 1), considers the grounds proposed by Goshen-Gottstein for identification to be inadequate. In spite of the colophon he insists that the pointing of the manuscript cannot be ascribed to Aaron ben Asher.

לֹ֫ אוֹדִיעֵ֫ם יָדַ֫עְתָּ נֵ֫ר חֲ֫ זַ֫ יְדַ֫נַ֫ נַ֫ יִ֫רְעַ֫י זַ֫ל קָרִ֫יאֵ֫ל רְבוּתַ֫אר
בְּו נִ֫ם חַ֫ר וַי֫ן יְחִ֫ידַ֫או וַיִ֫אמֵ֫ר עֶ֫שֶׂר מֵלַ֫אמֵ֫ר יָכַ֫ל ב

וְהַעִ֫ידָה בָּ֫ם אֶת־הַשָּׁמַ֫יִם וְאֶת־הָאָ֫רֶץ כִּ֫י יְ יָדַ֫עְתִּי יְ
אַחֲרֵ֫י מוֹתִ֫י יְי כִּ֫י־ הַשְׁחֵ֫ת יְ תַּשְׁחִת֫וּן יְ יְ וְסַרְתֶּ֫ם יְ יְ מִן
הַדֶּ֫רֶךְ יְ אֲשֶׁ֫ר יְ עִוִּ֫יתִי יְ אֶתְכֶ֫ם יְ וְקָרָ֫את יְ יְ אֶתְכֶ֫ם יְ יְ הָרָעָ֫ה ס
בְּאַחֲרִ֫ית יְ הַיָּמִ֫ים יְ כִּ֫י תַעֲשׂ֫וּ יְ אֶת־הָרַ֫ע יְ בְּעֵינֵ֫י יְ יְחֹנָ֫ה ס
לְהַכְעִיס֫וֹ יְ בְּמַעֲשֵׂ֫ה י וִידֵיכֶ֫ם וַיְדַבֵּ֫ר יְי מֹשֶׁ֫ה יְ יְ בְּאָזְנֵ֫י יְ כָּל־ ס
קְהַ֫ל יִשְׂרָאֵ֫ל אֶת־דִּבְרֵ֫י הַשִּׁירָ֫ה הַזֹּ֫את עַ֫ד תֻּמָּֽם:

וְתִשְׁמַ֫ע הָאָ֫רֶץ אִמְרֵי־פִֽי׃	הַאֲזִ֫ינוּ הַשָּׁמַ֫יִם וַאֲדַבֵּֽרָה
תִּזַּ֫ל כַּטַּ֫ל אִמְרָתִ֫י	יַעֲרֹ֫ף כַּמָּטָ֫ר לִקְחִ֫י
וְכִרְבִיבִ֫ם עֲלֵי־עֵֽשֶׂב׃	כִּשְׂעִירִ֫ם עֲלֵי־דֶ֫שֶׁא
הָב֫וּ גֹ֫דֶל לֵאלֹהֵֽינוּ׃	כִּ֫י שֵׁ֫ם יְיָ֫ אֶקְרָ֫א
כִּ֫י כָל־דְּרָכָ֫יו מִשְׁפָּ֫ט	הַצּ֫וּר תָּמִ֫ים פָּעֳל֫וֹ
צַדִּ֫יק וְיָשָׁ֫ר הֽוּא׃	אֵ֫ל אֱמוּנָ֫ה וְאֵ֫ין עָ֫וֶל
דּ֫וֹר עִקֵּ֫שׁ וּפְתַלְתֹּֽל׃	שִׁחֵ֫ת ל֫וֹ לֹ֫א בָּנָ֫יו מוּמָ֫ם
עַ֫ם נָבָ֫ל וְלֹ֫א חָכָ֫ם	הֲ־לַיְיָ֫ תִּגְמְלוּ־זֹ֫את
ה֫וּא עָשְׂךָ֫ וַֽיְכֹנְנֶֽךָ׃	הֲ־לֹא־ה֫וּא אָבִ֫יךָ קָּנֶ֫ךָ
שְׁאַ֫ל אָבִ֫יךָ וְיַגֵּ֫דְךָ זְקֵנֶ֫יךָ וְיֹ֫אמְרוּ לָֽךְ׃	זְכֹר֫ יְמ֫וֹת עוֹלָ֫ם בִּ֫ינוּ שְׁנ֫וֹת דֹּר־וָדֹ֫ר
בְּהַפְרִיד֫וֹ בְּנֵ֫י אָדָ֫ם	בְּהַנְחֵ֫ל עֶלְיוֹן֫ גּוֹיִ֫ם
לְמִסְפַּ֫ר בְּנֵ֫י יִשְׂרָאֵֽל׃	יַצֵּ֫ב גְּבֻלֹ֫ת עַמִּ֫ים
יַעֲקֹ֫ב חֶ֫בֶל נַחֲלָתֽוֹ׃	כִּ֫י חֵ֫לֶק יְיָ֫ עַמּ֫וֹ
וּבְתֹ֫הוּ יְלֵ֫ל יְשִׁמֹ֫ן	יִמְצָאֵ֫הוּ בְּאֶ֫רֶץ מִדְבָּ֫ר
יִצְּרֶ֫נְהוּ כְּאִיש֫וֹן עֵינֽוֹ׃	יְסֹבְבֶ֫נְהוּ יְב֫וֹנְנֵֽהוּ
יִפְרֹ֫שׂ כְּנָפָ֫יו יִקָּחֵ֫הוּ יִשָּׂאֵ֫הוּ עַל־אֶבְרָתֽוֹ׃	כְּנֶ֫שֶׁר יָעִ֫יר קִנּ֫וֹ עַל־גּוֹזָלָ֫יו יְרַחֵ֫ף
וְאֵ֫ין עִמּ֫וֹ אֵ֫ל נֵכָֽר׃	יְיָ֫ בָּדָ֫ד יַנְחֶ֫נּוּ
וַיֹּאכַ֫ל תְּנוּבֹ֫ת שָׂדָ֫י	יַרְכִּבֵ֫הוּ עַל־בָּ֫מֳתֵי אָ֫רֶץ
וְשֶׁ֫מֶן מֵחַלְמִ֫ישׁ צֽוּר׃	וַיֵּנִקֵ֫הוּ דְבַשׁ֫ מִסֶּ֫לַע
עִ֫ם חֵ֫לֶב כָּרִ֫ים וְאֵילִ֫ים	חֶמְאַ֫ת בָּקָ֫ר וַחֲלֵ֫ב צֹ֫אן
עִ֫ם חֵ֫לֶב כִּלְי֫וֹת חִטָּ֫ה	בְּנֵי־בָשָׁ֫ן וְעַתּוּדִ֫ים

אֶ֫רֶץ יְיָ֫ פֹ֫עַל וְעָשָׂ֫ה וַיִּשְׁמַח֫וּ וַיִּשְׂמֵ֫חוּ אֶ֫ל לֵ֫ב הַטּוֹבַ֫ה וַאֲנִ֫י וַיֹּ֫אמְרוּ הִ֫ינֵ֫ה יְהֹוָ֫ה בְּהַר֫עֵ֫ם בְּרַחֲמֵ֫ם מַ֫ה טוֹבַ֫ם לֹ֫אֵ֫ם פְּסִילֵ֫ם ו֫דַ֫ל יְדַ֫בֵֽ֫ל
בֵּ֫ית חַ֫ הַ֫לַ֫ לַ֫בַ֫ עָ֫רַ֫ל תָּ֫מַ֫ר וְאָ֫חַ֫ י וְ֫ל רַ֫ב וַ֫י יִ֫כַ֫תַ֫ו וַ֫י֫וֹן וַ֫ל וֹ֫ל אָ֫מַ֫ריַ֫ו֫ דַ֫ל יְ֫כַ֫ן חַ֫מַ֫לַ֫ יַ֫דַ֫רַ֫י בְּעֹ֫זוֹ לֵ֫ רֵ֫ינו ו ׃
רַ֫עַ֫י יְ֫לַ֫ נַ֫שַ֫ר יְ֫ו֫ן לַאֲחָ֫רִ֫ינַ֫ ב֫ כַ֫ בָ֫מַ֫דַ֫ל שָׁלֹ֫נַ֫ן לַ֫יהַ֫מַ֫ן ל֫י֫כַ֫מַ֫י קָ֫דִ֫יר֫י בַּעֹ֫זוֹ לַ֫ בַ֫י֫נֵֽו ׃

22. *BRITISH MUSEUM CODEX OR. 4445*

Cf. p. 39, n. 73. Illustration in reduced size (Num. 26:12-27) with the kind permission of the British Museum.

This manuscript of the Pentateuch is pointed and accented: the defective portions at the beginning (Gen. 1–39:19) and end (from Deut. 1:34 on), as well as Num. 7:46-73 and 9:12–10:18, are lacking or have been supplied by a later hand. The manuscript is written in a good, clear hand with three columns to a page, the Masora parva in the side margins, and the Masora magna in the upper and lower margins. Ginsburg (*Introduction to the Massoretico-Critical Edition of the Hebrew Bible*, 1897, pp. 469-474) recognized this as the oldest manuscript and dated the consonantal text and its pointing about A.D. 820-850; he thought the Masora was added about a century later by a Nakdan (cf. p. 14) who also revised the text. It may be assumed that the Masora was written while Ben Asher was still alive, because he is mentioned without the form of blessing usual for one who has died. Kahle, however, places the origin of the entire manuscript within the lifetime of Ben Asher: "[that] Ben Asher was obviously the great authority for the copyist, and that he really copied a Ben Asher text, is confirmed by the book of Mishael b. 'Uzziel" (Kahle, *VT* 1, 1951, p. 167; cf. also *Masoreten des Westens* 1, 1927, pp. 17f.; on Mishael ben 'Uzziel cf. pp. 24f. above and BHK, pp. xxixf.).

כל הברכ׳ עמד אעבד רגלך בני אם כל רבין יאמפלשתה וחורי ועלי עדר זדבר מפעד ולראשי בתראש טרחיות אמר
ירברית משכפרי רוח מלאן מאלה אלך כה לי ... אחר יד ... יהוה אלך בית הרכמכטואל ובזי ותרכ תאוון ...

משפחת הנמואלי	משפחת בני גד	בני נפתלי למשפחתם
לימין משפחת	לפקדיהם ארבעים	ליחצאל משפחת
הימיני לידו משפחת	אלף וחמש מאות	היחצאלי לגוני
הידכיני לזרח משפחת	בני יהודה	משפחת הגוני
הזרחי לשאול משפחת	ער ואונן וימת ער	לישוב משפחת
השאולי · אלה	ואונן בארץ כנען	הישבי לשלם
משפחת בני שמעון	ויהיו בני יהודה	משפחת השלמי
שנים ועשרים אלף	למשפחתם לשלה	אלה משפחת נפתלי
ומאתים · בני	משפחת השלני	וישב... לפקדיהם
גד למשפחתם	לפרץ משפחת	ארבעה וחמשים
לצפון משפחת	הפרצי לזרח ·	אלף ושלש מאות
הצפוני לחגי ·	משפחת הזרחי	
משפחת החגי	ויהי בני פרץ	בני יוסף למשפחתם
לשוני משפחת	לחצרון משפחת	לסכד משפחתי
השוני · לאזני ·	החצרני להמול	תסרדי לאלון ·
משפחת האזני	משפחת החמולי	משפחת האלוני
לערי משפחת	אלה משפחת	לנחלאל משפחת
הערי · לארודי	יהודה לפקדיהם	הנחלאל · אלה
משפחת הארודי	ששה ושבעים	משפחת הזבולדני
לאראלי משפחת	אלף וחמש מאות	לפקדיהם ששים
הארארלי · אלה	פ	אלף וחמש מאות

ג בטעם בני פלוא בעינה ... ותומנתהן ושושכי נפתנל דן ס חבולין ג. וכל ל. וטמנתהן אלה משתפחא חבולן אבלין
חדבולוני וחבלתו ... בן ... ז בטע בעתעא גד יהורה שמעון ובוין אשר אפרים בונמין ב ... דן ... וכת ... ס סיוקינעלה.
בן חפר ... ולחברה בן חפר גן גו עד מחלה ונעה חנלה מלכה ותרינת ... ותקרבנה מנת יתריעד מלבן ...

23. *A TORAH MANUSCRIPT FROM THE YEAR A.D. 930*

Codex 17 of the second Firkowitsch collection (cf. p. 30). Illustration (Deut. 9:15-23) from P. Kahle, *Masoreten des Westens* 1 (1927).

At the end of the codex, which comprises 241 folios with three columns of text per page, the scribe and the Masorete of the codex, two brothers, give separate accounts of their activities.

The scribal colophon: "I, Shelomo ha-Levi, son of Buya'a,[1] pupil of Sa'id the son of Fargai also called Balquq, have written this book of the Torah of Moses, as the good hand of my God is upon me, for our lord Barhon and for our lord Salich, the sons of our lord Maimun . . ."

The Masorete writes: "I, Ephraim, son of Rabbi Buya'a, have pointed and provided the Masora, completing this Torah and verifying it as the good hand of my God is upon me, and if there is a fault in it, may God not count it against me as a sin. I completed it on Friday, the eighth day of Kislev in the year 1241 of the [Seleucid] era for our lord Abraham and our lord Salich, the sons of our lord Maimun. May this Torah be for them, as well as for us and for all Israel, a good sign, a sign of blessing for salvation and for help, for the coming of the Messiah and the building of Jerusalem and for the gathering of the captivity of Israel, as it is promised to us by our Creator, the Builder of Jerusalem. Yahweh will gather the scattered of Israel, and raise up a banner for the nations and gather the scattered of Israel and the destroyed of Judah he will gather from the four corners of the earth (Isa. 11:12)."[2]

1. Shelomo ben Buya'a also wrote the Ben Asher codex in Aleppo (cf. p. 162).
2. Text from P. Kahle, *Masoreten des Westens* 1 (1927), pp. 58f. The Hebrew text (in H. Strack, *Dikduke ha-Te'amim*) was not available to me.

אתה עגל	־סלא אבדתי	־והדר
לקחתי ואשרף	־מים לא שתתי	בגרבאש וישן
אתו באש ואכת	על כל חטאתכם	לוחתהברית על
אתו טחון היטב	אשר חטאתם׳	שתמודי ואדא
עד אשר דק	לעשות הרע ־׳	והמה חטאתם ׳
לעפר ואשלך	בעיני יהוה ׳־	ליהוה אלהיכם
את עפרו אל	להכעסו כי ׳׳	עשיתם לכם ־׳
הנחל הירד מן	ואגרתי מפני האף	עגל מסכה ל׳
ההר ובתבערה	והחמה אשר	סרתם מהר כמו
ובמסה ובקברת	קצף יהוה עליכם	הדרך אשר צוה
התאוה מקצפם	להשמיד אתכם	יהוה אתכם
הייתם את יהוה	וישמע יהוה ׳־	ואתפש בשנ
ובשלח׳ יהוה	אלי גם בפעם	הלוחת ואשלכם
אתכם מקדש	ההוא ובאהרן	מעל שתי ידי
ברנע לאמר	התאנף׳ יהוה	ואשברק לעיניכם
עלו ורשו את	מאד להשמידו	ואתנפל לפני
הארץ אשר	ואתפלל גם בעד	יהוה כראשנה
נתתי לכם ותמרי	אהרן בעת החוא	ארבעם יום
את פי יהוה׳	ואת חטאתכם	וארבעם לילה
אלהיכם ולא	אשר עשיתם׳	

24. *CODEX LENINGRADENSIS*

Cf. p. 35. Illustration (Gen. 28:18–29:22) from a photograph kindly provided by P. Kahle.

The date of the manuscript is described in the following colophon:[1]

"This codex, the whole of the Holy Scriptures, was written and completed with pointing and Masora and carefully corrected in the Metropolis of Egypt [Cairo]. It was completed (a) in the month of Siwan of the year 4770 of the Creation of the world. (b) This is the year 1444 of the Exile of King Jehoiakin. (c) This is the year (1)319 of the Greek Reign, according to the reckoning of the Seleucid era and the Cessation of Prophecy. (d) This is the year 940 after the destruction of the second Temple. (e) This is the year 399 of the Reign of the Small Horn [cf. Dan. 8:9; Islam is intended]. It was acquired by Meborach ben Nathaniel, known as Ben Osdad, priest . . ."

The dating indicates the following years: (a) A.D. 1010, (c) 1008, (d) 1009, (e) 1008. The date (b) falls wide of this period and probably derives from erroneous assumptions. The date (e) A.D. 1008 is probably the most trustworthy because the writer lived in an Islamic country.

The following colophon refers to Ben Asher: "Samuel ben Jacob wrote and pointed and provided with Masora this codex of the Holy Scriptures from the corrected and annotated books prepared by Aaron ben Moses ben Asher the teacher, may he rest in the Garden of Eden! It has been corrected and properly annotated." Its dependence on the Ben Asher tradition, which has been questioned on occasion, has been confirmed by recent research (cf. BHK, pp. xxix-xxxiii).

---

1. The text of the colophon is printed and translated in part by A. Harkavy and H. L. Strack, *Catalog der hebräischen Bibelhandschriften der Kaiserlichen Öffentlichen Bibliothek in St. Petersburg* (1875), pp. 265ff.

25. *A MANUSCRIPT WITH DISTINCTIVE POINTING (OXFORD, BODLEIAN LIBRARY)*

Cf. p. 25. Illustration (Ps. 112:2–114:3) from P. Kahle, *Masoreten des Westens* 2 (1930).

The folio illustrated, one of the six surviving folios of a Psalter manuscript, exhibits certain peculiarities that are characteristic of a particular group of manuscripts. This group of manuscripts differs clearly from the Ben Asher manuscripts, and was earlier associated by Kahle (*op. cit.*, pp. 57*f.) with Ben Naphtali. Recent research has shown, however, that it is not related to Ben Naphtali, but represents a separate group with a distinctive pointing (cf. p. 25 above).

In the text illustrated the following peculiarities may be observed in contrast with the Ben Asher text:

1. When the א is pronounced as a consonant it has a dot in its center: בארץ Ps. 112:2; אור 112:4; איש 112:5; יראה 112:8; תאות 112:10; את 113:1; אם 113:9. When it is not pronounced a stroke is placed above it: לא 112:6-8.

2. The Mappiq in the final ה which indicates its consonantal value is placed *under* the ה: הללויה 113:1, 9.

3. When a final ו is pronounced as a consonant it has a Shewa placed within the letter: בצריו 112:8.

4. The ח and ע have a Shewa when in final position: בטוח 112:7; רשע 112:10.

5. The Pathah furtive is lacking where we would expect it: בטוח 112:7.

6. The Shewa of the composite Shewa with ה and ח is found over and not beside the vowel sign: יחרק 112:10.

7. The relative pronoun אשר is not pointed: 112:8. Proper nouns of frequent occurrence are similarly left unpointed or only partially pointed: ישראל 114:2.

The manuscript illustrated was further worked over by a second hand which added mainly the accents of the textus receptus (Kahle, *op. cit.*, p. 52*).

גִּבּוֹר בָּאָרֶץ יִהְיֶה זַרְעוֹ · דּוֹר יְשָׁרִים יְבֹרָךְ
הוֹן וָעֹשֶׁר בְּבֵיתוֹ · וְצִדְקָתוֹ עֹמֶדֶת לָעַד
זָרַח בַּחֹשֶׁךְ אוֹר לַיְשָׁרִים · חַנּוּן וְרַחוּם וְצַדִּיק
טוֹב אִישׁ חוֹנֵן וּמַלְוֶה · יְכַלְכֵּל דְּבָרָיו בְּמִשְׁפָּט
כִּי לְעוֹלָם לֹא יִמּוֹט · לְזֵכֶר עוֹלָם יִהְיֶה צַדִּיק
מִשְּׁמוּעָה רָעָה לֹא יִירָא · נָכוֹן לִבּוֹ בָּטֻחַ בַּיהוָה
סָמוּךְ לִבּוֹ לֹא יִירָא · עַד אֲשֶׁר יִרְאֶה בְצָרָיו
פִּזַּר נָתַן לָאֶבְיוֹנִים צִדְקָתוֹ עֹמֶדֶת לָעַד · קַרְנוֹ תָּרוּם בְּכָבוֹד
רָשָׁע יִרְאֶה וְכָעָס שִׁנָּיו יַחֲרֹק וְנָמָס · מַאֲוַת רְשָׁעִים תֹּאבֵד

הַלְלוּיָהּ
הַלְלוּ עַבְדֵי יְהוָה · הַלְלוּ אֶת שֵׁם יְהוָה
יְהִי שֵׁם יְהוָה מְבֹרָךְ · מֵעַתָּה וְעַד עוֹלָם
מִמִּזְרַח שֶׁמֶשׁ עַד מְבוֹאוֹ · מְהֻלָּל שֵׁם יְהוָה
רָם עַל כָּל גּוֹיִם יְהוָה · עַל הַשָּׁמַיִם כְּבוֹדוֹ
מִי כַּיהוָה אֱלֹהֵינוּ · הַמַּגְבִּיהִי לָשָׁבֶת
הַמַּשְׁפִּילִי לִרְאוֹת · בַּשָּׁמַיִם וּבָאָרֶץ
מְקִימִי מֵעָפָר דָּל · מֵאַשְׁפֹּת יָרִים אֶבְיוֹן
לְהוֹשִׁיבִי עִם נְדִיבִים · עִם נְדִיבֵי עַמּוֹ
מוֹשִׁיבִי עֲקֶרֶת הַבַּיִת · אֵם הַבָּנִים שְׂמֵחָה הַלְלוּיָהּ

בְּצֵאת יִשְׂרָאֵל מִמִּצְרַיִם · בֵּית יַעֲקֹב מֵעַם לֹעֵז
הָיְתָה יְהוּדָה לְקָדְשׁוֹ · יִשְׂרָאֵל מַמְשְׁלוֹתָיו
הַיָּם רָאָה וַיָּנֹס · הַיַּרְדֵּן יִסֹּב לְאָחוֹר

26. *THE SECOND RABBINIC BIBLE OF JACOB BEN CHAYYIM*

Cf. pp. 37f. Illustration (Gen. 21:33b–22:4a) from a copy at the Bodleian Library, Oxford, by the kind permission of the Bodleian Library.

Rabbinic Bibles (מקראות גדולות) are printed copies of the Old Testament produced from the sixteenth century onward in which the Hebrew text, Targum, Masora, and Rabbinic commentaries are brought together. The illustration shows the arrangement: in the center is the Hebrew text (with Masora) and the Targum, and around it are the commentaries (here of Ibn Ezra and Rashi).

The first Rabbinic Bible, as yet without Masora, was published by Felix Pratensis of the Order of Augustinian Hermits in 1516/17 at the Bomberg press in Venice. As the son of a Rabbi, Felix was familiar with Hebrew studies from his youth. After his conversion to Christianity (*ca.* 1506) he became familiar with the scientific methods of classical philology. He applied these to the text of the Hebrew Bible—just as the editors of the Complutensian polyglot were doing at about the same time (cf. pp. 214f.). He attempted to prepare a correct text on the basis of his study of manuscripts—"an extremely difficult task, and for this reason one which had never been attempted by others."[1] In his dedication to the Pope he explains with pride that he has restored to the Hebrew text its true and original splendor, in contrast to the many defective manuscripts in circulation at the time (probably these were actually manuscripts of a different Masoretic school; cf. pp. 24f.). He was the first to indicate in a printed Bible the Kethib and the Qere, to introduce the *puncta extraordinaria,* and to observe the Masoretic rules about the special forms of particular letters, such as the *litera majusculae, suspensae, inversae,* etc., as well as to record variant readings from the manuscripts he used.

The work of Felix Pratensis exercised a far-reaching influence because his critical edition provided in large measure the groundwork for the second Rabbinic Bible here illustrated, the work of Jacob ben Chayyim, who may have been less significant as a scholar, but whose work became in turn the standard basis for many later editions (cf. pp. 37f. above).[2]

Further Rabbinic Bibles were published in Venice (1546/48, 1568, 1617/19), Basel (1618/19, edited by Johan Buxtorf the Elder), Amsterdam (1724/25), and Warsaw (1860/66, with thirty-two commentaries).[3]

1. "Rem equidem perdifficilem nec ob id ab aliis hactenus tentatam."
2. P. Kahle, *WdO* 1 (1947/52), pp. 32-36; *idem, Essays presented to Leo Baeck on the occasion of his eightieth birthday* (1954), pp. 50-74 (*Opera Minora,* 1956, pp. 128-150).
3. *Encyclopaedia Judaica* 4 (1929), col. 547f., "Rabbinic Bibles."

אבן עזרא

27. *THE SAMARITAN TRIGLOT*

Cf. pp. 42f. Illustration (Deut. 31:15-19) from P. Kahle, *Die Handschriften aus der Höhle* (1951).

The illustration shows a folio acquired by P. Kahle from a valuable triglot in Nablus (Shechem), the Torah Finchasiye, which was written in the year 601 of the Mohammedan era, i.e., A.D. 1204/5. The Hebrew, Aramaic, and Arabic texts are all written in Samaritan script from right to left in three columns. This script was developed from the Old Hebrew script. Comparing this folio with the fragment of Leviticus in Old Hebrew script found by de Vaux (cf. pl. 14), Kahle comments: "Of course the forms of the letters are somewhat more developed, and certain principles in the method of transcribing Biblical manuscripts show signs of evolution through the years. But with it all, it is simply amazing how constant the Old Hebrew script has remained over a period of 1000 to 1500 years" (Kahle, *op. cit.*, pp. 19f.).

Note the following characteristics in the manuscript: the individual words are separated by dots. The first letter and the last two letters in each line are written precisely under each other. There is also a tendency to write similar letters in successive lines directly under each other (cf. lines 7 and 8, 11 and 12). As a rule, manuscripts of the Samaritan Pentateuch are written without vowel points.

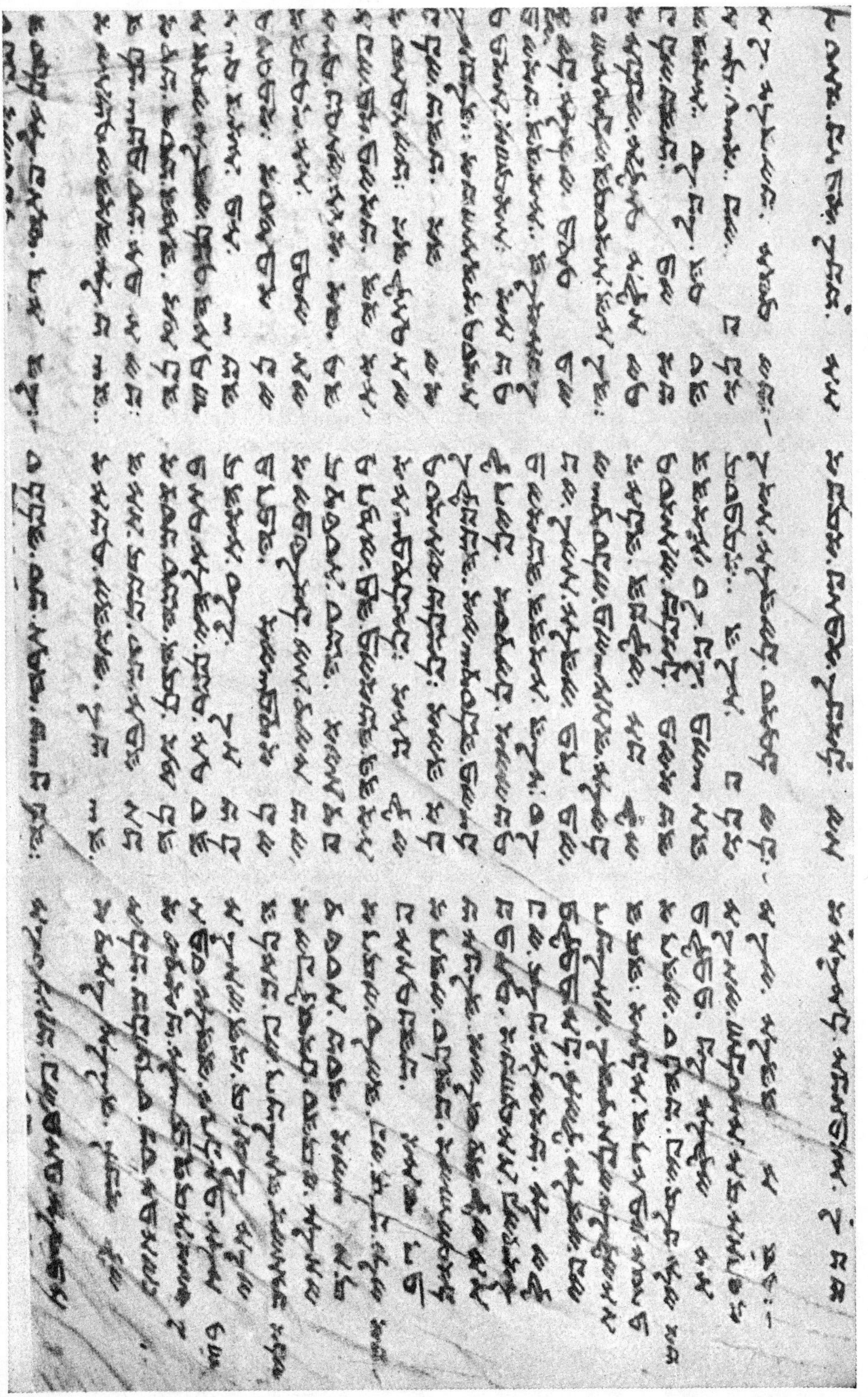

28. THE RYLANDS GREEK PAPYRUS 458

Cf. p. 68. Illustration from a photograph kindly provided by the John Rylands Library, Manchester.

Contents: (a) Deut. 23:24(26)–24:3. (b) Deut. 25:1-3. (c) Deut. 26:12. (d) Deut. 26:17-19. (e) Deut. 28:31-33. (f) Deut. 27:15(?). (g) Deut. 28:2(?). (h) ?

These fragments were found in the wrappings of a mummy acquired by Dr. Rendel Harris for the John Rylands Library in 1917. They presumably came from the Fayyum where we know there were two Jewish synagogues. Date: mid-second century B.C. The reverse of the Deuteronomy scroll from which the fragments are derived was later used for accounts or notes.

Of special interest is the system of spacing which is quite rare: "As can be seen from the photograph of fragment (b) the writer regularly leaves a space not only at the end of a verse or sentence, but at the end of a κῶλον or group of words. At the end of a verse (cf. frag. (a), line 14, after αὐτοῦ in the illustration) a wider space is left and a high point added; otherwise the writer's principle seems to be to leave a fairly large space at the end of a sentence or clause (cf. frag. (b)), and a smaller one at the end of a group of words" (C. H. Roberts, *Two Biblical Papyri in the John Rylands Library,* Manchester, 1936, p. 25). Is this division of the text related to its use in public reading, or does it reflect Aramaic influence? Otherwise the papyrus is like all other Greek manuscripts in ignoring word division.

It is particularly significant that the papyrus agrees in some readings with later Lucianic manuscripts. "This shows that late manuscripts may often contain very early elements, and that the Lucianic recension may have very old foundations."[1]

1. A. Vaccari, *Bibl* 17 (1936), p. 504: "Hinc patet iuniores codices quam antiqua elementa saepe contineant et quam profunda habeat fundamenta Luciani recensio."

29. *PAPYRUS FOUAD 266*

Cf. p. 68. Société Royale de Papyrologie, Cairo; first published by W. G. Waddell, *JTS* 45 (1944), pp. 158-161. Illustration (Deut. 31:28–32:6) from P. Kahle, *Handschriften aus der Höhle* (1951).

This papyrus is probably from the first or even the second century B.C., and is therefore the second oldest witness to the Greek text of the Old Testament after the Rylands Greek Papyrus 458. It was obviously written by a Jew. The treatment of the divine name Yahweh is of particular interest. Jerome reports in the *Prologus Galeatus* on the writing of this name in Greek manuscripts (Migne, 28, pp. 594f.): "Even today we find the tetragrammaton name of God written in archaic letters in some Greek manuscripts."[1] And in *Epistula 25 ad Marcellam* (*Corpus Scriptorum Ecclesiasticorum Latinorum* 54, 1910, p. 219): "(The name of God is) a tetragram which they considered *anekphōnēton* (i.e., unpronounceable) and wrote with the letters *yodh, he, waw, he*. Those who did not understand this would pronounce them PIPI when they read them in Greek books, because of their similarity to the Greek letters."[2]

Thus Jerome was aware of the custom of writing Yahweh in Hebrew letters in Greek manuscripts. The papyrus shown here is evidence for this in pre-Christian times: in col. 2, lines 7 and 15, Yahweh is written in the Hebrew square script in the middle of the Greek text. In fact, the scribe of the Greek text left a space, and the Hebrew letters added by the second scribe are so small that they do not fill the allotted space. Cf. also the form of the divine name in the Habakkuk Commentary (pl. 13) and the related discussion on p. 146.

Publication: F. Dunand, *Papyrus Grecs Bibliques (Papyrus F. Inv. 266), Volumina de la Genèse et du Deutéronome*, L'Institut Français d'Archéologie Orientale, *Recherches d'Archéologie, de Philologie, et d'Histoire* 27 (1966), introduction; *Extraits des Etudes de Papyrologie* 9 (1966), pp. 81-150, text, apparatus, and plates.

1. "Nomen Domini tetragrammaton in quibusdam Graecis volumnibus usque hodie antiquis litteris invenimus."
2. "(Dei nomen est) tetragrammum quod ἀνεκφώνητον, id est ineffabile, putaverunt et his litteris scribitur: iod, he, vau, he. Quod quidam non intelligentes propter elementorum similitudinem, cum in Graecis libris repererint, ΠΙΠΙ legere consueverunt."

ΠΡΟCΕΧΕΟΥΡΑ
ΚΑΤΑΚΟΥΕΤΩ
ΠΡΟCΔΟΚΕΙCΩ
ΚΑΙΚΑΤΑΒΗ
ΩCΕΙΟΜΒΡΟCΕ
ΚΟCΕΝΙΩ
ΟΝΟΜΑ
ΤΕΜΕΓΑΚΩ
CΑΛΗΘΙΝΑ
ΠΑCΑΙΑΟΔΟ
ΟCΠΙCΤΟCΚΑ
CΑΙΟC
ΥΤΟCΑΝΟ
ΕΑCΚΟΛΙΑ
ΓΑ ΑΙ
ΕΤΩICΛΛΟCΜ
ΟΥΚΑΥΤΟCΟΥ
ΕΙΠΗCΑΤ
Μ

ΛΑΙΤΥ
CΑΙΤΗΝ
ΧΤΗCΕΜΟΥ
ΝΕΚΚΛΙΝΕΤΕ
ΙΥΜΙΝΚΑ
ΚΑΕCΧΑΤΩΝ
CΤΟΠΟΝΗΡΩΝ
CΤΟΝΕΝΤΟΙC
ΝΕΝ

ΟΥ
ICIC
ΝΑΔΙΚΙ

30. A GREEK SCROLL OF THE MINOR PROPHETS

Cf. pp. 54, 68. Illustration (Hab. 1:14–2:5 and 2:13-15) from D. Barthélemy, *RB* 60 (1953).

This scroll which we have referred to often was found by the Taamire bedouin in August, 1952 in the Judean desert in a cave that was not at first identified; in 1952 and 1953 it was acquired by the Palestinian Archaeological Museum in Jerusalem. Israeli excavators were later successful in identifying the cave in Naḥal Ḥever, and in finding nine more small fragments.[1] The surviving parts of the scroll which were published by D. Barthélemy (cf. p. 6, n. 10 for bibliography) are from the books of Jonah, Micah, Nahum, Habakkuk, Zephaniah, and Zechariah. In his first report in *RB* 60 (1953), pp. 18-29, Barthélemy dated the scroll toward the end of the first century A.D., while C. H. Roberts assigned it to the century between 50 B.C. and A.D. 50—a position essentially supported by W. Schubart (cf. P. Kahle, *The Cairo Geniza,* 1959², p. 226).[2] In his edition of the text Barthélemy now indicates the mid-first century A.D. as most probable. The scroll therefore represents a Greek Biblical text written by Jews and for Jews. From the plentiful archaeological evidence (including coins) found together with the fragments by the bedouin and Israeli excavators in Naḥal Ḥever, it is clear that the scroll was placed in the cave during the Bar Kochba rebellion (A.D. 132-135), and at that time it was already well worn.

The discussion which has continued unabated since this amazing discovery is evidence of the great significance of this scroll (cf. pp. 62f.).

1. B. Lifschitz, *Yedi'ot* 26 (1962), pp. 183-190 = "Greek Documents from the Cave of Horror," *IEJ* 12 (1962), pp. 201-207.

2. P. Katz, *Studia Patristica* 1, *Texte und Untersuchungen zur Geschichte der altchristlichen Literatur* 63 (1957), pp. 343-353, supported Barthélemy's first dating and evaluation of the scroll: "As B. has well seen, it cannot be understood otherwise than as the work of Jewish scholars working after, perhaps very soon after, 70 A.D." (p. 349). But can the palaeographical evidence be so easily dismissed?

ΙСΘΑΛ
ΛΗΓΟΖΜΕΝΟΝ
ΛΕСΠΑСΕΝ ΚΑΙΕΥΡΕΝ
ΖΙΒΛΗСΤΡΩΑΥΤΟΥ ΚΑΙСΥΝΗΓΑ
ΓΑΓΩΝΗΑΥΤΟΥ ΔΙΑΤΟΥΤΟΕΥ
ΚΑΙΧΑΡΕΙΖΛ ΔΙΑΤΟΥΤΟΑΥΤΟΥ
ΓΩΑΥΤΟΥ ΚΑΙΘΥΜΙΑСΕΙΤΗСΑ
ΚΑΙΑΥΤΟΙСΕΛΙΠΑΝΘΗΑΡΤΟС
ΤΟС ΜΑΛΑΑΥΤΟΥΕΤΕΡΕΘΝ ΕΙΔΙΑΤΟΥ
ΙСΕΙΛΛΑΧΑΙΓΑΘΑΥΤΟΥ ΚΑΙΔΙΑΠΑΝ
ΗΝΗΡΥΦΩСΕΤΛ
ΛΟΥСΤΗС
ΛС ΚΑΙΑΠΟСΚ
ΜΕΛΛΟΙΚΑΤΙ
ΚΑΙΑСΙΕΚΡΙSΗ
ΙΟΡΑСΙΗΚΑΙΕΚΦΛ
ΗΑΠΛССΙΝШСΚШΝ
ΑΙΡΟΝ ΚΑΙΕΠΦΑΝΗСΕ
ΑΨΕΥСΕΤΑΙ ΕΛΝСΤΡΑС
ΤΟΝ ΟΤΙΕΡΧΟΜΕΝΟСΕ
ΟΤΙΛΟΓΚΕΥΘΑΛΛΙ ΑΥΤΟΙ
ΛΙΟСЕΝΠΕ ΙΑΥΤΟΥΛΗСС
ΟСΑΝΗΓΡΑΛΑΖШΝ ΚΑΙΟΥ
ΛΑΓ СΟΛΛΙСΤΥΧΗ
ΓΟΟΖΚΕΝΠΙΠΛΛ
ΣΝΠΛΝΤΑΤΛΓΘΗΚΑΙ

31. *CHESTER BEATTY PAPYRUS 967*

Cf. pp. 68f. Illustration (Ezek. 16:57–17:1) from the edition by F. G. Kenyon (cf. p. 69, n. 72).

After a thorough examination of the Chester Beatty-Scheide Papyrus 967 (34 leaves = 68 pages of a codex of Ezekiel from the first half of the third century), J. Ziegler comes to the following conclusions which we cite here because of their importance for the problems of ⑤:

"1. Papyrus 967 supports the oldest, pre-Hexaplaric, original readings hitherto attested by Codex B alone . . . Further, these readings of 967 and B are usually found also in the Old Latin, and frequently in the Coptic text. Therefore the tradition represented by 967 B 𝔏 (Old Latin) 𝔎 (Coptic) provides the earliest attainable form of the Greek text of Ezekiel.

"2. In some instances 967 *alone* has preserved the original reading.

"3. Papyrus 967 is important chiefly for demonstrating that in the pre-Hexaplaric period (perhaps even in the first century A.D.) the Septuagint text of Ezekiel was being corrected toward the Hebrew text. Its agreements with 𝔐 do coincide frequently with the Hexaplaric readings which have been corrected from 𝔐, and consequently also with the renderings of the later Greek translators Aquila, Symmachus, and Theodotion, but this does not indicate dependence upon them. They do not reflect a process of thoroughgoing revision, but rather merely occasional corrections.[1]

"4. The vocabulary of Papyrus 967 shows that the revision of the text of Ezekiel occurred at such an early date that it has affected the entire manuscript tradition, and is consequently difficult to detect. The translator was far more consistent in his rendering of the Hebrew exemplar than has long been suspected . . . Even his rendering of the divine name κύριος seems to have been consistent. This makes it less likely that several (three) translators shared in its preparation.

"5. The occasional agreement of Papyrus 967 with readings of Alexandrian manuscripts (A and related minuscules), the Lucianic recension (*L*), and the Catena group (*C*) shows that these witnesses frequently drew upon early pre-Hexaplaric sources, and that their value should not be underestimated."[2]

---

1. Cf. p. 55, n. 20. Kahle, who traces the process of assimilation back to the pre-Christian era, considers it certain "that a text of Ezekiel which had been revised by Jews must have been the basis for the emendations in this valuable papyrus of Ezekiel to the extent that they represent assimilation to the Hebrew original and to the Jewish parallel versions which Ziegler has noted" *(TLZ* 79, 1954, col. 89).

2. *ZAW* 61 (1945/48), pp. 93f.

ΤΟΝ ΝΥΝ ΟΝ ΕΙ . . .
ΡΩΝ ΣΥΡΙΑΣ ΚΑΙ ΠΑΝ . . . . ΚΑΙ
. . . Ν ΚΥΚΛΩ ΑΥΤΗΣ ΘΥΓΑΤΕ
ΡΩΝ ΑΛΛΟΦΥΛΩΝ ΤΩΝ ΠΕΡΙΕ
ΧΟΥΣΩΝ ΣΕ ΚΥΚΛΩ ΤΑΣ ΑΣΕΒΕΙ
ΑΣ ΣΟΥ ΚΑΙ ΤΑΣ ΑΔΙΚΙΑΣ ΣΟΥ ΣΥ
ΚΕΚΟΜΙΣΑΙ ΑΥΤΑΣ ΛΕΓΕΙ Κ̅Σ̅
ΚΑΙ ΠΟ . ΗΣΩ ΕΝ ΣΟΙ ΚΑΘΩΣ ΕΠΟΙΗ
ΣΑΣ ΩΣ ΗΤΙΜΩΣΑΣ ΤΑΥΤΑ ΤΟΥ
ΠΑΡΑΒΗΝΑΙ ΤΗΝ ΔΙΑΘΗΚΗΝ ΜΟΥ
ΚΑΙ ΜΝΗΣΘΗΣΟΜΑΙ ΕΓΩ ΤΗΣ ΔΙ
ΑΘΗΚΗΣ ΜΟΥ ΤΗΣ ΜΕΤΑ ΣΟΥ ΕΝ
ΗΜΕΡΑΝ ΝΗΠΙΟΤΗΤΟΣ ΣΟΥ Κ̅Ν̅ ΑΝΑ
ΝΑΣΤΗΣΩ ΣΟΙ ΔΙΑΘΗΚΗΝ ΑΙΩΝΙ
ΟΝ ΚΑΙ ΜΝΗΣΘΗΣΗ ΤΗΝ ΟΔΟΝ ΣΟΥ
ΚΑΙ ΕΞΑΤΙΜΩΘΗΣΗ ΕΝ ΤΩ ΑΝΑ
ΛΑΒΕΙΝ ΜΕ ΤΑΣ ΑΔΕΛΦΑΣ ΣΟΥ ΤΑΣ
ΠΡΕΣΒΥΤΕΡΑΣ ΣΟΥ ΣΥΝ ΤΑΙΣ ΝΕ
ΩΤΕΡΑΙΣ ΣΟΥ ΚΑΙ ΔΩΣΩ ΑΥΤΑΣ
ΣΟΙ ΕΙΣ ΟΙΚΟΔΟΜΗΝ ΚΑΙ ΟΥΚ ΕΚ
ΔΙΑΘΗΚΗΣ ΣΟΥ ΚΑΙ ΑΝΑΣΤΗΣΩ
ΕΓΩ ΤΗΝ ΔΙΑΘΗΚΗΝ ΜΟΥ ΜΕ
ΤΑ ΣΟΥ ΚΑΙ ΕΠΙΓΝΩΣΗ ΟΤΙ ΕΓΩ
Κ̅Σ̅ Ο Θ̅Σ̅ ΟΠΩΣ ΜΝΗΣΘΗΣ ΚΑΙ ΑΙ
ΣΧΥΝΘΗΣ ΚΑΙ ΜΗ ΗΙ ΣΟΙ ΕΤΙ ΑΝΟΙ
ΞΑΙ ΤΟ ΣΤΟΜΑ ΣΟΥ ΑΠΟ ΠΡΟΣΩ
ΠΟΥ ΤΗΣ ΑΤΙΜΙΑΣ ΣΟΥ ΕΝ ΤΩ Ε
ΞΙΛΑΣΚ . ΣΘΑΙ ΜΕ ΣΟΙ ΚΑΤΑ ΠΑ
ΤΑ ΟΣΑ ΕΠΟΙΗΣΑΣ ΛΕΓΕΙ Κ̅Σ̅ Κ̅Ν̅
ΕΓΕΝΕΤΟ ΛΟΓΟΣ Κ̅Υ̅ ΠΡΟΣ ΜΕ ΛΕ

32. *THE BERLIN GENESIS*

Cf. p. 69. Illustration (Gen. 34:11-25) from H. A. Sanders and C. Schmidt, *The Minor Prophets in the Freer Collection and the Berlin Fragment of Genesis* (1927).

This papyrus codex was bought by Professor C. Schmidt in 1906 in Akhmim in Upper Egypt and donated to the Prussian State Library in Berlin. The well-known papyrologist Dr. Hugo Ibscher applied his skill to opening the codex, which had suffered severely from its long burial in the ground, and to preparing it for study. A variety of circumstances delayed its publication until 1927, when it appeared together with the related papyrus codex of the Minor Prophets in the Freer Collection.

The manuscript is in codex form, comprising sixteen sheets folded once to make a single quire of thirty-two folios; the outer sheet has been lost. The script is an early cursive, revealing a variety of stylistic traits, yet from a single hand. Fitting the text within the limits of the available number of pages proved rather constrictive: the scribe's hand became a little cramped toward the end (cf. illustration). Judging from the general impression and the forms of particular letters, the hand "may be safely dated toward the end of the third century A.D." (Sanders, *op. cit.*, p. 238).

Sanders observed a number of assimilations to the Hebrew text which occurred in the period before Origen: "Origen did not start this form of corruption in the text, though he doubtless increased it" (p. 265).

33. *CODEX SINAITICUS*

Cf. p. 70. Illustration (1 Macc. 9:12f.; 9:20-22; Jer. 9:2f.; 9:9f.; Tob. 6:5-7; 6:11f.) from Milne and Skeat, *Scribes and Correctors of the Codex Sinaiticus* (1938).

The illustration shows samples of the writing of three scribes who wrote this codex, according to the study mentioned above. As we noted on p. 70, many correctors worked on this manuscript. In this connection a sixth- or seventh-century note at the end of Ezra and of Esther is particularly interesting. It states that the codex had been collated with a very old manuscript which had itself been corrected by the martyr Pamphilus from a manuscript of the Hexapla which Origen himself had corrected.

The discovery of this important manuscript, the last of the great Greek codices to be found, may be described briefly. In 1844, on the first of his research journeys to libraries in the east, Konstantin von Tischendorf visited the monastery of St. Catherine on Sinai. When he was in the library there he saw 129 leaves of an ancient manuscript in a waste basket, put there by the ignorant monks to be burned. He was given 43 of the leaves (later known as Codex Frederico-Augustanus) before the monks realized their value and refused to part with more. In 1853 Tischendorf visited the monastery again, hoping to obtain or make copies of the remaining leaves, but he was unsuccessful. The monks themselves had forgotten about them and could not find them. In 1859 Tischendorf went once more in quest of them, this time as an envoy of the Russian Tsar, the protector of Orthodox Christendom. Again all Tischendorf's efforts seemed in vain until the eve of his departure, when the steward of the monastery, whom he had told about his search, showed him a codex in his cell. It contained not only the 86 leaves he had seen in 1844, but 112 further leaves of the Old Testament. It also contained the complete New Testament and two early Christian writings which had been lost for centuries: the Letter of Barnabas and the Shepherd of Hermas. After lengthy negotiations the codex was placed in the Imperial Library at Petersburg, and in 1933 it was acquired by the British Museum from the Russian government for the amount of £100,000.

It was reported recently that eight more leaves of the manuscript were found in the Sinai monastery in 1976 during structural repairs of the building. They have not yet (1978) been made available to the scholarly world.[1]

---

1. Cf. S. Agourides and J. H. Charlesworth, "A New Discovery of Old Manuscripts on Mt. Sinai: A Preliminary Report," *BA* 41 (1978), pp. 29-31.

CΑλΠΙΓΞΙΝΚΑΙΕϹΑλ
ΠΙϹΑΝΟΙϹΑΛΠ·Υ
λΑΚΑΙΑΥΤΟΙΠΑΙ·Cλ
ΠΙΓΞΙΝΚΑΙΕϹΑλΠ
ΘΗΓΓΗΑΙΤΟΤΗϹΦω
ΝΗϹΤωΝΠΑΡΕΜΚ·
λωΝΚΑΙΕΓΕΝΕΤΟ
ΟΠΟΛΕΜΟϹϹΥΝΗΜ
ΜΕΝΟϹΑΠΟΠΡωΙ
ΘΕΝΜΕΧΡΙΕϹΠΕΡΑϹ·

ΠΟλλΑϹΕΚΑΙΕΠΙ·Ν
ΠΙωϹΕΙΤΕϹΕΝΑΥΝΑ
ΤΟϹϹωΖωΝΤΟΝ·Χ
ΚΑΙΤΑΠΕΡΙϹϹΙΑΓ̄
λΟΓωΝΙΟΥΔΑΚΑΙ
ΤωΝΠΟΛΕΜωΝ·ΗϹ
ΤωΝΑΝΔΡΑΓΑΘΙωΝ
ωΝΕΠΟΙΗϹΕΝΚΑΙ
ΤΗϹΜΕΓΑΛωϹΥΝΗ·
ΑΥΤΟΥΟΥΚΑΤΕΓΡΑ

ϹΟΝ·ΨΕΥΛΟϹΚΑΙΟΥ
ΠΙϹΤΙϹΕΝΙϹΧΥϹΕΝ
ΕΠΙΤΗϹΓΗϹΟΠΕΚ
ΚΑΚωΝΕΙϹΚΑΚΑΕ
ϹΗλΘΟϹΑΝ·ΚΑΙΕ·
ΜΕΟΥΚΕΓΝωϹΑΝ·
ΕΚΑϹΤΟϹΑΠΟΤΟΥ
ΠλΗϹΙΟΝΑΥΤΟΥ
ΦΥλΑϹΞΕϹΘΑΙΚΑΙ
ΕΠΑΔΕλΦΟΙϹΑΥΤῑ

ΓΑϹΤΡΙΚΟΥϹΤΗϹΕ
ΡΗΜΟΥΘΡΗΝΟΝΟ
ΤΙΕΞΕλΑΠΟΝΠΑΡΑ
ΤΟΜΗΕΙΝΗΑΝΟΥϹ·
ΟΥΚΗΚΟΥϹΑΝΦω
ΝΗΗΝΥΠΑΡΞΕωϹ
ΑΠΟΠΕΤΙΝωΝΤου
ΟΥΡΑΝΟΥΚΑΙΕωϹ
ΚΤΗΝωΝΕΞΕϹΤΗ
ϹΑΝωΧΟΝΤΟΚΝ

ΚΑΙΤΟΠΠΙΑΡ·ΚΑΙω
ΠΙΤΗϹΕΝ·ΤΟΥΙΧΟΥ
ΟϹΚΑΙΕΦΑΙΕΝ·ΚΑΙ
λΦΠΙΚΕΝΕϹΑΥΤΟΥ
ΠΑΙϹΜΕΝΟΝ·ΚΑΙΕ
ΠΙΟΡΕΥΘΗϹΑΝΑΜ·
ΦΟΤΕΡΟΙΚΟΙΝωϹ
ΕωϹΘΗΓΓΙϹΑΝΕΙϹ
ΜΗλΙΑΝ·
ΚΑΙΤΟΤΕΠΡωΤΗϹΕ
ΤΟΠΑΙλΑΡΙΟΝ·ΤΟΝ

ΜΑϹΑΥλΙϹΟΗΠΝΑΙ
ΚΑΙΟΑΝΘΡωΠΟϹ
ϹΥΠΓΕΝΗϹϹΟΥΓΕ·
ϹΤΙΝΚΑΙΕϹΤΙΝΑΥ
·ΤωΟΥΓΑΤΗΡΗΟΝΟ
ΜΑϹΑΡΡΑΚΑΙΥΙΟϹ·
ΑΡϹΗΝΟΥλΕΘΥΙΑ̈
ΥΠΑΡΧΕΙΑΥΤωΠλΗ
ϹΑΡΡΑϹΜΟΝΗϹΚΑΙ
ϹΥΕΠΙϹΤΑλΥΓΗϹ
ΕΠΠΑΡΑΠΑΝ·ΤΑϹ·

34. THE HEXAPLA FRAGMENTS OF MILAN

Illustration and transcription (Ps. 28[27]:6f.) from the edition mentioned on p. 56, with the Hebrew column added from 𝔐.

𝔐	Transliteration	Aquila	Symmachus	Septuagint	Quinta
יְהֹוָה	יהוה	יהוה	יהוה	יהוה κς	יהוה
כִּי	χι	ὅτι	ὁ	ὅτι	ὅτι
שָׁמַע	σαμας	ἤκουσε	ἐπακούσας	εἰσήκουσε	εἰσήκουσε
קוֹל	κωλ	φωνῆς	τῆς φωνῆς	τῆς φωνῆς	τῆς φωνῆς
תַּחֲנוּנָי	θανουναι	δεήσεώς μου.	τῆς ἱκεσίας μου	τῆς δεήσεώς μου.	τῆς δεήσεός μου.
עֻזִּי	δζει	κράτος μου	ἰσχύς μου	βοηθός μου	βοηθός μου
וּמָגִנִּי	οὐμαγεννυ	(καὶ) θυράός μου	καὶ ὑπερασπιστής μου·	καὶ ὑπερασπιστής μου·	καὶ ὑπερασπιστής μου·
בּוֹ	βω.	ἐν αὐτῶι	αὐτῶι	ἐν αὐτῶι	ἐν αὐτῶι
בָטַח	βατε	ἐπεποίθησεν	ἐπεποίθησεν	ἤλπισεν	ἤλπισεν
לִבִּי	λεββι	καρδία μου,	ἡ καρδία μου,	ἡ καρδία μου,	καρδία μου,
וְנֶעֱזָרְתִּי	ου · νάζερθι	(καὶ) ἐβοηθήθην,	καὶ ἐβοηθήθην,	καὶ ἐβοηθήθην,	(καὶ) ἐβοηθήθην,
וַיַּעֲלֹז	ουαιαλεζ	καὶ ἠγαυριάσατο	(καὶ) ἱλαρύνθ(η)	καὶ ἀνέθαλεν	καὶ ἐκραταιώθ(η)
לִבִּי	λεββι	καρδία μου·	ἡ καρδία μου·	ἡ σάρξ μου·	ἡ καρδία μου·
וּמִשִּׁירִי	οὐμισσιρω	(καὶ) ἀπὸ αἴσματό(ς) μου	καὶ ἐν ᾠδαῖς μου	καὶ ἐκ θελήματό(ς) μου	(καὶ) ἀπὸ τοῦ ᾄσματός μου
אֲהוֹדֶנּוּ	ααθοδεννου	ἐξομολογήσομ(αι) αὐτ(ῷ.) μοι	ὑμνήσω αὐτόν.	ἐξομολογήσομαι αὐτ(ῷ.) μοι	ἐξομολογήσομ(αι)μοι αὐτ(ῷ.)
יְהֹוָה	יהוה	יהוה	יהוה	יהוה κς	יהוה
עֻזִּי	δζει	κράτος μου	ἰσχύς μου	βοηθός μου	βοηθός μου
וּמָגִנִּי	οὐμαγεννι	καὶ θυρεός μου	καὶ ὑπερασπιστής μου·	καὶ ὑπερασπιστής μου·	καὶ ὑπερασπιστής μου·
בּוֹ	βω	ἐν αὐτῶι	αὐτῶι	ἐν αὐτῶι	ἐν αὐθῶ

35. *CODEX COLBERTO-SARRAVIANUS*

Cf. p. 70. Illustration (Josh. 10:12-19) from G. M. Perella, *Introduzione Generale alla Sacra Biblia* (1948).

The illustration shows the beauty of the manuscript, which has two columns to each page. It probably dates from the fifth century A.D., although some scholars assign it to the fourth century. It is distinctive among the uncials for preserving the Hexaplaric text with many of the Hexaplaric signs. On the page shown an obelos marks the words (left column, lines 1-5): ηνικα συνετριψεν αυτους εν γαβαων και συνετρειβησαν απο προσωπου ιηλ (ισραηλ). This indicates that Origen found these words in G, but that they are not in the Hebrew text.

Several passages in the illustration are marked with an asterisk: this indicates that Origen did not find them in G and supplied them from other Greek versions. When such a passage extends over several lines the Aristarchan sign is repeated before each line: cf. for example v. 15, which is lacking in G and is given here with an asterisk (lower left to upper right column): και επεστρεψεν ιϛ (ιησους) και πας ιηλ μετ αυτου εις την παρεμβολην εις γαλγαλαν.

ΗΛΙΤΙΝΙΚΑCΥΝΕΤΡΙ
ΕΝΑΥΤΟΥCΕΝΙΑΚΑ
ΩΝ·ΚΑΙCΥΝΕΤΡΕΙΒΑ
CΑΝΑΠΟΠΡΟCΩΠΟΥ
ΙΗΛ·ΚΑΙΕΠΙΓΕΝΙCΟΗΝ
ΟCΚΑΤΑΓΑΒΑΩΝCΤΗ
ΤΩΚΑΙΗCΕΛΗΝΗΚΑ
ΤΑΦΑΡΑΓΓΑΛΛΑCΩΝ
ΚΑΙΕCΤΗΟΗΛΙΟCΚΑΙΗ
CΕΛΗΝΗΕΝCΤΑCΕΙC
ΩCΗΜΥΝΑΤΟΟΘΟC·Θ
ΕΧΟΡΟΥCΑΥΤΩΝ·ΟΥ
ΧΙΤΟΥΤΟΓΕΓΡΑΜΜΕ
ΝΟΝΕΠΙΒΙΒΛΙΟΥΤΟΥ
ΕΥΟΟΥC·ΚΑΙΕCΤΗΟ
ΗΛΙΟCΚΑΤΑΜΕCΟΝΤΟΥ
ΟΥΡΑΝΟΥΟΥΠΡΟCΕ
ΠΟΡΕΥΕΤΟΕΙCΔΥCΜΑC
ΕΙCΤΕΛΟCΗΜΕΡΑCΜΙ
ΑC·ΚΑΙΟΥΚΕΓΕΝΕΤΟ
ΗΜΕΡΑΤΟΙΑΥΤΗΟΥΔΕ
ΤΟΠΡΟΤΕΡΟΝΟΥΔΕ
ΤΟCΕCΧΑΤΟΝΩCΤΕC
ΠΑΚΟΥCΑΙΟΝ·ΦΩ
ΝΗC·ΑΝΟΥΟΤΙΚCCΥ
ΝΕΠΟΛΕΜΗCΕΝΤΩ
ΙΗΛ·ΚΑΙΕΠΕCΤΡΕΦΕ
ΙCΚΑΙΠΑCΙΗΛΑΜΕΤΑΥ

ΤΟΥΕΙCΤΗΝΠΑΡΕΝΙΚ
ΛΗΝΕΙCΜΑΑΓΔΑΝ·
ΚΑΙΕΦΥΓΟΝΟΙΕΒΑCΙ
ΛΕΙCΟΥΤΟΙΚΑΙΚΑΤΕ
ΚΡΥΒΗCΑΝΕΙCΤΟCΠΗ
ΛΑΙΟΝΤΟΕΙCΜΑΚΗΔΑ
ΚΑΙΑΠΗΓΓΕΛΗΤΩΙΩ
ΛΕΓΟΝΤΕCΕΥΡΗΝΤΑΙ
ΟΙΕΒΑCΙΛΕΙCΚΕΚΡΥ
ΜΜΕΝΟΙΕΝΤΩCΠΗ
ΛΑΙΩΤΩΕΝΜΑΚΗΔΑ
ΚΑΙΕΠΕΝΙCΚΥΛΙCΑΤΕ
ΛΙΘΟΥCΜΕΓΑΛΟΥC·
ΕΠΙΤΟCΤΟΜΑΤΟΥCΠΗ
ΛΑΙΟΥΚΑΙΚΑΤΑCΤΗ
CΑΤΕΕΠΑΥΤΟΥΑΝΔΡΑ
ΤΟΥΦΥΛΑCCΕΙΝΕΠΙ
ΤΟΥCΥΜΕΙCΔΕΜΗΕC
ΕCΤΗΚΑΤΕΚΑΤΑΛΙCΩ
ΚΟΝΤΕCΟΠΙCΩΤΩ
ΕΧΟΡΩΝΥΜΩΝΚΑΙ
ΚΑΤΑΛΑΒΕΤΑΓΓΗΝΟΥ
ΡΑΓΙΑΝΑΥΤΩΝ·ΚΑΙΜ
ΑΦΗΤΕΑΥΤΟΥC·ΕΙCΕ
ΟΓΙCΙCΕΙCΤΑCΠΟΛΕΙC
ΑΥΤΩΝΠΑΡΑΔΛΩ
ΚΕΝΓΑΡΑΥΤΟΥCΚCΟ
ΘCΗΜΩΝΕΙCΤΑCΧ

36. CODEX MARCHALIANUS (VAT. GR. 2125)

Cf. p. 71. Illustration (Jer. 24:11-19 [𝔐 35:11-19]) from *Specimina Codicum Graecorum Vaticanorum collegerunt P. Franchi de' Cavalieri et I. Lietzmann* (1929²).

The illustration gives a clear example of the peculiar features of this manuscript: a corrector has supplied in the margin the Hexaplaric readings which assimilate 𝔊 to 𝔐 together with their Hexaplaric signs. It demonstrates how frequently Origen had to supplement the Greek text of Jeremiah which is so much shorter than the Hebrew text. In Codex Marchalianus the source of these additions is sometimes given: the words εως της ημερας ταυτης οτι ηκουσαν της εντολης του πατρος αυτω are from Aquila (α΄ [A]) and Theodotion (θ΄ [Θ]), while the phrase which 𝔊 lacks in v. 17 has been supplied from Theodotion's version.

J. Ziegler has demonstrated in his edition of Ezekiel that there are two stages of Hexaplaric influence in Codex Marchalianus: "The first was present in the exemplar copied by Q, whose scribe accepted the Hexaplaric additions without marking them as such; the second was the work of a corrector who identified the Hexaplaric elements already in the text with an asterisk and added missing ones in the margin of Q from another source which was also used by 88-Sy^h (BH: Syh [S^h]; *Septuaginta, Ezechiel*, 1952, pp. 34f.). The original form of Q in Isaiah and the Minor Prophets, however, represents the Alexandrian group.

Note also in the illustration the omission of vv. 16-18 due to homoioteleuton (the omitted passage has been added in the lower margin), the corrections in the text (lines 14, 19, 24), and the abbreviation of frequently occurring words. The readings of Codex Marchalianus are noted in the apparatus of Swete's edition of the Septuagint, q.v.

CωΜΕΘΑΕΙCΙΕΡΟΥCΑΛΗΜΑΠΟΠΡΟCω
ΠΟΥΤωΝΧΑΛΔΑΙωΝ·ΚΑΙΑΠΟΠΡΟCω
ΠΟΥΤΗCΔΥΝΑΜΕωCΤωΝΑCCΥΡΙω
ΚΑΙωΙΚΗCωΜΕΝΕΚΕΙ·ΚΑΙΕΓΕΝΕΤΟ
ΛΟΓΟCΚΥΠΡΟCΜΕΛΕΓωΝΟΥΤωCΛΕΓ
ΚCΠΟΡΕΥΟΥΚΑΙΕΙΠΟΝΑΝωΙΟΥΔΑ·
ΚΑΙΤΟΙCΚΑΤΟΙΚΟΥCΙΝΙΛΗΜΟΥΜΗ
ΛΑΒΗΤΕΠΑΙΔΕΙΑΝΤΟΥΑΚΟΥΕΙΝΤΟΥCΛΟ
ΓΟΥCΜΟΥ·ΕCΤΗCΑΝΡΗΜΑΥΙΟΙΙωΝΑ
ΔΑΒΥΙΟΥΡΗΧΑΒ·ΟΝΕΝΕΤΕΙΛΑΤΟΤΟΙCΤΕ
ΚΝΟΙCΑΥΤΟΥΠΡΟCΤΟΜΗΠΙΕΙΝΟΙΝΟ·
ΚΑΙΟΥΚΕΠΙΟΝ·ΚΑΙΕΓωΕΛΑΛΗCΑΠΡΟC
ΥΜΑCΟΡΘΡΟΥ·ΚΑΙΕΛΑΛΗCΑΚΑΙΟΥΚΗΚΟΥ
CΑΤΕ·ΚΑΙΑΠΕCΤΕΙΛΑΠΡΟCΥΜΑCΤΟΥC
ΔΟΥΛΟΥCΜΟΥΤΟΥCΠΡΟΦΗΤΑCΛΕΓω·
ΑΠΟCΤΡΑΦΗΤΕΕΚΑCΤΟCΑΠΟΤΗCΟΔΟΥ
ΑΥΤΟΥΤΗCΠΟΝΗΡΑC·ΚΑΙΒΕΛΤΙΟΝΑ
ΠΟΙΗCΑΤΕΤΑΕΠΙΤΗΔΕΥΜΑΤΑΥΜωΝ·
ΚΑΙΟΥΠΟΡΕΥCΕCΘΕΕΠΙCωΘΕωΝΕΤΕΡω
ΤΟΥΔΟΥΛΕΥΕΙΝΑΥΤΟΙC·ΚΑΙΟΙΚΗCΕΤΕ
ΕΠΙΤΗCΓΗCΗCΕΔωΚΑΥΜΙΝ·ΚΑΙΤΟΙC
ΠΑΤΡΑCΙΝΥΜωΝ·ΚΑΙΟΥΚΕΚΛΙΝΑΤΕ
ΤΑωΤΑΥΜωΝ·ΚΑΙΟΥΚΗΚΟΥCΑΤΕ
ΚΑΙΕCΤΗCΑΝΟΙΥΙΟΙΙωΝΑΔΑΒΥΙΟΥΡΗΧΑΒ·
ΤΗΝΕΝΤΟΛΗΝΤΟΥΠΡΑΥΤωΝΕΠΟΙΕΙ·
ΚΑΙΟΤΙΕΝΕΤΕΙΛΑΤΟΑΥΤΟΙCΟΠΗΡΑΥ
ΤωΝΟΥΜΗΕΚΛΙΠΗΑΝΗΡΤωΝΥΙω
ΙωΝΑΔΑΒΥΙΟΥΡΗΧΑΒΠΑΡΕCΤΗΚωC
ΚΑΤΑΠΡΟCωΠΟΝΜΟΥΠΑCΑCΤΑCΗΜΕΡΑC

ΔΙΑΤΟΥΤΟΟΥΤωCΕΙΠΕ
ΚCΙΔΟΥΕΓωΦΕΡωΕΠΙΙΟΥΔΑΝ·ΚΑΙΕΠΙΤΟΥCΚΑΤΟΙ
ΚΟΥΝΤΑCΙΛΗΜΠΑΝΤΑΤΑΚΑΚΑ·ΕΛΑΛΗCΑΕΠΑΥΤΟΥC
ΔΙΑΤΟΥΤΟΟΥΤωCΕΙΠΕΝΚCΕΠΕΙΔΗΗΚΟΥCΑΝΥΙΟΙΙω
ΝΑΔΑΒΥΙΟΥΡΗΧΑΒΤΗΝΕΝΤΟΛΗΝΤΟΥΠΑΤΡΟCΙΤω

241

37. *A SYRO-HEXAPLAR MANUSCRIPT OF A.D. 697*

Cf. p. 57. Illustration (Exod. 27:10-15) from E. Tisserant, *Specimina Codicum Orientalium* (1914).

This manuscript (British Museum Ms. Add. 12134), like the one shown in pl. 39, is one of the hundreds of manuscripts brought to the British Museum in the years following 1839 from the monastery of St. Maria Deipara in the Nitrian desert of Lower Egypt. From the beginnings of Christian monasticism there has been a colony of monks in the Nitrian desert; toward the end of the fourth century they numbered into the thousands, and at times they exhibited a very lively intellectual life. The Syrian monastery of St. Maria Deipara in particular had a fine library which was considerably increased in the tenth century through the efforts of Abbot Moses of Nisibis. Later the monastery declined, and the books lay unused and largely neglected although they were zealously guarded by the few remaining uneducated monks until 1839, when an Englishman named Henry Tattam, and later others, acquired hundreds of manuscripts to take to England. An immediate result was a significant increase in Syriac studies.

The manuscript contains the book of Exodus, and according to its colophon it was written by a scribe named Lazarus in the year 1008 of the Seleucid era (i.e., A.D. 697); this is fairly close in time to the translation by Bishop Paul of Tella (616/617). As the illustration shows, the Hexaplaric signs are preserved in the text (obelos in lines 7, 13, 14f., 20; asterisk in line 12). The versions of Aquila, Symmachus, and Theodotion are noted in the margin. The long marginal note following line 2 gives an explanation of ψαλιδος (Syriac: *psalidis*); και ψαλιδος is written in the upper margin in red ink.

38. *A CATENA MANUSCRIPT (NINTH CENTURY A.D.)*

Cf. p. 60, n. 35. Illustration (Job 6:5) from *Specimina Codicum Graecorum Vaticanorum collegerunt P. Franchi de' Cavalieri et I. Lietzmann* (1929²).

"In contrast to the more general term florilegium, catena refers to a compilation where exegetical excerpts from various authors are placed in a connected sequence like links in a chain to provide a commentary on a Biblical book. This format enables the reader to formulate his own thoughts after becoming acquainted with the views of the most important exegetes of the Church in a minimum of time."[1] The Catenae are important for patristic as well as for textual studies: they preserve for the patristic scholar fragments of patristic writings that would otherwise be completely lost, and for the textual scholar they provide material relevant to the history of the text. Rahlfs has demonstrated that there was a special Catena recension of the Septuagint (cf. pp. 60f.).

Marginal catenae and text catenae are distinguished by their formats. "The most elegant and perhaps the oldest form of the catena commentary is that of the marginal catena: the scribe wrote the sacred text in a closely confined space in the center of the page, leaving margins far wider than the space devoted to the text, in which the commentary was added in closely written lines"[2] (cf. illustration). "In the second principal form of catena commentary the Scripture verses were followed by their corresponding commentary so that while text and commentary alternated in sequence, they were written in the same area of the page."[3]

In the page illustrated the headings (lemmata) of the individual excerpts stand out because they are written in red ink (e.g., line 30 Διδύμου; line 33 καὶ μετ' ὀλίγα).[4]

1. H. Lietzmann, *Catenen: Mitteilungen über ihre Geschichte und Handschriftliche Überlieferung* (1897), p. 1.
2. *Ibid.*, p. 9.
3. *Ibid.*, p. 11.
4. G. Karo and H. Lietzmann published a *Catenarum Graecarum Catalogus* in *Nachrichten der Gesellschaft der Wissenschaften zu Göttingen, Phil.-hist. Klasse* (1902); cf. esp. p. 322.

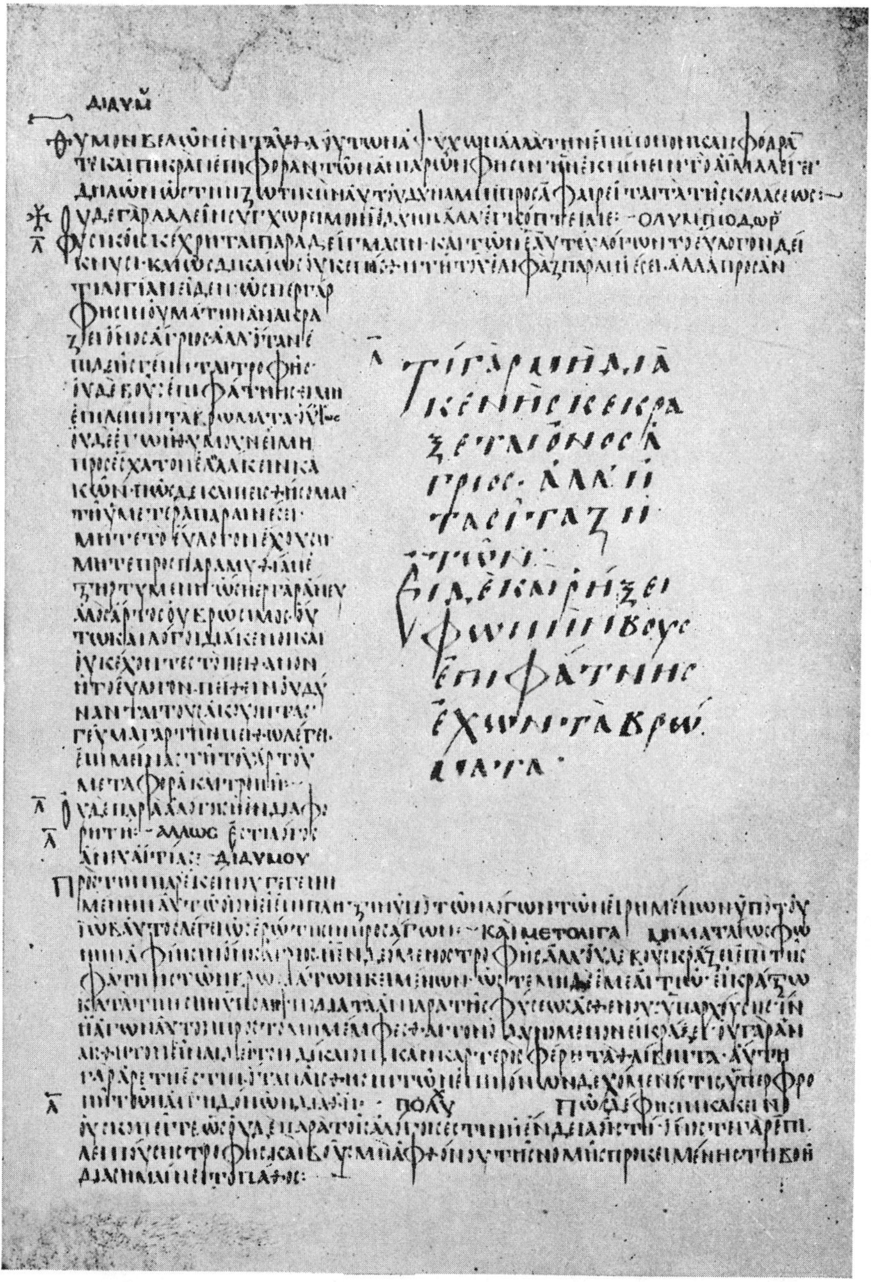
ΔΙΔΥΜ
ΟΛΥΜΠΙΟΔΩΡ
ΑΛΛΩΣ
ΔΙΔΥΜΟΥ
ΠΟΛΥ

39. *A PESHITTA MANUSCRIPT OF THE YEAR A.D. 464*

Cf. p. 82. Illustration (Exod. 13:8-17) from The Palaeographical Society, *Facsimiles of Manuscripts and Inscriptions* (Oriental Series), edited by W. Wright (1875-1883).

This West Syriac manuscript on parchment (British Museum Ms. Add. 14425) is one of the manuscripts from the Nitrian desert (cf. p. 194), and contains the books of Genesis, Exodus, Numbers, and Deuteronomy written in the Estrangela script. The first two books were written in Amida (Diyarbekr) in the year 775 of the Seleucid era (i.e., A.D. 464) by a certain John. The other two books are probably from the same period but were written by a different scribe. This is the oldest known Biblical manuscript to contain a dated colophon. It is approximately the same age as the Greek codex Alexandrinus.

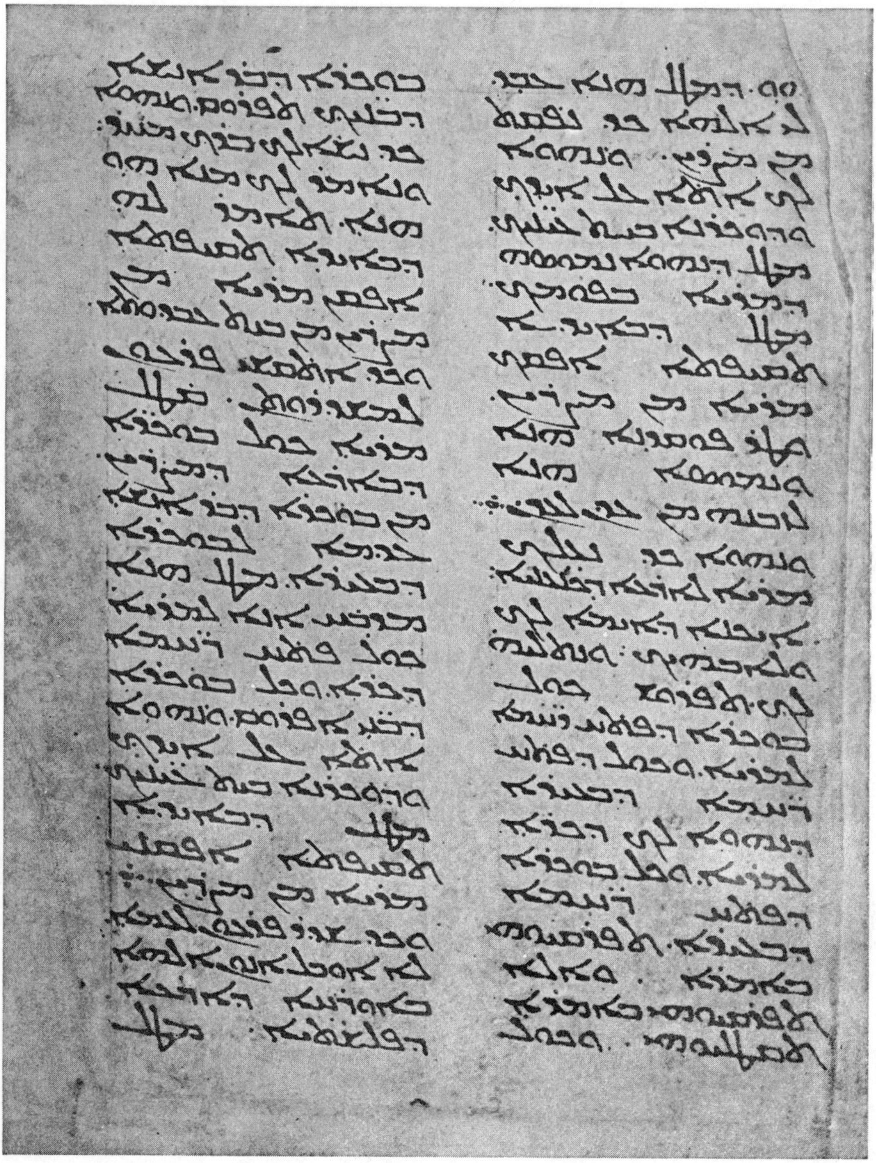

40. THE CONSTANCE FRAGMENTS OF THE OLD LATIN PROPHETS

Cf. pp. 88f. Illustration (Ezek. 20:43-47 𝔙) with the kind permission of A. Dold.

Illustrated is a fragment of a sumptuous manuscript of the Prophets in Old Latin found by A. Dold in the binding of Codex 191 of the Court Library of Fürstenberg at Donaueschingen. This manuscript of the Prophets, which was probably written in northern Italy in the fifth century, came into the Cathedral Library of Constance where it was taken apart (probably around 1450) and used in the binding of various parchment manuscripts. Fragments of this manuscript have been found in the bindings of twenty-six different manuscripts in Fulda, Darmstadt, Stuttgart, Donaueschingen, and the Benedictine monastery of St. Paul at Kärnten. In view of the scarcity of surviving Old Latin texts these fragments are of great importance: before their discovery the only known examples of the Latin Prophets before Jerome were the fragments of the Würzberg palimpsest (cf. p. 89). A. Dold has published further fragments of the Old Latin Prophets from St. Gall (Ezekiel, Daniel, Minor Prophets) in the appendix of the book mentioned on p. 88.

Note the marginal glosses in a later hand (sixth century) which include Greek readings and other material.

MINJULLIF
UESTRIS
DIAUESTRA
QUIBUSCO...UI
NABAMIN...N
EISETCED...
FACIESUE...

INONH...ES
IMALOITISUESTRIS
ETCOGNOSCE
TISQUIACCISUN
DMSDUNTX...
FACIOUIIISUN
NOMENDEUN
NONFE...DE
TURSECUN...
UNSUEETA...
MALASE...

...MINASOL
...DICON
TUXO...EQUIRERHT
NA...ASPICE
...EN ET

IMNABEG
CESSALTO
BEG
DICITDMS
...ECAXGEN
NIEIENEM
...MEDCIIN
...ENIUMCII
...IM ETOM
...CRUNTA
...IION

41. *CODEX LUGDUNENSIS*

Cf. p. 89. Illustration (Gen. 27:46–28:11) from a photograph kindly provided by A. Dold.

Codex Lugdunensis contains an Old Latin text, and is among the Old Latin evidence which has been discovered since Sabatier. It has had a checkered history. Originally in the Chapter Library of the Canon Counts of Lyons, it was later in the Municipal Library of Lyons. At some time it was divided into two parts, and the second part (now Ms. 1964) was removed from Lyons but recovered in 1895 and returned to Lyons. From the first part (now Ms. 403) seventy-nine leaves were stolen in 1847 and sold to Lord Ashburnham, whose son learned of these circumstances in 1880 and generously returned them to the Library.

According to U. Robert the manuscript was written by three different scribes. It "was used for liturgical reading, hence the variety of marginal notes in various hands from various periods, yet all probably native to Lyons. Two whole readings have been inserted: at 1 Kgs. for the Traditio Symboli, and at 1 Pet. 2 for the Cathedra Petri; these follow the Vulgate text. Similarly the numerous corrections in the individual sections made by later hands (partly in Tironian notes, a form of Latin shorthand) are largely assimilations to the Vulgate" (*Vetus Latina, Genesis,* edited by B. Fischer, 1951, p. 6). These assimilations are significant for the history of the Old Latin, which was eventually supplanted by the Vulgate.

DIXITAUTEMREBECCA
ADISACDESTINAUIAM
MONICOPROPTERFI
LIASFILIORUMCHET
SIACCEPERITIACOB
UXOREMAFILIABUS
TERRACHUIIUSUIQUO
MIHIUIUERE
UOCAUITAUTEMISAC
IACOBADSEETBENE
DIXITCUMEIPRAECE
PITEIDICENSNON
ACCIPIESUXOREM
AFILIABUSCHANNA
NEORUMSEDSURCE
ETUADEINMESOPO
TAMIAMHNDOMU
BATHUELISPATRIS
MATRISTUAEETACCI
PEINDUCTIBIUXORE
EXFILIAB LABENFRATRIS
MATRISTUAEETAC
CIPETIBIINDEUXORE
DSAUTEMMEUSBE
NEDICATTEETAUGEAT
TEETREPLEATTEET

ERISINECCLESIISGEN
TIUMETDETTIBIBE
NEDICTIONEMPATRIS
MEIABRAHAEETISC
MINITUOPOSTTE
HEREDITARETERRA
HABITATIONISTUAE
QUAMDEDITISAB
RAHAE
ETDIMISITISACIACOB
ETABIITINMESOPO
TAMIAMADLABAN
FILIUMBATHUELIS
SYRIFRATREMREBEC
CAEMATRISIACOB
ETESAU
UIDITAUTEMESAUQUIA
BENEDIXITISACIACOB
ETQUIAABIITINMESO
POTAMIAMSYRIAE
ACCIPERESIBIINDE
UXOREMNEOQUOD
BENEDIXERITEUM
ETPRAECEPERITEI
DICENS NONACCIPIES
UXOREMAFILIABUS

CHANNANEORUMEO
QUODAUDIERITIACOB
PATREMSUUMETMA
TREMSUAMETABIE
RITINMESOPOTAMIA
ETTUNCPOSTQUAM
UIDITESAUQUIAMA
LIGNASUNTFILIAE
CHANNANEORUM
ANTEISACPATREM
SUUMABITADISMA
HELETACCEPITMULIE
FILIAMISMAELFILII
ABRAHAESOROREM
NABEOTHADUXITSIE
RESSUASSIBIUXORE
ETEXIITIACOBAPUTEO
IURAMENTIUTIRET
INCHARRAMETPER
UENITINQUENDAM
LOCUMETMANSIIBI
OCCEDERATENIM
ACCEPITLAPIDEUM
EXLAPIDIBUSLOCIIIII
ETPOSUITSUBCAPIT
SUUMETUNDORMIUIT

42. *A VULGATE PALIMPSEST FROM THE FIFTH CENTURY A.D.*

Cf. pp. 91ff. Illustration (Judg. 5:15-18) from a photograph kindly provided by A. Dold, with the permission of the Herzog August Library, Wolfenbüttel.

Among the books once treasured by the monastery of Bobbio in northern Italy there were two fifth-century manuscripts of Isidore, one of which found its way into the Vatican Library and the other into the Herzog August Library at Wolfenbüttel. These manuscripts were written on the parchment leaves of older manuscripts whose texts had been erased, one of which was a fifth-century Bible in uncial script, and another a sixth-century Bible in half-uncials. These older manuscripts followed the Vulgate text; A. Dold published their texts after deciphering them with the aid of photographic techniques developed for the study of palimpsests at the Abbey of Beuron.[1]

The illustration shows a page of the old uncial manuscript, "probably one of the finest manuscripts of the Bible, or more precisely of a part of the Bible, remaining from antiquity" (Dold). The greater part of Judges and thirteen verses of Ruth have survived. The manuscript may have contained only these books. It was most likely written in Italy. A comparison of this earliest known text of Jerome's version with the official Vulgate (Vg) and with Codex Amiatinus (A) yields the following results: "In about 600 passages our manuscript agrees with (A) in a difference from the Vulgate about 200 times, it agrees with the (Vg) where (A) differs about 180 times, and in 220 passages it differs from both (Vg) and (A) with a reading of its own which differs distinctly although admittedly only slightly."[2]

This uncial and the above-mentioned half-uncial manuscript (Job 1:1–15:24) are of great importance for the recovery of the earliest form of Jerome's text. "These two manuscripts of such great age provide us with a most valuable link between the lost original of Jerome and the Codex Amiatinus, which was hitherto the earliest known witness of the Vulgate text. The total impression of the writing suggests further that in these two manuscripts we have copies which were executed with incomparable concern and devotion, which is itself the best guarantee of textual quality and fidelity."[3]

1. *Zwei Bobbienser Palimpseste mit frühestem Vulgatatext, herausgegeben und bearbeitet von P. A. Dold. Texte und Arbeiten herausgegeben durch die Erzabtei Beuron* 1, 19–20 (1931).
2. *Ibid.*, p. IL.
3. *Ibid.*, p. LVII.

BORAELBARAACLIESTICIASUN

SEQUITI   QUIIUIIASIITPRAE

CEPSAARATRUAISEDIACRI

IUAICHOEDIT

DIUISOCONTRASCRIBENDAGNA

AMIDORUMREPERIA

CONTENTOR

QUIAEHABITASINTERDUOSICROII

NOSUIAUDIASSIENOTORECUM

DICTISOCONTRASCRUBENDIAGNA

LANIOIORUMREPERIA

RECONTENTIOEST

EXTAAIIIRANSTOROANEMQUIES

CEGHATEIDANUACABATIIILAUBUS

ASERTHABITABATURLITORECMARIS

ETINFORTUBUSMORABATUR

BULLOUUIEROMINETALIN

OBTCITERENISANITISABSCUS

43. *CODEX AMIATINUS*

Illustration (Ps. 22 [v 21]:25–25[24]:5) from a photograph kindly provided by the Biblioteca Medicea-Laurenziana.

This well-known and highly valued codex of the Vulgate, which is named after the Abbey of Monte Amiata where it once belonged, is of English origin. It was commissioned by Ceolfrid, abbot of the monasteries of Jarrow and Wearmouth in Northumberland, which were under the direct control of the Holy See. Ceolfrid intended to take it on his last journey to Rome as a gift to the Pope. The abbot died on his journey at Langres (A.D. 716), but some of his companions delivered the codex to Rome. It is the only codex to survive of the three which Ceolfrid commissioned to be written in his monasteries between 690 and 716: all three were in "the new translation," i.e., the translation by Jerome.[1]

In its outer form and in its artistic decoration Codex Amiatinus follows the example of the great codex of Cassiodorus, an illuminated manuscript with illustrations and tables which contained Jerome's revision of the Hexaplar text in the Old Testament. It was bought by Benedict Biscop and Ceolfrid while in Rome in 678, and brought to Jarrow. Contrary to earlier belief, neither the text nor the auxiliary material in Amiatinus is related to Cassiodorus.[2]

B. Fischer says of the text of Amiatinus:

> Several different manuscripts served as exemplars. A demonstrably inferior Irish text served for the Psalms, a good Neapolitan manuscript for the Gospels, and one with local color for the Catholic Epistles; for most books of the Bible there were good manuscripts available, probably from Italy. The monks at Jarrow edited their material deliberately. They were quite capable of recognizing good texts and choosing their models. Where only inferior texts were available they would attempt to improve them; cf. especially Tobit, also Psalms and Acts, and occasionally even books with good texts.
>
> These corrections of the Biblical text may be understood in connection with the commentaries of the Venerable Bede, who was also among the monks at Jarrow when Amiatinus and its sister codices were in production there."[3]

1. Single leaves of one of these two lost codices have been found since 1909 (some had been used as "wrappers for estate papers") and are now in the British Museum.
2. Cf. also B. Fischer, "Codex Amiatinus und Cassiodor," *BZ* n.s. 6 (1962), pp. 57–79.
3. *Ibid.*, pp. 78f.

qm non dispexit neque contempsit
modestiam pauperis
et non abscondit faciem suam a me
et cum clamaret ad eum exaudiuit
apud te laus mea in ecclesia multa
uota mea reddam in conspectu
timentium eum.
Comedent mites et saturabuntur
laudabunt dñm quaerentes eum
uiuet cor uestrum in sempiternu
recordabuntur et conuertentur
ad dñm omnes fines terrae
et adorabunt coram eo uniuersae
cogitationes gentium
quia dñi est regnum et domina
bitur gentibus
comederunt et adorauerunt
omnes pingues terrae
ante faciem eius curbabunt genu
uniuersi qui discendunt in puluere
et anima eius ipsi uiuet
et semen seruiet ei
narrabunt dño in generatione
uenient et adorabunt iustitiam eius
populo qui nascitur quas fecit
psalmus dauid uox ecclesiae
post baptismum
22 Dns pascit me nihil mihi deerit
in pascuis herbarum adclinauit me
super aquas refectionis
enutriuit me
animam meam refecit
duxit me super semitas iustitiae
propter nomen suum
sed et si ambulauero in ualle mortis
non timebo malum qm tu mecum es
uirga tua et baculus tuus ipsa
consolabuntur me
pones coram me mensam
aduerso hostium meorum
inpinguasti oleo caput meum
calix meus inebrians
sed et benignitas et misericor
dia subsequitur me
omnibus diebus uitae meae
et habitabo in domo dñi
in longitudine dierum
psalmus prima sabbati
confirmatio populi credentis
portae quas dicit peccata uel
inferni uox xpi diligentib; se
23 Dñi est terra et plenitudo eius
orbis et habitatores eius
qui ipse super maria fundauit eu
et super flumina stabiliuit illu
quis ascendet in montem dñi
et quis stabit in loco sco eius
innocens manib; et mundo corde
qui non exaltauit frustra
animam suam
et non iurauit dolose
accipiet benedictionem a dño
et misericordiam a do salutari suo
haec est generatio quaerentium eu
quaerentium faciem iacob semper
leuate portae capita uestra
et eleuamini ianuae sempiternae
et ingreditur rex gloriae
quis est iste rex gloriae
dns fortis et potens dns
fortis in proelio
leuate portae capita uestra
et erigite ianuae sempiternae
et ingreditur rex gloriae
quis est iste rex gloriae
dns exercituum ipse est rex gloriae semp
psalmus dauid canticum
24 Ad te dñe animam meam leuabo
ds meus in te confisus sum
ne confundar
ne laetentur inimici mei
sed uniuersi qui sperant in te
non confundantur
confundantur qui iniqua gerunt
frustra
uias tuas dne ostende mihi
semitas tuas doce me
deduc me in ueritate tua

44. *A COPTIC PAPYRUS CODEX*

Cf. pp. 96f. Illustration (Deut. 34:11f.; Jonah 1:1-4) from E. A. Wallis Budge, *Coptic Biblical Texts in the Dialect of Upper Egypt* (1912).

In 1911 the British Museum acquired this papyrus codex found in Upper Egypt; it contains extensive parts of Deuteronomy, the whole book of Jonah, and the larger part of the Acts of the Apostles. It is to be dated in the fourth century A.D., and is thus of very great age.

The illustration shows the conclusion of the book of Deuteronomy: the title is written in large letters at the end of the book. Following it is a blessing in Greek on scribe and reader, and then the beginning of the book of Jonah.

ϨⲘϨⲀⲢⲦⲏⲢ· ... ...ⲏ̄ⲨⲔⲀⲎⲚ
ⲚⲞϬⲚϢϢⲡⲏⲢⲉⲀ... ...ⲟⲓⲭⲉⲦ
ⲭⲞⲞⲢⲉⲚⲦⲀⲘϢⲨⲤⲏⲤⲀⲗⲨⲘ
ⲡⲉⲘⲦⲞⲉⲃⲟⲗⲘ̄ⲡⲓⲤⲢⲀⲏⲗ
ⲦⲏⲢϤ̄ ⳩⳩⳩⳩⳩⳩⳩⳩⳩
⳩⳩⳩⳩⳩⳩ · · · · · · · · ⳩⳩⳩⳩⳩⳩

ⲦⲡⲉⲨⲦⲉ
ⲢⲞⲚⲞⲘⲓⲞⲚ

ⲉⲓⲢⲏⲚⲏⲦⲱⲅⲢⲀⲯⲀⲚⲦⲓ
ⲕⲀⲓⲦⲱ
ⲀⲚⲀⲅⲓⲚⲱⲥⲕⲟⲚⲦⲉ

ⲓ̄ⲱⲚⲀⲥ

ⲡϤⲁⲝⲉⲙ̄ⲡⲭ̄ⲥ̄ⲉⲓⲥⲁⲩϣⲱⲡⲉϣⲁ
ⲓ̄ⲱⲚⲀⲥⲡϣⲏⲣⲉⲛ̄ⲁⲙⲁⲑⲉⲉⲉϫⲱ
Ⲙ̄ⲙⲟⲥϫⲉⲦⲱⲟⲩⲛⲅ̄ⲃⲱⲕⲉϩⲣⲁⲓ
ⲉⲦⲚⲓⲚⲉⲨⲏⲦ̄ⲛⲟϬⲙ̄ⲡⲟⲗⲉⲓⲥ
ⲕⲏⲣⲝⲥⲥⲉϩⲢⲀⲓ̈ⲛ̄ϩⲏⲧ̄ϫⲉⲁⲡⲉⲥⲟ
ⲉⲓ̈ϣⲛ̄ⲦⲉⲥⲕⲁⲕⲓⲁⲉⲓⲉϩⲢⲀⲓ̈Ⲙ̄ⲡⲀ
Ⲧⲟⲉⲃⲟⲗ· ⲀⲨⲱⲁⲨⲦⲱⲟⲩⲛⲚ̄Ϭⲓ
ⲓ̄ⲱⲚⲀⲥⲉⲡⲱⲧⲉⲃⲁⲢⲥⲓⲥⲚ̄ϩⲁ
Ⲣⲛ̄ⲦϨⲟⲘ̄ⲡϫⲟⲉⲓⲥ· ⲀⲨⲱⲀϤⲃⲱⲕ
ⲉϩⲢⲀⲓ̈ⲉⲓⲟⲡⲏ· ⲀϤϬⲚ̄ⲟⲩⲭⲟⲉⲓⲉⲛⲁ
ⲥⲟ̄ⲏⲢⲉⲃⲟⲗ̄ⲦⲉⲓⲤⲁⲨ̄ⲧⲉⲥⲏⲙⲉϣ
ⲦⲀⲗⲉⲃⲢⲟϤⲉⲥⲟ̄ⲏⲢⲛ̄Ⲙ̄ⲙⲁϥⲉⲃⲁⲢⲥⲓⲥ
Ⲙ̄ⲛⲁϩⲢⲏ̄Ⲙ̄ⲡϫⲟⲉⲓⲥ· ⲀⲨⲱⲀϤ
ⲉⲓⲁϤ̄ϩ̄ⲁⲅⲓⲉⲟⲩⲚⲟϬ̄Ⲛ̄Ⲧⲏⲟⲩ
ⲉϩⲢⲀⲓ̈ⲥⲓⲉⲃⲀⲗⲗⲁⲥⲥⲁ· ⲁⲩⲛⲟϬⲚ̄

45. *AN ETHIOPIC MANUSCRIPT* (Paris, Bibliothèque
Nationale, Eth. 11, fol. 70a)

Cf. p. 98. Illustration (Sus. 1-5) from O. Löfgren, *Die äthiopische Übersetzung des Propheten Daniel* (1927).

The manuscript from which this illustration is taken contains the books of Job and Daniel. Löfgren describes it in this way: "Palaeographically this manuscript is of great interest. Its general appearance and many details bespeak its antiquity. The large (about 6 mm. high) angular script which differs little from the lapidary style of inscriptions; the simple decoration, limited to rows of dots, St. Anthony's cross, and similar designs in the margin; the two-column page format—these all place S (i.e., this manuscript) in the relatively small group of ancient Ethiopic manuscripts which was succeeded about the middle of the fifteenth century by a new type with a more beautiful style of writing and a richer ornamentation" (*op. cit.,* p. xxii). It was probably written between 1300 and 1400. "The care with which this manuscript was written, and its freedom from any substantial correction or revision suggests that we have in it a valuable witness to the text as it circulated about 1300, probably not yet revised" (*op. cit.,* p. xxv).

While this manuscript preserves the original Ethiopic version, in later manuscripts the traces of various processes of revision may be observed: some indicate revision from Syro-Arabic sources, beginning in the fourteenth century; some point to a Hebrew base for revision in the fifteenth or sixteenth century. Naturally for the textual criticism of the Septuagint only those manuscripts are significant which preserve the original, Old Ethiopic form of this daughter text of the Septuagint.

ዘዳንኤልልነ	ደ፡አነጠልዓሬ
ቢዩ፨	ቤቱ፨
ወሀሎ፡ለሕዩ	ወደወጸኡነ
ብእሲ፡ዘዌነ	በሁ፡ኢዬሁዩ
ብሬ፡ዓቢሎ፥	እክሉ፡ወእቱ
ወክሙ፡ኢዮስ	ይኪብር፡አሥኣ
ቄዎ፡ወእወከ	ሎሙ፨
ቦ፡ዘእኪተ፡ኤ	ወእክተርእዩ
ንተ፡ክሙ፡ስከና።	ክልኤቱ፡ሬባና
ወለቱ፡ኪልዊ	ት፡መደልዎንዘ
ቹ፡ዉሠ ጓዬት፨	ወእቱ፡ዴሞት
ጠቀወትፈርሀ	እሉ፡በእንቲ፡አሁ
እግዚአ፡ብሔ	ው፡ንገሬ፡እግ
ር፨ ወእዝ ጣዴ	ዚእ፡ብሔር፨
ሀኑ፡ጸድቃኑ፡	ክሙ፡እ ፱ባቢ
ወመሀርዋበ	ሎነ፡ወ ፱ስተ፡
ወለቹ መ፡እሬ	ንዊእት፡ኢስ
ተ፡ሉኤ፡ወኢዬ	ሬባናተ፡መደል
ዋ ቄ ም፡ብ ቅል፨	ዋ ን፡ኢ ለ ይ ብእ
ጠ ቀ፡ወ ቦ፡ ዐ ጸ	ነ ወ ቅ ብ ሉ ለ

46. AN ARABIC MANUSCRIPT (British Museum arab. 1475 [Add. 26116])

Cf. p. 100. Illustration (Job 22:12–23:2) from The Palaeographical Society, *Facsimiles of Manuscripts and Inscriptions* (Oriental Series), edited by W. Wright (1875-1883).

The variety of Arabic versions of Job, of which a page of the oldest is shown here, is representative of Arabic versions of the Bible as a whole.

There are at least four different versions of Job, one of which is among the earliest documents of Christian Arabic literature. The manuscript Brit. Mus. arab. 1475, which contains extensive portions of it, was written in the first half of the ninth century, probably at the monastery of St. Sabas. The version itself is from a Syro-Hexaplar base.

The author of another version of Job is known: Pethion (Fatyun ibn Aiyub), who was active as a translator in Baghdad probably about the middle of the ninth century; he is also credited with translations of Sirach and the Prophets. Pethion's text of Job is divided into fifteen chapters and (according to the London manuscript) claims to be translated from the Hebrew; actually the translator worked from a Syriac exemplar. Other versions of Job go back to the Peshitta and to the Coptic (G. Graf, *Geschichte der christlichen arabischen Literatur* 1, *Die Übersetzungen*, *Studi e Testi* 118, 1944, p. 126).

العلماء كنه والدير يفلقون بالعزه يد لهم واب ملئت
مزايرات ودى الهود وصنف ان الصاب حول شك
وسو الغط وان الخاب كل سر اعمالك لا زلازج
وعلمك لما طراف الادحر مزبد وسالكى العمله
من حمط اليد بمتقكم الصاكحيز ولم يد رد
انك نوحد بلاوقت من الد يكحمل الانهاد على
الحمال كدلك يمنك المنيرين الدين يمولوا
ما اليد يضع نا الرب واسر كلب علينا الكبت
كل الدين ملوا ابوتهم من الحير وهوا مرد الما
يهبر بعده من الرب والطا حيز سطر وان
اليهم ويجحكوا ومن كان عبر مد لب لسمع
لهم بار سريع بملك قواممم ومن كنهم ناكل
القار واطرح من فمك ما لا يبغا واكد يقول
الرب على قلبك لانك رحمت وجمعم بوريد
الرب بما عد مرصعا مك الاوجاع وكمسك
على حره قوبه نكوطابك اوديم الحير والعسد
تابك الكل وخلصد من العدوا ونصور
نبيا سله فضه مسلوكه ولعوم سريدى الرب
مسلمحرا وبطر الى السما قوك صاحبه واذا
طلب اليه يسمعك ويعطيك وبدرله الانذار
وبر دعليك طعام الصلاح ولتكور الصوادى
لعمرى طوبك بانك اصمع بيعسك بوريده
وبطرح عند الحوه وبطا من عبد ينزيد نه
وهو ليعلمك وهو سلم الركى وبرد علبك هو انك
احاب ابوب وقال
اما اعلم بان نوحى بويد يد من صادت نبيله

47. THE COMPLUTENSIAN POLYGLOT

Illustration (Gen. 21:28–22:3) from the Bodleian copy, with the kind permission of the Bodleian Library, Oxford.

The polyglots formed a useful tool for textual criticism by printing the original text with translations of the Bible in parallel columns to facilitate their comparison. The earliest polyglot, named the Complutensian after Complutum (Alcala de Henares), its place of publication, was edited in 1514-1517 by Francisco Ximenez, Archbishop of Toledo and founder of the University of Alcala; it was not published until 1522 due to a delay of papal authorization. Jewish converts were engaged to work on the Old Testament because at that time they alone had the training necessary for the work: among them was the renowned Alfonso de Zamora, Professor of Oriental languages at Alcala from 1512.

The Hebrew text of the Complutensian Polyglot reveals some interesting deviations from normal usage. The Tiberian accent system is represented only by the athnah, yet here it is not used for the principal caesura alone, so that it may occur more than once in a verse (e.g., Gen. 22:3 [cf. illustration, lines 24-26]); nor is it written with the accented syllable, but after the word. The maqqeph is completely lacking. Hatephs appear only rarely: usually the vowel is written without the shewa; cf. in the illustration אֱלֹהִים, אֲשֶׁר [line 27], עֲצֵי [line 26], etc. These peculiarities do not reflect any editorial caprice, as might be suspected. Rather it is the usage of ancient manuscripts that the editors appeal to as their precedent. Since the peculiarities mentioned are characteristic of the simple Babylonian pointing system (cf. pp. 22f.), we may infer that the editors of the polyglot made use of Hebrew manuscripts of the Bible with Babylonian pointing along with manuscripts of the Ben Asher tradition These may have been intended by the "*vetustissima exemplaria* (most ancient copies)" used by the editors, which have influenced the form of the Hebrew text printed in the polyglot.[1] These manuscripts are not lost: they were probably destroyed in ignorance of their value. For the Greek text of the Complutensian polyglot, cf. p. 72.

Of the later polyglots, the most comprehensive is the London Polyglot, edited by Brian Walton in 1654-1657.

1. P. Kahle, *The Hebrew Text of the Complutensian Polyglot, Homenaje a Millás-Vallicrosa* (Barcelona, 1954) 1, pp. 749f.

et statuit abraā septē agnas ouiū
καὶ ἔστησεν ἀβραὰμ ἑπτὰ ἀμνάδας προβάτων
solas. et dixit abimelech abraam. quid
μόνας. καὶ εἶπεν ἀβιμέλεχ τῷ ἀβραάμ. τί εἰ-
sunt septē agne ouiū harū: quas
σιν αἱ ἑπτὰ ἀμνάδες τῶν προβάτων τούτων, ἃς
statuisti solas. et dixit qz septē agnas
ἔστησας μόνας. καὶ εἶπεν ὅτι τὰς ἑπτὰ ἀμνά-
accipies a me: vt sint mihi in testimoniū:
δας λήψη παρ' ἐμοῦ, ἵνα ὦσί μοι εἰς μαρτύριον,
qz ego fodi puteū hunc. ppter hoc vo-
ὅτι ἐγὼ ὤρυξα τὸ φρέαρ τοῦτο. διὰ τοῦτο ἐπω-
cauit nomē loci illius: puteū iu-
νόμασε τὸ ὄνομα τοῦ τόπου ἐκείνου, φρέαρ ὁρ-
ramenti. qz illic iurauerūt ambo: et posuerūt
κισμοῦ. ὅτι ἐκεῖ ὤμοσαν ἀμφότεροι, καὶ ἔθηκαν
fedus sup puteū iuramēti. surrexit ãt abi
διαθήκην ἐπὶ τὸ φρέαρ τοῦ ὁρκισμοῦ. ἀνέστη δὲ ἀβι-
melech et ochozad pronubus eius et phi
μέλεχ καὶ ὀχοζὰθ ὁ νυμφαγωγὸς αὐτοῦ καὶ ὁ φι-
chol princeps exercitus eius: et re
χὼλ ὁ ἀρχιστράτηγος τῆς δυνάμεως αὐτοῦ, καὶ ἀ-
uersi sunt in terrā philistijm. et plan-
πέστρεψαν εἰς τὴν γῆν τῶν φυλιστιείμ. καὶ ἐφύ-
tauit abraam agrū sup puteū iu
τευσεν ἀβραὰμ ἄρουραν ἐπὶ τῷ φρέατι τοῦ ὁρ-
ramēti. et inuocauit ibi nomē dñi: deus
κισμοῦ. καὶ ἐπεκαλέσατο ἐκεῖ τὸ ὄνομα κυρίου, θεὸς
etern⁹. habitauit ãt abraā in terra phi-
αἰώνιος. παρῴκησε δὲ ἀβραὰμ ἐν τῇ γῇ τῶν φυ-
listiim dies multos.
λιστιείμ ἡμέρας πολλάς.

Ca. 22.

A Et factū ē post verba hec: deus
Καὶ ἐγένετο μετὰ τὰ ῥήματα ταῦτα, ὁ θεὸς
tentauit abraā. et dixit ei: abraam
Judith 8.c. ἐπείρασε τὸν ἀβραάμ. καὶ εἶπεν αὐτῷ, ἀβραὰμ
Heb. 11 d. abraā. et dixit. ecce ego. et dixit: accipe fi-
ἀβραάμ. καὶ εἶπεν, ἰδοὺ ἐγώ. καὶ εἶπεν, λάβε τὸν υἱ-
liū tuū dilectū: quē dilexisti isaac: et
όν σου τὸν ἀγαπητόν, ὃν ἠγάπησας τὸν ἰσαάκ, καὶ
vade in terrā excelsā. et offer eū
πορεύθητι εἰς τὴν γῆν τὴν ὑψηλήν. καὶ ἀνένεγκε αὐ-
ibi in holocaustū sup vnū montiū: quos
τὸν ἐκεῖ εἰς ὁλοκάρπωσιν ἐφ' ἓν τῶν ὀρέων, ὧν ἄν
tibi dixero. surgēs ãt abraā mane strauit
σοι εἴπω. ἀναστὰς δὲ ἀβραὰμ τὸ πρωῒ ἐπέσαξεν
asinā suā. assumpsit ãt secū duos pue-
τὴν ὄνον αὐτοῦ. παρέλαβε δὲ μεθ' ἑαυτοῦ δύο παῖ-
ros: et isaac filiū suū. et scindēs ligna in
δας, καὶ ἰσαὰκ τὸν υἱὸν αὐτοῦ. καὶ σχίσας ξύλα εἰς
holocaustū: surgens abijt. et venerūt in
ὁλοκάρπωσιν, ἀναστὰς ἐπορεύθη. καὶ ἦλθον εἰς
locū quē dixit ei deus: die
τὸν τόπον ὃν εἶπεν αὐτῷ ὁ θεός, τῇ ἡμέρᾳ

Et statuit abraam septem agnas gregis seorsū. Cui dixit abimelech. Quid sibi volunt septem agne iste: quas stare fecisti seorsum? At ille. Septem inquit agnas accipies de manu mea: vt sint mihi in testimoniū: qm ego fodi puteū istū. Idcirco vocatus ē locus ille bersabee: quia ibi vterqz iurauit. Et inierunt fedus p puteo iuramēti. Surrexit aūt abimelech & phicol princeps exercitus eius: reuersiqz sūt ī terrā palestiorū. Abraā vero plātauit nemus in bersabee: & inuocauit ibi nomen dñi dei eterni: & fuit colonus terre palestiorū diebus multis.

Ca.22.

Que postquā gesta sunt: tentauit deus abraam: & dixit ad eū. Abraam abraam. At ille rñdit. ad sū. ait illi. Tolle filiū tuū vnigenitum quem diligis isaac: & vade in terrā visionis: atqz ibi offeres eū in holocaustum sup vnū montiū: quem monstrauero tibi. Igitur abraā de nocte consurgens strauit asinū suum ducens secum duos iuuenes & isaac filiū suum. Cumqz concidisset ligna in holocaustum: abiit ad locum quem preceperat ei deus. Die autem

ויצב אברהם את שבע כבשת
הצאן לבדהן: ויאמר אבימלך אל
אברהם מה הנה שבע כבשת
האלה אשר הצבת לבדנה:
ויאמר כי את שבע כבשת תקח
מידי בעבור תהיה לי לעדה כי
חפרתי את הבאר הזאת: על כן
קרא למקום ההוא באר שבע כי
שם נשבעו שניהם: ויכרתו
ברית בבאר שבע ויקם אבימלך
ופיכל שר צבאו וישבו אל ארץ
פלשתים: ויטע אשל בבאר
שבע ויקרא שם בשם יהוה אל
עולם: ויגר אברהם בארץ
פלשתים ימים רבים:

Cap.xxii.

ויהי אחר הדברים האלה
והאלהים נסה את אברהם
ויאמר אליו אברהם ויאמר הנני:
ויאמר קח נא את בנך את יחידך
אשר אהבת את יצחק ולך לך אל
ארץ המריה והעלהו שם לעלה
על אחד ההרים אשר אמר
אליך: וישכם אברהם בבקר
ויחבש את חמרו ויקח את שני
נעריו אתו ואת יצחק בנו ויבקע
עצי עלה ויקם וילך אל המקום
אשר אמר לו האלהים: ביום

בדד
יצב
עבר היה
קום
שבע
קום
שור שוב
נטע
קרא
עלם גור
יום רבה
היה
אמר
לקח יחד
הלך
עלה
הרר
שכם
חבש שנה
בקע
קום הום

Transla.Chal.

ואקים אברהם ית שבע חורפאן דעאן בלחודיהון: ואמר אבימלך לאברהם מה
אינין שבע חורפאן האלין דאקימת בלחודיהון: ואמר ארי ית שבע חורפאן תיסב
מן ידי בדיל דתהא לי לסהיד ארי חפרית ית בירא הדין: על כן קרא לאתרא
ההוא באר שבע ארי תמן קיימו תרויהון: וגזרו קיים בבאר שבע וקם אבימלך
ופיכל רב חיליה ותבו לארע פלשתאי: ונצב נצבא בבירא דשבע וצלי תמן בשמא
Ca.xxij. דיי אלה עלמא: ואתותב אברהם בארע פלשתאי יומין סגיאין:
והוה בתר פתגמיא האילין ויי נסי ית אברהם ואמר ליה אברהם ואמר הא אנא:
ואמר דבר כען ית ברך ית יחידך דרחימתא ית יצחק ואיזיל לך לארעא פולחנא
ואסקיה קדמי תמן לעלתא על חד מן טוריא דאימר לך: ואקדים אברהם בצפרא
וזריז ית חמריה ודבר ית תרין עולימוהי עמיה וית יצחק בריה וצלח אעי דעלתא
וקם ואזל לאתרא דאמר ליה יי: ביומא

Interp.chal.

Et statuit abraham septē agnas ouium seorsum. Dixitqz abimelech ad abraham. Que sunt iste septem agne quas statuisti seorsum. Et ait. Quoniaz septem agnas accipies de manu mea: vt sit mihi in testimonium quoniā fodi puteuz istum. Propterea vocauit locum illū bersabee: quia ibi iurauerūt ambo: et inierunt pactū in bersabee. Surrexitqz abimelech et phicol princeps exercitus eius: et reuersi sunt in terram philistinoz. Et plantauit plantationem in bersabee: et orauit ibi in nomine domini dei eterni. Et peregrinatus est abraham in terra philistinorum diebus multis.

Cap. 22.

Et factū est post verba hec: et deus tentauit abraham: et dixit ei. Abraham. Et ait: ecce ego. Et dixit. Tolle nunc filium tuū vnicum tuū quez diligis isaac: et vade in terram diuini cultus: et offer illum coram me ibi in holocaustum super vnū montium quē dixero tibi. Et surrexit abraham mane et strauit asinum suum: et tulit duos pueros suos secum: et isaac filium suum: et concidit ligna in holocaustum: et surrexit et abijt in locum quē dixerat ei deus. Die autem

Primitiua chal.

קום חד
אל נסב
היה
קום קום
דבב תוב צלא
יתב
אל נסה
אזל
נסק עלה קדם
אעא
קום

	Gezer	Inscriptions	Cursive	Literary	Coins	Samaritan	Square
1							א
2							ב
3							ג
4							ד
5							ה
6							ו
7							ז
8							ח
9							ט
10							י
11							כ
12							ל
13							מ
14							נ
15							ס
16							ע
17							פ
18							צ
19							ק
20							ר
21							ש
22							ת

A. Sylvester

49. *THE IZBET ṢARṬAH ABECEDARY*[1]

Cf. p. 4. Photo by Moshe Weinberg, *Biblical Archaeology Review* 4 (1978), p. 22, with the kind permission of *Biblical Archaeology Review*.

In 1974, during the excavations at Izbet Ṣarṭah (the Biblical Ebenezer?) sponsored by Tel Aviv University and Bar Ilan University, an ostracon in two pieces preserving the longest Old Hebrew inscription yet discovered was found by Aryeh Bornstein, a Tel Aviv University student. It measures 8.8 x 15 cm., and contains five lines of writing. The first four lines appear to be random letters (a writing exercise?), but the last line presents an abecedary with minor variations, written from left to right, evidently witnessing to a period before the right-to-left direction of Hebrew writing became established.

Archaeologically the find may be dated 1200-1000 B.C., but the writing has been ascribed on palaeographic grounds to the twelfth/eleventh century B.C., making it a century older than the Gezer calendar, and the oldest Hebrew abecedary yet discovered, as well as the most complete (the מ is no longer fully visible, although a trace of the letter remains).

It is interesting to note that the order of the letters עפ agrees with the pattern found in Pss. 9f. and Lam. 2–4, in contrast to the more usual order found in Pss. 25, 34, 37, 111f., 119, 145, Prov. 31, and Lam. 1.

For discussion, see M. Kochavi, "An Ostracon of the Period of the Judges from Izbet Ṣarṭah," *Tel Aviv* 4 (1977), pp. 1-13; A. Demsky, "A Proto-Canaanite Abecedary Dating from the Period of the Judges and its Implications for the History of the Alphabet," *Tel Aviv* 4 (1977), pp. 14-27; also A. Demsky and M. Kochavi, "An Alphabet from the Days of the Judges," *Biblical Archaeology Review* 4 (1978), pp. 22-30.

1. Added by translator.

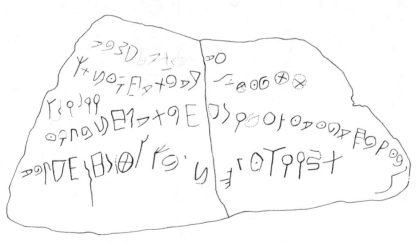

SELECTED BIBLIOGRAPHY

Bibliographical references mentioned in the text and footnotes are generally not repeated here for reasons of space.

GENERAL WORKS

Einleitung in das Alten Testament by C. Steuernagel (1912), by J. Goettsberger (1928), by O. Eissfeldt (1964³; Eng. trans. by P. R. Ackroyd, 1965), by A. Weiser (1966⁶; Eng. trans. of 1957⁴ by Dorothea M. Barton, 1961), by Sellin-Fohrer (1969¹¹; Eng. trans. of 1965¹⁰ by D. E. Green, 1968), by A. Bentzen (1959⁵; Eng. trans. 1957³). *Introduction to the Old Testament* by R. H. Pfeiffer (1948²). *Die Welt des Alten Testaments* by M. Noth (1964; Eng. trans. by V. I. Gruhn, *The Old Testament World*, 1966).

Geiger, A. *Urschrift und Übersetzungen der Bibel in ihrer Abhängigkeit von der inneren Entwicklung des Judenthums* (1857; reprint 1928).

Driver, S. R. *Notes on the Hebrew Text of the Books of Samuel with an Introduction on Hebrew Palaeography and the Ancient Versions* (1913²).

Kenyon, F. G. *Our Bible and the Ancient Manuscripts*, revised by A. W. Adams (1958⁵).

Thomas D. W. "The textual criticism of the Old Testament." In H. H. Rowley, ed., *The Old Testament and Modern Study* (1958), pp. 238-263.

Roberts, B. J. *The Old Testament Text and Versions* (1951), with a 29-page bibliography.

Goshen-Gottstein, M. *Text and Language in Bible and Qumran* (1960).

The Cambridge History of the Bible (= *CHB*). 1, edited by P. R. Ackroyd and C. F. Evans (1970). 2, edited by G. W. H. Lampe (1969).

Further bibliography by subject in *Internationale Zeitschriftenanschau für Bibelwissenschaft und Grenzgebiete* (1952ff.).

CHAPTER 1

Driver, G. R. *Semitic Writing*, Schweich Lectures 1944 (1948; revised 1954; revised by S. A. Hopkins, 1976).

Diringer, D. *The Alphabet*. 2 vols. (1968³).

―――――. *The Story of the Aleph Beth* (1958).

Bea, A. *Die Entstehung des Alphabets: eine kritische Übersicht. Studi e Testi* 126 (1946), pp. 1-35.

Blau, L. *Studien zum althebräischen Buchwesen* (1902).

Schubart, W. *Das Buch bei den Griechen und Römern* (1921²).

————. *Einführung in die Papyruskunde* (1918).

Wendel, C. *Die griechisch-römische Buchbeschreibung verglichen mit der des Vorderen Orients* (1949).

Jensen, H. *Die Schrift in Vergangenheit und Gegenwart* (1958²).

Gelb, I. J. *Von der Keilschrift zum Alphabet* (1958).

CHAPTER 2

Ginsburg, C. D. *Introduction to the Massoretico-Critical Edition of the Hebrew Bible* (1897; reprint 1966).

Kahle, P. *Der masoretische Text des Alten Testaments nach der Überlieferung der babylonischen Juden* (1902).

————. *Masoreten des Ostens* (1913).

————. "Untersuchungen zur Geschichte des Pentateuchtextes." *Theologische Studien und Kritiken* 88 (1915), pp. 399-439 (= *Opera Minora,* 1956, pp. 3-37).

————. Par. 6-9 in Bauer-Leander, *Historische Grammatik der hebräischen Sprache* (1922).

————. "Die Punktation der Masoreten." *BZAW* 41 (1925), pp. 167-172 (= *Opera Minora,* 1956, pp. 48-53).

————. *Masoreten des Westens* 1 (1927), 2 (1930).

————. *Die Handschriften aus der Höhle* (1951).

————. "The Hebrew Ben Asher Manuscript." *VT* 1 (1951), pp. 161-67.

————. *The Cairo Geniza* (1947; revised 1959).

————. *Der hebräische Bibeltext seit Franz Delitzsch* (1961).

Aptowitzer, V. *Das Schriftwort in der rabbinischen Literatur. Sitz.-Ber. Ak. Wiss. Wien, Phil.-hist. Kl.* 153/6 (1906); 160/7 (1908); *Jahresbericht der Isr.-Theol. Lehranstalt Wien* 18 (1911), pp. 1-173; 22 (1915), pp. 1-82.

Ehrentreu, E. *Untersuchungen über die Masora. Beitr. zur semit. Philologie und Linguistik* 6 (1925).

Lipschütz, L. *Ben Ašer–Ben Naftali; Der Bibeltext der tiberischen Masoreten. Bonner Orientalist. Studien* 25 (1937).

Gerleman, G. "Synoptic Studies in the Old Testament," *Lund Univ. Årskrift* n.s. 1, 44 (1948).

Teicher, J. L. "The Ben Asher Bible Manuscripts." *JJS* 2 (1950/51), pp. 17-25.

Textus: Annual of the Hebrew University Bible Project 1-8 (1960-1973).

DEAD SEA SCROLLS

For the older literature see W. Baumgartner, *ThR* 17 (1948/49); 19 (1951); also the progress reports by O. Eissfeldt, P. Kahle, and others in *TLZ* (1949ff.), *BA* (1948ff.), *BASOR* (1948ff.), *Revue de Qumran* (1958ff.).

Burchard, C. *Bibliographie zu den Handschriften vom Toten Meer* 1, *BZAW* 76 (1957); 2, *BZAW* 89 (1965); supplement by H. Stegemann, *ZDPV* 83 (1967), pp. 95-101 (to 1966).

Fitzmyer, J. A. *The Dead Sea Scrolls: Major Publications and Tools* (1975, with Addendum 1977).

LaSor, W. S. *Bibliography of the Dead Sea Scrolls* (1958).

Burrows, M. *The Dead Sea Scrolls* (1956).

_____. *More Light on the Dead Sea Scrolls* (1958).

Milik, J. T. *Dix ans de découvertes dans le Désert de Juda* (1957); Eng. revision, *Ten Years of Discovery in the Wilderness of Judaea* (1959).

Bardtke, H. *Die Handschriftenfunde am Toten Meer I* (1953²).

Cross, F. M. *The Ancient Library of Qumran and Modern Biblical Studies* (1961).

Martin, M. *The Scribal Character of the Dead Sea Scrolls* 1, 2 (1958).

Brownlee, W. H. *The Meaning of the Qumran Scrolls for the Bible* (1964).

Cross, F. M., and Talmon, S., ed. *Qumran and the History of the Biblical Text* (1975).

CHAPTER 3

Gesenius, W. *De Pentateuchi Samaritani origine, indole et auctoritate commentatio philologica-critica* (1815).

Geiger, A. *Urschrift und Übersetzungen der Bibel* (1857; reprint 1928).

Kahle, P. "Aus der Geschichte der ältesten hebräischen Bibelhandschrift." *BZAW* 33 (1918), pp. 247-260.

CHAPTER 5

Swete, H. B. *An Introduction to the Old Testament in Greek* (1914²).

Pretzl, O. "Septuagintaprobleme im Buche der Richter." *Bibl* 7 (1926), pp. 233-269, 353-383.

Sperber, A. "Probleme einer Edition der Septuaginta." In *Kahle-festschrift* (1935), pp. 39-46.

Rehm, M. *Textkritische Untersuchungen zu den Parallelstellen der Samuel-Königsbücher und der Chronik* (1937).

Allgeier, A. *Die Chester-Beatty-Papyri zum Pentateuch. Studien zum Geschichte und Kultur des Altertums* 21/2 (1938).

Stegmüller, O. *Berliner Septuagintafragmente. Berliner Klassikertexte* 8 (1939).

Seeligmann, I. L. "Problemen en Perspectieven in het moderne Septuaginta-Onderzoek." *Jaarbericht van het vooraziatisch-egyptisch Gezelschap 'Ex Oriente Lux'* 6/8 (1943), pp. 359-90ᵉ, 763-66. (A comprehensive survey of the problems and literature.)

_____. *The Septuagint Version of Isaiah* (1948).

Gerleman, G. *Studies in the Septuagint* 1, *The Book of Job* (1946). 2, *Chronicles* (1946). 3, *Proverbs* (1956).

Mercati, G. "Il problema della colonna II dell' Esaplo." *Bibl* 28 (1947), pp. 173-215.

Jellicoe, S. *The Septuagint and Modern Study* (1968).

Katz, P. *Philo's Bible: The Aberrant Text of Bible Quotations in Some Philonic Writings and its Place in the Textual History of the Greek Bible* (1950).

_____. "Septuagintal studies in the mid-century." *Dodd-Festschrift* (1956), pp. 176-208.

Soisalon-Soininen, I. *Die Textformen der Septuaginta-Übersetzung des Richter-buches. Annales Acad. Scient. Fennicae* 72 (1951).

―――. *Der Charakter der asterisierten Zusätze in der Septuaginta* (1959).

Wevers, J. W. "Septuaginta-Forschungen," *ThR* n.s. 22 (1954), pp. 85-138, 171-190; n.s. 33 (1968), pp. 18-76.

Ziegler, J. *Die Septuaginta. Würzberger Universitätsreden* 33 (1962).

Tov, E., and Kraft, R. A. "Septuagint." *IDBS* (1976), pp. 807-815.

O'Connell, K. G. "Greek versions (minor)." *IDBS* (1976), pp. 377-381, with bibliography.

Walters (formerly Katz), P. *The Text of the Septuagint, Its Corruptions and Their Emendations.* Edited by D. W. Gooding. (1973).

CHAPTER 6

Wohl, S. *Das Palästinische Pentateuch-Targum: Untersuchungen zu den Geniza-Fragmenten und ihrem Verhältnis zu den Übrigen Targumen und der Peshitta,* Diss. Bonn (1935).

Peters, C. "Vom palästinischen Targum und seiner Geschichte." *Das Heilige Land* 2 (1940), pp. 9-22.

Stenning, J. F. *The Targum of Isaiah* (1953²).

Goldberg, L. *Das samaritanische Pentateuch-Targum: Eine Untersuchung seiner handschriftlichen Quellen. Bonner Orient. Studien* 11 (1945).

Levine, E. *The Aramaic Version of Jonah* (1975).

McNamara, M. J. "Targums." *IDBS* (1976), pp. 856-861, with bibliography.

CHAPTER 7

Haefeli, L. *Die Peschitta des Alten Testaments mit Rücksicht auf ihre textkritische Bearbeitung und Herausgabe* (1927).

Baumstark, A. "Pešîttâ und palästinensisches Targum." *BZ* 19 (1931), pp. 257-270.

―――. "Neue orientalische Probleme biblischer Textgeschichte." *ZMDG* 89 (1935), pp. 89-118.

Peters, C. "Peschitta und Targumim des Pentateuchs." *Le Muséon* 48 (1935), pp. 1-54.

―――. "Pešitta-Psalter und Psalmentargum." *Ibid.* 52 (1939), pp. 275-296.

Schneider, H. "Wenig beachtete Rezensionen der Peschitta." *ZAW* 62 (1950), pp. 168-199.

van Puyvelde, C. "Versions Syriaques." In L. Pirot, *et al.,* ed., *Dictionnaire de la Bible,* Suppl. 6 (1960), col. 834-884.

Vööbus, A. "Syriac versions." *IDBS* (1976), pp. 848-854, with bibliography.

CHAPTER 8

Allgeier, A. *Die altlateinischen Psalterien* (1928).

Botte, B. "Itala." In *Dictionnaire de la Bible,* Suppl. 4 (1949), col. 777-782; "Latines (Versions) Antérieures à S. Jérome." 5 (1957), col. 334-339.

Schneider, H. *Die altlateinischen biblischen Cantica. Texte und Arbeiten* 29/30 (1938).

Schildenberger, J. *Die altlateinischen Texte des Proverbienbuches. Texte und Arbeiten* 32/33 (1941).
Cf. also the publications of the Vetus Latina Project: *Aus der Geschichte der lateinischen Bibel* (1957ff.).
Gribomont, J. "Latin versions." *IDBS* (1976), pp. 527-532, with bibliography.

CHAPTER 9

Stummer, F. "Die neue römische Ausgabe der Vulgata zur Genesis." *ZAW* 45 (1927), pp. 141-150.

————. "Spuren jüdischer und christlicher Einflüsse auf die Übersetzung der Grossen Propheten durch Hieronymus." *Journal of the Palestine Oriental Society* 8 (1928), pp. 35-48.

————. "Hauptprobleme der Erforschung der alttest. Vulgata." *BZAW* 66 (1936), pp. 233-39.

————. "Griechisch-römische Bildung und christliche Theologie in der Vulgata des Hieronymus." *ZAW* 58 (1940/41), pp. 251-269.

————. "Beiträge zur Exegese der Vulgata." *ZAW* 62 (1950), pp. 152-167.
Lietzmann, H. "Die neue römische Vulgata." *TLZ* 65 (1940), col. 225-230.
Ziegler, J. *Antike und moderne lateinische Psalmenübersetzungen* (1960).

CHAPTER 10

Budge, E. A.W. *Coptic Biblical Texts in the Dialect of Upper Egypt* (1912).
Vaschalde, A. "Ce qui a été publié des versions coptes de la Bible: textes sahidique." *RB* (1919-22), also separately: *Le Muséon* (1930-33).
Till, W. C. "Coptic Biblical Texts published after Vaschalde's Lists." *BJRL* 42 (1959), pp. 220-240.
Hallock, F. H. "The Coptic Old Testament." *American Journal of Semitic Languages* 49 (1932/33), pp. 325-335.
Botte, B. "Versions Coptes." In *Dictionnaire de la Bible,* Suppl. 6 (1960), col. 818-825.

CHAPTER 11

Littmann, E. "Geschichte der äthiopischen Litteratur." In C. Brockelmann, *et al., Geschichte der christlichen Litteratur des Orients* (1909²), pp. 223-28.
Harden, J. *An Introduction to Ethiopic Christian Literature* (1926).
Guidi, J. *Storia della letteratura etiopica* (1932).
Gleave, H. C. *The Ethiopic Version of the Song of Songs* (1951).
Botte, B. "Versions Ethiopiennes." In *Dictionnaire de la Bible,* Suppl. 6 (1960), col. 825-29.

CHAPTER 12

Finck, F. N. "Geschichte der armenischen Litteratur." In *Geschichte der Christlichen Litteratur des Orients* (1909²), pp. 75-130.
Leloir, L. "Versions Arméniennes." In *Dictionnaire de la Bible,* Suppl. 6 (1960), col. 810-18.

CHAPTER 13

Kahle, P. *Die arabischen Bibelübersetzungen* (1904).

Graf, G. *Geschichte der christlichen arabischen Litteratur* 1. *Studi e Testi* 118 (1944), pp. 85-297.

Botte, B. "Versions Arabes." In *Dictionnaire de la Bible,* Suppl. 6 (1960), col. 807-810.

Ecker, R. *Die arabische Job-Übersetzung des Gaon Saadja Ben Josef al-Fajjumi* (1962).

CHAPTER 14

Cantorowicz, H. *Einführung in die Textkritik* (1921).

Maas, P. *Textkritik, Einleitung in die Altertumswissenschaft* 1/2 (1927).

Nyberg, H. S. "Das textkritische Problem des Alten Testaments am Hoseabu   demonstriert." *ZAW* 52 (1934), pp. 241-254.

———. *Studien zum Hoseabuche. Uppsala Univ. Årsskrift* (1935).

Begrich, J. "Zur Frage der alttestamentlichen Textkritik." *Orientalistische Literaturzeitung* 42 (1939), col. 473-483.

Thomas, D. W. *The Recovery of the Ancient Hebrew Language* (1939).

Coppens, J. "La critique du texte hébreu de l'Ancien Testament." *Bibl* 25 (1944), pp. 9-49; 2nd ed. separately (1955).

———. "La critique textuelle de l'Ancien Testament: Solutions anciennes et données nouvelles." *EThL* 36 (1960), pp. 466-475.

Driver, G. R. *L'interpretation du texte masorétique à la lumière de la lexicographie hébraique. ALBO,* Ser. 2, 18 (1950).

Barthélemy, D. *Etudes d'Histoire du Texte de l'Ancien Testament. Orbis Biblicus et Orientalis* 21 (1978), especially pp. 365-381.

ABBREVIATIONS

ALBO	*Analecta Lovaniensia Biblica et Orientalia*
ALQ	F. M. Cross, *The Ancient Library of Qumran and Modern Biblical Studies* (1961²)
ANET	J. B. Pritchard, ed., *Ancient Near Eastern Texts Relating to the Old Testament* (1969³)
AOS	*American Oriental Series*
BA	*Biblical Archaeologist*
BASOR	*Bulletin of the American Schools of Oriental Research*
BH	*Biblia Hebraica* (= BHK and BHS)
BHK	*Biblia Hebraica,* edited by R. Kittel and P. Kahle
BHS	*Biblia Hebraica Stuttgartensia,* edited by K. Elliger and W. Rudolph
Bibl	*Biblica*
BJRL	*Bulletin of the John Rylands Library*
BWAT	*Beiträge zur Wissenschaft vom Alten Testament*
BZ	*Biblische Zeitschrift*
BZAW	*Beihefte zur Zeitschrift für die alttestamentliche Wissenschaft*
CHB	*Cambridge History of the Bible*
DOTT	D. W. Thomas, ed., *Documents from Old Testament Times* (1958)
EHT	J.-D. Barthélemy, *Etudes d'Histoire du Texte de l'Ancien Testament* (1978)
EThL	*Ephemerides Theologicae Lovanienses*
HUCA	*Hebrew Union College Annual*
IDBS	*Interpreter's Dictionary of the Bible, Supplement* (1976)
IEJ	*Israel Exploration Journal*
JAOS	*Journal of the American Oriental Society*
JBL	*Journal of Biblical Literature*
JJS	*Journal of Jewish Studies*
JNES	*Journal of Near Eastern Studies*
JQR	*Jewish Quarterly Review*
JSS	*Journal of Semitic Studies*
JTS	*Journal of Theological Studies*
NAG	*Nachrichten der Akademie der Wissenschaften in Göttingen*

QHBT   F. M. Cross and S. Talmon, ed., *Qumran and the History of the Biblical Text* (1975)
RB   *Revue Biblique*
SAM   *Sitzungsberichte der Bayerischen Akademie der Wissenschaften, München*
TDNT   *Theological Dictionary of the New Testament*
ThBl   *Theologische Blätter*
ThR   *Theologische Rundschau*
ThWNT   *Theologisches Wörterbuch zum Neuen Testament*
ThZ   *Theologische Zeitschrift*
TLZ   *Theologische Literaturzeitung*
VT   *Vetus Testamentum*
VTS   *Supplements to Vetus Testamentum*
WdO   *Die Welt des Orients*
ZAW   *Zeitschrift für die alttestamentliche Wissenschaft*
ZDMG   *Zeitschrift der Deutschen Morgenländischen Gesellschaft*
ZDPV   *Zeitschrift des deutschen Palästina-Vereins*
ZNW   *Zeitschrift für die neutestamentliche Wissenschaft und die Kunde der älteren Kirche*

LIST OF SIGLA

Occasionally manuscripts cited in BHK are not designated individually in BHS but indicated simply by the group sigla which include the particular witnesses. Such group sigla are shown in parentheses in the following list.

BHK	BHS	
A	α′	Aquila
E′	ε′	Origen's Quinta
Θ	θ′	Theodotion
	ο εβρ	see below: BHK Hᵒ
	οι γ′ ⎫	the three later Greek versions
	οι λ′ ⎭	Samaritan Pentateuch, A. von Gall's edition
ɯ	ɯ, ɯMs(s)	Samaritan Pentateuch manuscript(s) in A. von Gall's critical apparatus
ɯT	ɯT	Samaritan Targum
	ɯW	Samaritan Pentateuch, B. Walton's London Polyglot
Σ	σ′	Symmachus
𝔄	𝔄	Arabic version
𝔄	𝔄	Ethiopic version
	Ambr	Ambrose
Arm	Arm	Armenian version
𝔅	𝔅	Second Rabbinic Bible by Jacob ben Chayyim
	Bo	Bohairic version
C	C	Codex Cairensis of the Prophets
	ℭ	Cairo Geniza Hebrew codex fragment
	ℭ2.3 etc.	Cairo Geniza Hebrew codex fragments
	cit(t)	Citations in Rabbinic and Medieval Jewish literature following V. Aptowitzer
	Cyr	See below: BHK 𝔊Cyr
E′		See above: E′
Ea 1–27 ⎫		
Eb 1–30 ⎬ (ℭ)		Fragments with simple Babylonian pointing
Ec 1–24 ⎭		

229

	Ed(d)	Editions of the Hebrew text by Kennicott, de Rossi, and Ginsburg; cf. Ms(s)
	Eus	Eusebius Pamphilius of Caesarea
	Eus Onom	Eusebius' *Onomasticon*
Ginsb(urg Mass)	G	C. D. Ginsburg, *The Massorah compiled from Manuscripts*
𝔊	𝔊	Septuagint
	𝔊*	Original Greek text
𝔊ᴺ	𝔊ˢ	Codex Sinaiticus
𝔊ᴺ c.a, c.b, c.c	𝔊ˢ 1.2.3	Correctors of Codex Sinaiticus
𝔊ᴬ	𝔊ᴬ	Codex Alexandrinus
𝔊ᴮ	𝔊ᴮ	Codex Vaticanus
𝔊Beatty		Chester Beatty Papyri
𝔊Γ	(𝔊Ms)	Codex rescriptus Cryptoferratensis
𝔊ᶜ	𝔊ᶜ	Codex Ephraemi Syri rescriptus
	𝔊ᶜ	Greek text of the Catenae
𝔊C(om)pl		Septuagint in the Complutensian Polyglot
𝔊Cyr	Cyr	Septuagint in Cyril of Alexandria
𝔊ᴰ	(𝔊Ms)	Codex Cottonianus of Genesis
𝔊ᴱ	(𝔊Ms)	Codex Bodleianus of Genesis
𝔊ᶠ	𝔊ᶠ	Codex Ambrosianus
𝔊ᴳ	(𝔊Ms)	Codex Colberto-Sarravianus
𝔊Θ	(𝔊Ms)	Codex Freer
𝔊ʰ	𝔊ᴼ	Hexaplaric recension of the Septuagint
	𝔊ᴼᵖ	𝔊ᴼ in part
𝔊Mss(Holmes-) Parsons	𝔊Ms(s)	Manuscripts in Holmes-Parsons's edition
𝔊62.147(Parsons)	(𝔊min)	Minuscules 62 and 147 in Holmes-Parsons
	𝔊22.26,etc.	Minuscule manuscripts in A. Rahlfs, *Verzeichnis der griechischen Handschriften des AT*
𝔊ˣᴵ	(𝔊maj)	Uncial no. XI in Holmes-Parsons
𝔊ᴷ	(𝔊Ms)	Codex Lipsiensis
𝔊ᴸ		Largarde's edition
𝔊Luc	𝔊ᴸ	Lucian's recension
	𝔊ᴸᵖ	𝔊ᴸ in part
	𝔊ˡ.ᴵ.ᴵᴵ	Lucianic Subgroups I and II
𝔊ᴹ	(𝔊ᴹ)	Codex Coislinianus
𝔊ᴺ	(𝔊ᴹ)	Codex Basiliano-Vaticanus
𝔊Pap Lond	𝔊ᵁ	British Museum Papyrus 37
𝔊Q	𝔊Q	Codex Marchalianus
	𝔊ᴿ	Codex Veronensis
𝔊ⱽ	𝔊ⱽ	Codex Venetus
𝔊ⱽⁿ		Aldine edition
𝔊ᵂ	(𝔊Ms)	Codex Atheniensis
	𝔊ᵂ	Septuagint fragment edited by H. Hunger
	𝔊-ˢetc.	Greek tradition except for 𝔊ˢ etc.
	Ga	Psalterium Gallicanum
	Gn R	Genesis rabba, see cit(t)

אֲ°O	ο εβρ′	Origen's Hebrew text
Hie(r)	Hier	Jerome
Hill	Hill(el)	Codex Hillel
	jJeb	Jerušalmi Jebamot, see cit(t)
	Jos Ant	Flavius Josephus, *Antiquities of the Jews*
Jerich	Jericho	Codex Jericho
	Just	Justin Martyr
K	K	Kethib
K^Occ	K^Occ	Kethib of the Western Masoretes
K^Or	K^Or	Kethib of the Eastern Masoretes
𝔎	𝔎	Coptic version
Ka 1–22		
Kb 1–15	(ℭ)	Fragments with complex Babylonian pointing
Kc 1–14		
L	L	Codex Leningradensis
𝔏	𝔏	Old Latin versions
	𝔏 91	Codex Legionensis
	𝔏 93	Copy of Codex Legionensis
	𝔏 94	Incunabulum 54 marginalia
	𝔏 115	Naples Codex Lat. 1 (formerly Vindob. 17)
	𝔏 116	Fragmenta Quedlinburgensia and Magdeburgensia
	𝔏 117	Fragmenta Vindobonensia
𝔏(Berger)		Old Latin version edited by Berger
	𝔏 CY	Cyprian's Testimonia
𝔏D		Old Latin version edited by Dold
	𝔏G	Codex Parisinus Latinus
	𝔏 gl	Old Latin Glossarium
𝔏h		Old Latin version in the Würzburg palimpsests
𝔏L		Codex Lugdunensis
𝔏Lg	𝔏 Lg	Codex Legionensis margin
	𝔏R	Codex Veronensis
	𝔏S	Fragments from St. Gall
	𝔏 TE	Tertullian, *Adversus Marcionem*
𝔏Vind		Palimpsestus Vindobonensis
𝔐	𝔐	Masora, Masoretic text
Mas		Masora of Codex Leningradensis
Mm, Mas. M	Mm	Masora magna
Mp	Mp	Masora parva
MSS	Ms(s)	Hebrew manuscripts in the editions of Kennicott, de Rossi, and Ginsburg
	Mur	Manuscripts found in Wadi Murabba'at
	Naft	Ben Naftali
Occ	Occ	Western Masoretes
Ochla	Okhl	*Okhla weOkhla*, Frensdorff's edition
Or	Or	Eastern Masoretes
Orig	Orig	Origen
	Pes R	Pesiqta Rabba, see cit(t)

Q	Q	Qere
Q^{Occ}	Q^{Occ}	Qere of the Western Masoretes
Q^{Or}	Q^{Or}	Qere of the Eastern Masoretes
	ⵕ	Qumran manuscripts
	ⵕ^a	1QIsa^a
	ⵕ^b	1QIsa^b
	1QGenAp	1QGenesis Apocryphon
	1QM	1QMilhama
	4QPs^b	Ps. 91–118, edited in *CBQ* 26 (1964), pp. 313-322
S	S^W	Syriac Peshitta in the London Polyglot
	S	Syriac Peshitta, consensus of S^A and S^W
S^A	S^A	Codex Ambrosianus
S^{Aphr}		Syriac Bible quotations in Aphraates
	S^B	Codex Londoni British Museum Add. 14,431
	S^C	Codex Leningradensis Public Library No. 2
	S^D	Codex Londoni British Museum Add. 14,442
S^h	Syh	Syrohexaplaric text
S^L	SL	Syriac Peshitta edited by Lee
	S^M	Syriac Peshitta, Mosul edition
	S^{Mss}	Syriac Peshitta manuscripts
S^U	S^U	Syriac Peshitta, Urmia edition
	S$^{Jac\ edess}$	Syriac version of Jacob of Edessa
	S$^{Bar\ Hebr}$	Readings in the Scholii of Bar Hebraeus
Sah	Sa	Sahidic version
	Samar	Samaritan pronunciation according to P. Kahle
Seb	Seb	Sebir
Sev	Sev	Codex Severi
Sor	Sor	Soraei (= Masoretes of Sura)
T	T	Targum
	T$^{Ms(s),Ed(d)}$	Targum manuscripts or editions cited in Sperber's critical apparatus
T^B		Targum in the Second Rabbinic Bible
	T^{Buxt}	Targum, Buxtorf edition
	T$^{ed\ princ}$	Targum, editio princeps, Leiriae 1494
T^J	T^J	Targum Pseudo-Jonathan
T^{JII}	T^{JII}	Targum Jerušalmi II
T^L	T^f	Codex Reuchlinianus, edited by Lagarde (BHK) or from Sperber's critical apparatus (BHS)
T^M		Merx, *Chrestomathia targumica*
T^O	(T)	Targum Onkelos
T^P	T^P	Palestinian Targum
T^{Pr}		Targum, Praetorius edition
T^W		Targum, London Polyglot
	Tert	Tertullian
Tiq Soph	Tiq Soph	Tiqqune Sopherim
	Tyc	Tyconius
V	V	Latin Vulgate version

$\mathfrak{d}^A$		Codex Amiatinus
Var^B		Variants in Baer's edition
Var$^{E1.2.3}$		Variants in the three Erfurt codices
V(ar)^F		Variants in the first Firkowitsch collection
V(ar)^G		Variants in Ginsburg's edition
V(ar)^J		Variants in Yemenite manuscripts
V(ar)^{Ka}		Variants in Babylonian Mss collected by Kahle
V(ar)^{Ken}	V$^{Ken\ 96\ etc.}$	Variants cited in Kennicott's edition
V(ar)^M		Variants in Michaelis' edition
V(ar)^O		Variants in the Scholastic Odo
V(ar)^P	V^P	Variants in the Petersburg Prophets Codex
V(ar)^{pal}		Variants in fragments with Palestinian pointing
Var^S	V^S	Variants in Strack, *Grammatik*
V(ar)^W		Variants in Wickes
	Vrs	All or most of the versions

C ast	C ast	with asterisk
C ob	C ob	with obelos
conj		conjecture
dittogr	dttg	dittography
gl(oss)	gl	gloss
haplogr	hpgr	haplography
Hex, hex		Hexapla, Hexaplaric
homoeoarct	homark	homoioarcton
homoeotel	homtel	homoioteleuton

INDEXES

INDEX OF SUBJECTS

INDEX OF AUTHORS

238

INDEX OF BIBLICAL CITATIONS